EVEREST
1953

'Mick Conefrey painstakingly studied the vast volume of detail surrounding the British expedition and can claim to have filled in some significant blanks on the map.'

The Times

'[The] cliff-hanging chapter endings had me feverishly turning pages long after midnight, eager to follow the team through danger, despair, and delight. Hugely enjoyable and highly recommended.'

New Books

'Fascinating [and] poignant. Conefrey has consulted obscure documents, interviewed all the right people and written a magnificent book.'

Geographical Magazine

'A gripping narrative underpinned by meticulous research.'
Stephen Venables – first British mountaineer to summit Everest without oxygen and author of *Higher Than The Eagle Soars: A Path to Everest*

'Outstanding. Conefrey has found fascinating hitherto unpublished material and woven it cleverly into one of the most famous tales in mountaineering history. Eminently readable and valuable.'
Julie Summers – Chair of the Mountain Heritage Trust and author of *Fearless on Everest: The Quest for Sandy Irvine*

'A highly readable and comprehensive account of a landmark mountaineering achievement.'
Peter Gillman – author of *The Wildest Dream: Mallory – His Life and Conflicting Passions*

'A thorough and well-researched book which tells the "inside" story of an often misunderstood expedition. Essential reading for anyone with a fascination for Everest.'
Matt Dickinson – author of *The Death Zone: Climbing Everest Through the Killer Storm*

ABOUT THE AUTHOR

Mick Conefrey is the author of the award-winning *Adventurer's Handbook* and *How to Climb Mont Blanc in a Skirt*. An internationally recognised filmmaker, he has produced several BBC documentaries on mountaineering and exploration, including *The Race for Everest*. He lives in north Oxford with his family. For further details, please visit his website at mickconefrey.co.uk

EVEREST
1953

THE EPIC
STORY OF
THE FIRST
ASCENT

**MICK
CONEFREY**

ONEWORLD

A Oneworld Book
First published by Oneworld Publications 2012
The paperback edition published in 2013

ISBN 978-1-78074-230-4
ebook 978-1-78074-103-1

Typeset by Jayvee, Trivandrum, India
Printed and bound by Nørhaven, Viborg, Denmark

Cover design by Stuart Polson
Cover photographs: Everest team © Royal Geographical Society;
Everest © David Pearson / Alamy

Oneworld Publications
10 Bloomsbury Street, London WC1B 3SR, England

To
Stella Bruzzi

What a strange and thrilling thing we have let loose – a very wonderful experience awaits us, if we don't lose our heads.

John Hunt's Diary, 3 June 1953

Contents

Prologue

OUR MOUNTAIN

For British climbers of the 1920s and 1930s, Everest was, quite simply, 'our mountain'. It didn't matter that it was over 4500 miles away on the border of two of the most remote countries in the world, countries that weren't even part of the British Empire. To paraphrase the poet Rupert Brooke, it was a foreign field that would be forever England. The British had measured it, named it, photographed it, flown over it and died on it. And so they assumed that one day a British mountaineer would be first to its summit.

Everest was measured in the mid-nineteenth century. It stands in the middle of the Himalayas, on the border of Nepal and Tibet and like many mountains, marks both a physical and a political boundary. Even though none of the surveyors ever set foot on its slopes, the Great Trigonometric Survey of British India was able to measure its height with astonishing accuracy from observation points over one hundred miles away. They estimated it to be 29,002 ft, 27 ft shorter than the current official height.[1] Breaking with convention, instead of retaining its local name, Chomolungma, they christened it Mount Everest, in honour of George Everest, a former chief surveyor. Good geographer that he was, George Everest was not so keen on this act of cartographic piracy but the name stuck.

At about the same time, the sport of mountaineering was growing in the European Alps. British climbers were very competitive, making first ascents of many peaks in Switzerland and France and, in 1857, establishing the world's first mountaineering society, the Alpine Club. Within a few years most of the high mountains of the Alps had been climbed and the more enthusiastic mountaineers had begun to look further afield for new challenges.

In 1895, Albert Mummery led a small expedition to Nanga Parbat, in modern-day Pakistan, the ninth-highest mountain in the world. His pioneering attempt ended in disaster when he and two Ghurkha assistants were killed by an avalanche. Albert Mummery's death did not act as a deterrent. Soon thoughts turned to Everest, the highest mountain in the world and therefore the greatest prize.

For men like Lord George Curzon, the Viceroy of India between 1899 and 1905, climbing Everest was almost a national duty. He called Britain the home of 'the mountaineers and pioneers *par excellence* of the universe' and actively campaigned for a British expedition under the auspices of the Alpine Club and the Royal Geographical Society (RGS), which was set up in 1830 to promote exploration and advance geographical science. The two organisations joined forces to create the Everest Committee, to administer and raise funds for a British expedition.

Initially, it was hard to get permission from either Tibet or Nepal. Both, in theory, were closed kingdoms, which refused to allow foreigners to cross their borders. But such was Britain's military power and prestige in the region that eventually the Tibetan government agreed to allow a British team to make the first reconnaissance of the north side of Everest in 1921. And so began what Sir Francis Younghusband called the 'Epic of Everest'.

The reconnaissance expedition came back with mixed news. Everest was isolated, awesome and intimidating but not totally impossible. In 1922 and 1924 there were two large-scale attempts on the mountain. Both followed the same route to the northern side of Everest, via India and Tibet; both were remarkably successful, considering their very primitive equipment. In 1922 George Finch and Captain J.G. Bruce reached 27,300 ft and in 1924 Edward Norton reached 28,140 ft, less than 1000 ft from the summit. When two British climbers on the same expedition, George Mallory and Andrew Irvine, disappeared close to the top, there was speculation that they might have reached the summit and perished on the descent.

The deaths of Mallory and Irvine further reinforced the idea of Britain's special link to Everest, as Sir William Goodenough, the president of the RGS, wrote to the Secretary of State for India in 1931:

> The [Everest] Committee feel that the fact that two bodies of our countrymen lie still at the top, or very near it, may give this country a priority in any attempt that may be made to reach the summit.[2]

Tibet banned any attempts between 1925 and 1932 but granted permission for a fourth British Everest expedition in 1933. Once again it was remarkably successful, with three climbers reaching roughly the same point as Edward Norton. The final 1000 ft, however, proved to be a challenge too far. There were three more British expeditions in the 1930s but none got anywhere near the summit. A tone of desperation crept into British rhetoric, epitomised in a letter written by Sir Percy Cox, the Secretary of the Everest Committee, to the latest Secretary of State for India, in 1934:

> Owing to the number of assaults which have been made upon the mountain in the past exclusively by British expeditions, the final conquest of the mountain has become practically a national ambition ... correspondingly it would be a national humiliation were the final ascent

to be able to be allowed to pass to the nationals of any other country by
reason of any slackening of interest on our part or lack of vigilance.[3]

There was no official policy of banning anyone, nothing so crude, but effectively Britain had a monopoly over Everest because of its relationship with the Tibetan government and, perhaps more importantly, because it controlled travel through India. Climbers from other countries were welcome to try other Himalayan giants but no one ever succeeded in getting permission for Everest. Germany sent a series of expeditions to Nanga Parbat; Italians and Americans made attempts on K2 but Everest was 'our mountain'. It was the kind of gentlemen's agreement that favoured British gentlemen.

The Second World War changed everything. Britain emerged weakened and wounded. The new bipolar world had room for only two global superpowers: the United States and the Soviet Union. In 1947 the British Empire suffered a body blow when India, the so-called 'jewel in the crown', gained its independence. The British Raj gave way to the Republic of India and the Dominion of Pakistan. Within a decade Union Jacks were coming down all over the former British Empire. Britain's influence in Asia did not disappear overnight but its power was significantly diminished.

In the same year the Dalai Lama, Tibet's spiritual and political leader, announced that he was closing its borders after a very poor horoscope had predicted that he would be threatened by outsiders. Three years later the prophecy came true when his country was invaded by communist China. Mao's new revolutionary government was no friend to Britain and it would be many years before any British climbing party was allowed back into Tibet.

In the same period, however, something remarkable happened. Nepal, which had for decades been as hostile to foreigners as Tibet, tentatively began to open up to the outside world. In 1949 it allowed British and Swiss parties to make exploratory expeditions to its mountains and in 1950 a small American trekking party was given permission to visit the Everest region.

This book is the story of what happened next, beginning with the British Everest reconnaissance expedition of 1951 and the little-known training expedition to Cho Oyu in the following year, before focusing in detail on the events of 1953.

It is based on diaries, letters, memoirs and a variety of other archival material, as well as interviews with the participants and their families carried out over the last ten years. Its aim is two-fold: first to give the inside story of the expedition, both for the climbers and Sherpas on the mountain and the large number of other people who played crucial roles in the background. Second, it is an examination of the way that this major event was reported at the time and the myths and misconceptions that have grown up in the years since.

Foremost among the modern myths is that the first ascent of Everest was essentially made by two men: Edmund Hillary and Tenzing Norgay. No serious mountaineer has ever claimed this, and nor did Hillary or Tenzing, but over the years the rest of the team has been largely forgotten. Today newspapers and school textbooks regularly headline 'Hillary and Tenzing's ascent of Everest' and the others go unmentioned. Everest 1953 was a team effort, led by an exceptional leader, John Hunt. Hillary and Tenzing were at the apex of the pyramid but beneath them were the strong shoulders of many other men. They weren't even the first summit pair in 1953. If a small valve had not been damaged on an oxygen set, Charles Evans and Tom Bourdillon could well have beaten them to the prize.

The other myth that needs to be dispelled is that this was an expedition that ran with 'clockwork precision', 'like a military operation' as the clichés go. This again bears little resemblance to the truth. The British Everest expedition of 1953 was very well planned but far from being a smooth ride from conception to execution, it was marked by controversy at the beginning and at the end and by frequent crises in the middle.

Everest 1953 was also an exceptional media story, with no comparison to any previous mountaineering expedition in the Himalayas or elsewhere. Not only were a reporter from *The Times* and a freelance cameraman embedded within the climbing team but dozens of other journalists from all over the world were assigned to cover the expedition. Most stayed back in Kathmandu; some braved the slopes of Everest itself. All had one aim: to scoop their rivals. In particular they wanted to steal the story from *The Times*, the expedition's principal sponsor. This fevered competition led to some outrageously dishonest reporting, some of which had a significant impact on events. Though much of it was motivated by opportunism and occasionally sheer spite, the media circus was a testament to the importance of the expedition. The three countries most closely involved in the story – Britain, Nepal and India – were at turning points in their history and because of this the Everest expedition assumed an importance much greater than anyone had ever anticipated. Crucial to the British story was an event which had nothing at all to do with the expedition but mattered enormously to how it was received: the coronation of Queen Elizabeth II. The seemingly magical coincidence of the news of the first ascent being published on coronation day turned the expedition into a hugely symbolic event.

The story begins two years earlier, long before the Queen proceeded up the nave of Westminster Abbey and Hillary and Tenzing became two of the most famous men on the globe. A young mountaineer decided that it was about time that Britain staged another Everest expedition. His first step was to visit a world-famous institution.

Chapter 1

MR EVEREST

For almost a century the RGS has occupied an imposing Queen Anne-style mansion on the south side of Hyde Park in London. When it relocated in 1913 there were worries that the Society's new headquarters were too far from the gentlemen's clubs of Mayfair and St James to attract members. Since then London has grown so much that it seems almost central. Today the RGS is a busy hub of academic and cultural life but in the early 1950s it was a quiet geographical backwater, famous for its lectures, its map room and its collection of books and manuscripts. It was here in 1951 that a young British mountaineer came looking for information that was obscure even by the Society's standards. His name was Michael Ward and his mission was to find maps and photographs of the south side of Mount Everest.

Handsome, with dark bushy eyebrows, Michael was feisty, opinionated and tough. In 1951 he was in his second year of National Service with the Royal Army Medical Corps. He was very committed to medicine but his passion was climbing. When he read in a newspaper that 'foreign' mountaineers were on their way to Everest, his first reaction was that Britain had been 'caught napping' and that something had to be done. Everest was still 'our mountain', unfinished business for British mountaineers.

And so began his visits to the RGS, where he scoured the archives for maps, photographs and anything he could find on the history and geography of Nepal. There wasn't much. All the pre-war expeditions had approached Everest from the northern, Tibetan side and though a few British climbers had managed to look at the southern side of the mountain from vantage points in Tibet, they had been very negative about what they saw. George Mallory, whose name became so closely associated with Everest in the 1920s, described the huge icefall which controlled access to the south-west faces as 'one of the most awful and utterly forbidding scenes ever observed by man' and unsurprisingly, was very pessimistic about the chance of getting through it.

Everest was photographed from the air in 1933, during the Houston Everest Air expedition and again in 1945 and 1947, when Royal Air Force pilots based in India flew illicitly across Nepal and just happened to find themselves circling the world's highest mountain. A few of their photographs showed the southern side but they were too fragmentary and incomplete to provide any conclusive answers about a viable southern route. As Michael Ward knew from the outset, there was really only one way to find out: stage a proper reconnaissance expedition.

He set about persuading a small group of friends and young climbers to join him on an expedition to the Nepalese side of Everest. Bill Murray was a tough Scottish mountaineer, known for his pioneering winter climbs in Glen Coe and Ben Nevis and his penchant for meditation, a habit he acquired while interned in a prisoner-of-war camp during the Second World War. Campbell Secord was a tall, voluble Canadian who had come to England in the 1930s and stayed on to fly bombers for the RAF. Both he and Bill Murray had previously visited the Himalayas but the other two candidates had not climbed outside Europe. Alfred Tissières was a brilliant Swiss alpinist, then studying biology at Cambridge; Tom Bourdillon was a young British scientist, a proverbial 'man mountain', who in spite of being built like a rugby forward was a graceful and powerful climber. Their average age was thirty-two and their average weekly wage was far less in pounds sterling but nevertheless, they planned to finance the trip largely from their own pockets. Campbell Secord realised, however, that they would have to get some help with securing official permissions. He offered to approach the Himalayan Committee, the successor body to the Everest Committee of the 1920s, made up of grandees from the Alpine Club and the RGS.

Initially the Committee was a little sniffy but Campbell Secord was both persistent and persuasive and they eventually agreed to offer financial and administrative support. The Nepalese government approved their application and the War Office agreed Michael Ward's young pretenders could hire some army tents and climbing equipment. There were setbacks, however. Campbell Secord had to pull out of the expedition because of work commitments, although he agreed to continue to help with the organisation. Alfred Tissières, the Swiss scientist, decided that his research into molecular biology was much more important than his hobby and dropped out completely. The expedition was reduced to three men, only one of whom had any Himalayan experience. And then something remarkable happened.

In June 1951 Eric Shipton, the famous pre-war climber, returned to England unexpectedly, after being thrown out of China. Shipton was a fair-haired, blue-eyed, quintessentially British hero. During the 1930s he had spent almost all his time in the Himalayas, gaining a reputation as one of the world's pre-eminent mountaineers. He had been on all four of the British Everest expeditions, led one of them and reached almost 28,000 ft on another. Between attempts on Everest, he made the first reconnaissance of Nanda Devi in India, and two extraordinary journeys through the Karakoram region of modern-day Pakistan.

Eric Shipton was famously ascetic. His favourite snack was a raw onion and, rather than taking the kind of tinned luxuries that early Everest expeditions had been famous for, he invariably preferred to eat local food. But though he was incredibly tough, Eric Shipton was not just the clichéd strong, silent type. In some situations he could be diffident and taciturn but he could also be very sociable. Countless women fell for his pale blue eyes and his 'little boy lost expression' and wanted to mother him. He had a string of girlfriends and lovers, sometimes simultaneously. When not on the slopes of some hellish mountain, he loved lively conversation and, in his younger days, dancing. In spite of childhood dyslexia and difficult school days, he turned out to be an extremely good writer, whose books were read avidly by both armchair mountaineers and young climbers.

The Second World War put a temporary end to his wandering. For most of the 1940s he worked as a diplomat. His most recent posting, as the British Consul-General at Kunming in Eastern China, had ended ignominiously when he and the rest of the consular staff were expelled by the Communist authorities.

Eric Shipton had been back in England for barely a couple of weeks when he left his cottage in Hampshire and headed up to London to call on his old friend Campbell Secord, at his mews house near Trafalgar Square.

Shipton's description of their fateful meeting, in *The Mount Everest Reconnaissance Expedition 1951*, could have come out of the pages of a *Boys' Own* annual:

> *He (Secord) said:*
> *'Oh you're back, are you? What are you going to do now?'*
> *I told him I had no plans, to which he replied:*
> *'Well, you'd better lead this expedition.'*
> *I said:*
> *'What expedition?' and he explained the position.*[1]

For Campbell Secord it was pure serendipity. If Eric Shipton were to join the Everest reconnaissance expedition, the money would flow in, the press would sit up and take notice and the expedition would undoubtedly succeed.

Eric Shipton, however, did not immediately leap at the prospect. At the age of forty-three, he was not quite the carefree nomad of old. He had a wife and two children to support and no immediate job prospects. He didn't categorically reject Campbell Secord's offer but he was lukewarm. When a meeting was organised between Eric Shipton and Michael Ward, the young climber came away depressed and demoralised. As he recalled many years later:

> I told him everything and the thing that struck me was that he was rather
> uninterested; it surprised me at the time because I was red hot about it.[2]

Perhaps it wasn't all that surprising. Eric Shipton was barely off the boat and having just escaped Chairman Mao's shock troops, was hardly looking forward to returning to within a few miles of the Chinese border. He didn't feel fit, hadn't climbed for over a year and wanted nothing more than to spend a quiet English summer with his wife and family.

But then again …

Could he really say no?

Everest had been part of his life for so many years that to turn down the opportunity would be to deny a key part of his identity. Although he hadn't been in the Himalayas for over a decade he had never stopped thinking about Everest. In 1945, just a few months after the Second World War ended, he had been part of a plan to stage another British expedition to Everest, via Tibet. Four years later, he tried to get an expedition to Nepal off the ground, with his old climbing partner Bill Tilman. Neither plan had come to anything but Tilman went to Nepal in 1949 and 1950 and accompanied the

American party which first photographed the southern approach to Everest. Eric Shipton had a definite sense of unfinished business.

In particular he longed to see the Solu Khumbu,[3] the mountainous region of Nepal adjacent to Everest. It was the homeland of the Sherpas, who had served as porters on many British expeditions. Eric had heard so much about it from them that in his mind the Solu Khumbu had become what he called 'a kind of Mecca, the ultimate goal in Himalayan mountaineering'.[4]

As he considered Secord's offer, Eric found that his wife Diana was surprisingly positive. She had realised when she married him in 1942 that moments like this were bound to arise and was determined never to be a 'nuisance'. Even though they had been apart for the previous five months, she encouraged him to go. Eric Shipton put a proposition to the Himalayan Committee: if it agreed to look after finance and publicity, he would consider leading the expedition.

The Himalayan Committee became much keener on the whole thing, knowing that Shipton's involvement would raise the expedition's profile enormously. Michael Ward and Bill Murray had already done most of the organising and were happy to back out of the limelight and let him become leader. As soon as the press heard about it, they made straight for his cottage in Hampshire. On 4 July the first stories began to appear: Eric Shipton, 'Mr Everest', was back in the fray and once again Britain was on its way to the Himalayas. It was a key moment in the 1951 expedition and one that would have a major impact on the events of 1953.

In the days that followed there was a veritable bidding war for the expedition's story. Before the war almost every expedition had been sponsored by *The Times* but to everyone's astonishment, a popular newspaper, the *News Chronicle*, offered the enormous sum of £30,000 for the rights to cover the 1951 reconnaissance and future attempts.

The rather conservative members of the Himalayan Committee,

however, were not quite ready for the mass circulation market, however much money was on offer. They lived in constant fear of sensational reporting. *The Times* they regarded differently. It was a 'newspaper of record' and in their view could be trusted with the Everest story. They were very pleased, of course, when the threat of competition persuaded *The Times* to raise its initial offer of £2000 to £5000 for the exclusive rights. Looking ahead, *The Times* also took out an option for a future Everest expedition, if Shipton and his team were to return with positive news of the southern route.

That July was intensely busy. While Eric Shipton fended off the rest of the press and responded to letters from all manner of climbers and cranks, the others got on with assembling equipment and supplies at Campbell Secord's house. It was all a little chaotic and last minute but Eric Shipton had never been someone who enjoyed complex organisation. The whole caper reached a frenetic climax on

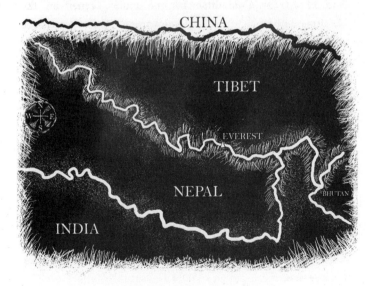

Map 1   Everest lies on the border of Nepal and Tibet

29 July, when they were forced, to their embarrassment, to make an emergency call to the Women's Voluntary Service (an organisation set up just before the Second World War to support civilians during and after air-raids), to plead for help with their packing. Within a few hours several efficient ladies had turned up to sort out the chaos. Three days later, on 2 August, Michael Ward and Bill Murray left Tilbury for India, with several dozen boxes loaded with tents, sleeping bags and climbing gear. Eric and Tom Bourdillon followed by air on 18 August and after a long train journey, caught up with them at a rain-soaked Jogbani, a small town on the border of Nepal and India.

On the following day the famous Sherpa Ang Tharkay arrived with twelve men from Darjeeling. He had worked on several of Eric Shipton's pre-war expeditions and was a well-respected *sirdar*, or head porter. Over the last decade Ang Tharkay had lost his pigtails and gained a smart new wardrobe but the other Sherpas were wild-looking men, short but sturdily built, dressed in a strange mixture of Western clothes from previous expeditions and their own local costume. Four were hired as high-altitude porters for the duration of the expedition. The other eight agreed to work as ordinary porters for the march to the Solu Khumbu.

As they unpacked the crates and inspected their baggage, Eric surprised Bill Murray and Michael Ward with some news. Before leaving England he had been contacted by the New Zealand Alpine Club, which had asked if some of its members could join the expedition. That summer four of them were climbing nearby, in the Garhwal Mountains of India, and were more than willing to come over to Nepal. For weeks Eric Shipton had been receiving applications from climbers wanting to join the team but he had turned them all down, good and bad, arguing that the smaller the party the better. However, on impulse he had said yes to two extra men, because he had fond memories of another New Zealand mountaineer, Dan Bryant, with whom he had climbed in the 1930s. Michael and Bill were bemused and a little annoyed that they had not been consulted but it was a typical Shiptonian decision that would have far-reaching consequences.

For the moment, they had other things to worry about. In front of them lay a two-week march across the spine of Nepal. They would follow the route that the American trekking party had taken in the previous year but whereas the Americans had travelled in late spring, Shipton's team would make the same journey at the tail end of the monsoon and encounter a lot more mud and mosquitoes.

The rains carried on relentlessly until, on 27 August, they loaded their gear into a huge Studebaker lorry and, accompanied by several stowaways and hangers-on, trundled across the border. The first hour was surprisingly good but thereafter they spent as much time carrying the vehicle as it did them. In 1951 Nepal had very few roads outside the Kathmandu valley where the capital city lay. Vehicles destined for Kathmandu were taken apart in India and carried in by hand, piece by piece.

Eventually, after five hours, the 'road' ended at Dharan, where they spent an uncomfortable night in a bug-filled guesthouse. The next day the real difficulties began when they attempted to hire porters for the second stage of the journey. No one travelled at this time of the year so it took a lot of haggling before Ang Tharkay managed to engage twenty-five Tamang villagers. Despite what Michael Ward called their 'graveyard coughs' and skeletal frames, they were incredibly tough, shouldering loads of more than 80 lb. However, none of them could be persuaded to make the whole journey to the Solu Khumbu. After the first stage Shipton had to stop at another small village, Dhankuta, and spend two more tedious days looking for replacements.

For Tom Bourdillon and Michael Ward, neither of whom had climbed in the Himalayas, this was a very intense introduction to the world of expedition mountaineering. Tom had married his university sweetheart, Jennifer, just six months earlier and was missing her badly.

He filled his diaries with descriptions of the semi-tropical landscape and the exotic creatures they encountered, always wishing that Jennifer could be there too. Michael Ward was more scientific in his appreciation; he noted that villages could invariably be smelt before they were seen and that the villagers were equally pungent.

In the sweltering heat they marched bare-chested, in shorts and plimsolls. Eric Shipton preferred pyjamas and shaved his head to keep cool; sunglasses and a permanently erect umbrella completed his outfit. At night they stopped in villages, sleeping in barns or the stables of peasant houses. As was Shipton's wont, they lived mainly on local food – rice and dhal and the occasional scrawny chicken.

Tom Bourdillon was fascinated to watch his famous leader at work:

> My respect for Shipton grows. He seems astonishingly casual, never quite sure about how many porters we have or where we are going for the day. But things work out smoothly.[5]

Eric Shipton was also intrigued by his young teammates. He instantly warmed to Tom Bourdillon, though as he wrote to his wife, Diana, he found Michael Ward a little 'undergraduate'. By instinct Eric preferred quieter companions and found it hard to deal with anyone he considered too outwardly ambitious (or organised).

The third stage of their journey ended at Dingla, a small town in the middle of the rain forest. They took a room in a village house and stayed put for three days, while Ang Tharkay sought out a new group of porters.

Then, on the night of 8 September, they heard heavy boots coming up the stairs. The door opened and in walked a pair of filthy, emaciated figures: Harold Earle Riddiford and Edmund Percival Hillary, the pride of the New Zealand Alpine Club. For the last three months they had been climbing with two other friends in the Garhwal Mountains and had found out about Shipton's offer of two places on the team by telegram.

For the thirty-two-year-old 'Ed' Hillary, this was a moment that he had been looking forward to with equal measures of excitement and trepidation. Back home in Auckland he ran a honey business with his father and his brother Rex. When he had first heard that Shipton was willing to take two New Zealanders along, he had not been sure if he could spend more time abroad but the thought of climbing with one of his childhood heroes had quickly persuaded him, as he confessed in a telegram to his family:

> Invited Shipton Everest expedition. Could not refuse. Please forgive erring son.[6]

Ed was nervous about meeting the British climbers. Would they be *pukka sahibs*: frightfully formal, gin and tonics, smoking jackets and stiff upper lips? Probably not … but you never knew with the Poms.

Fortunately, a week into their journey, Shipton's men were anything but *pukka*. Although they had not quite reached the New Zealanders' level of trek dirt, they all sported rough beards and looked to Ed Hillary's eyes attractively disreputable. Eric Shipton walked forward with an outstretched hand and began a friendship that would last until the end of their lives.

The first thing that the New Zealanders noticed was how well-fed they seemed. Over the previous two months of hard climbing, Ed Hillary had lost nineteen pounds and Earle Riddiford thirty, almost a quarter of his body weight. By comparison, Shipton's men looked almost rotund, particularly the huge man mountain, Tom Bourdillon. For his part, the first thing that Tom noticed was the length of the New Zealanders' axes, which looked to his eyes positively Victorian.

Ed's companion, Earle Riddiford, was a lawyer by trade. This was also his first trip to the Himalayas and he was enjoying himself hugely. Earle was very organised and ambitious and much more vocal than the laconic Ed Hillary. Eric Shipton did not warm to him.

The next day was spent getting to know each other, reorganising their supplies and continuing their porter recruitment drive. From Dingla onwards, the travelling would become even harder and because no one quite knew the route ahead, they had to carry more food, and that meant more porters and more delays.

The monsoon was coming to an end with a vengeance. With the rain came hundreds of leeches, hanging off branches, waiting to sink their suckers into delicate Caucasian skin. Many of the rivers were in spate, washing away bridges and forcing Shipton's party to make long detours. Even though they knew that they had to be close to their destination, they could see little but steaming forest and swirling mist.

Then, abruptly, the rains stopped and the mists cleared to reveal a dazzling array of huge peaks above them. The journey had taken them almost four weeks, twice as long as expected, but at last they were entering the fabled Solu Khumbu. The Sherpas could barely contain their excitement. As they climbed higher up the Dudh Kosi valley, at every turn there seemed to be a local family offering buckets of *chang*, the local home-brewed beer, and hot potatoes.

The young British climbers were shocked by the sudden beauty of the surroundings. In his diary Tom Bourdillon could barely contain himself, although everything as always was seen through the lens of his longing for his wife, Jennifer:

> I spent half an hour sitting in the sun on the river bank watching half a dozen white capped redstarts and one plumbeous redstart playing twenty yards away on the other side. It was an enchanted place. Am sure that Eden was in the Himalayan foothills. But now there is no Eve. And you would love it, I'm sure.[7]

For Eric Shipton, their arrival in the Solu Khumbu was a moment of nostalgia and revelation. After weeks of mud, mosquitoes and rainforest, they had emerged into a wondrous landscape of pine trees and towering peaks. Mountains that he had only known from the northern, Tibetan side now revealed their previously hidden southern aspects.

The local Sherpas greeted him like a returning hero, reminiscing about the adventures that they or their relatives had enjoyed with him during his expeditions of the 1930s. Tom Bourdillon wrote in his diary that he had never seen so much alcohol being consumed. Michael Ward called it one long party.

For three days they settled into Namche Bazaar, the Sherpa 'capital'. The celebrations continued relentlessly for everyone apart from Ed Hillary. He was ill when he joined Shipton's team and two weeks travelling in the monsoon had done nothing to improve his health. Stomach pains had developed into dysentery and a fever that wouldn't clear. While the others prepared to move on, he lay in his sleeping bag, with a temperature of 102.5°F (31.9°C). There was no chance that he could continue, so he reluctantly decided to stay in Namche until he recovered.

Eric Shipton's final stop before Everest was at the Thyangboche Monastery, the 'sister' institution of the famous Rongbuk Monastery on the Tibetan side of the mountain, about which the pre-war climbers had written so much. But whereas Rongbuk was high up on a rocky ridge in the middle of the barren Tibetan plain, the Thyangboche Monastery was in an idyllic pine-filled valley.

The monks were pleased to see the British team and showed them around their monastery's dark mysterious rooms, which were filled with paintings and prayer wheels. The tour climaxed with a hearty meal of yak milk; boiled potatoes; the local fire-water, 'rakshi'; and Tibetan tea, served with great ceremony in the main room. Then, much to the climbers' amusement, they were shown a gong that was sounded every evening to warn any women in the vicinity to leave before sunset. On inspection, it was discovered to be an empty oxygen cylinder from a pre-war British Everest expedition, salvaged from across the border.

From Thyangboche, the summit of Everest was just visible above the huge wall of rock that ran from Lhotse to Nuptse, the two mountains next to Everest. Soon they would reach the Khumbu Glacier and the legendary icefall that was the gateway to Everest's southern slopes. Would it be passable? Eric Shipton did not hold out much hope. Back in Britain, he had estimated that the odds were thirty-to-one against there being a viable route and more recently, he had confided to Ed Hillary that he was more interested in exploring the ground *around* Everest than wasting time on a futile attempt on the mountain itself. Michael Ward and Bill Murray were much more positive but they too had come with a Plan B: to investigate a nearby mountain, Cho Oyu, if the approach to Everest proved impossible. Everything depended on the state of the Khumbu Glacier. Three marches later, they arrived.

The landscape was entirely different. The lush valleys of the Solu Khumbu had been replaced by a harsh panorama of rock and ice. All around were huge rocky peaks and tall *seracs*, towers of ice, which poked from the surface of the glacier like enormous teeth. In the mornings the weather was fine but every afternoon there was a brutal snowstorm.

Ed Hillary caught up with them at their base camp in a small hollow on the west side of the Khumbu Glacier. After three days taking it easy, he was now completely recovered but just when they were most needed, the three young British climbers started to falter. As Eric Shipton wrote to his wife, Diana, they were showing the classic symptoms of altitude sickness:

> Bill has been like a pricked balloon ever since we got to the glacier ... Michael is feeling weak and is cheerfully frank about it. Poor Tom tries mightily and gets so disturbed that he is so feeble – he is such a nice person ... [8]

Leaving the others in the camp, Eric Shipton and Ed Hillary climbed up one of the glacier's huge terminal moraines, the enormous piles of rock spewed from its far end, to take a closer look at the task ahead.

The view was dominated by the Khumbu Icefall, a vast, chaotic mass of ice, 2000 ft high and roughly half a mile long. Formed by the movement of the Khumbu Glacier over steep rock, it was a surreal sight: a twisted giant's carpet, riven by huge crevasses and covered in apartment-sized blocks and vast tottering towers of snow and ice. Behind it was a high valley, formed in a depression between the slopes of Everest, Nuptse and Lhotse. In 1921 George Mallory had given it the incongruously Welsh name of the Western Cwm (valley). Towering above everything was Everest itself: 29,029 ft high, by over 700 ft the highest peak in the world.

Their first real opportunity to study the southern approach to Everest was far from encouraging. The summit was plastered with snow and looked un-climbable. The sight-lines weren't good enough to see properly into the Western Cwm but it looked inaccessible. They were very aware of the huge avalanches that regularly bombarded the Khumbu Icefall from the flanks of Everest and Nuptse, obliterating everything in their path. If this was the only way into Everest from the south, then perhaps they should now start thinking seriously about Plan B.

The next day Eric Shipton announced a three-pronged attack. He sent Earle Riddiford and Pasang to explore the centre of the icefall and the recovering Michael Ward and Tom Bourdillon to investigate the right-hand side. Meanwhile, he and Ed Hillary took some binoculars and headed for a rock buttress leading to Pumori, a beautifully-shaped mountain that offered the best view of the southern approach to Everest.

A year earlier Eric Shipton's former climbing partner, Bill Tilman, and the American mountaineer Charles Houston had climbed a nearby peak,[9] to take the first photographs of the Western Cwm from the south. They came away feeling very pessimistic about the chance of there being a viable route up Everest but while Houston and Tilman had stopped at 18,000 ft, Eric and Ed kept on going for another 2000 ft. This made an enormous difference, providing them with quite a different view.

From this new vantage point the whole of the North-West Face of Everest was visible in its savage splendour – their powerful binoculars enabled them to follow the final stages of the pre-war route from the Tibetan side: the North Col, the high pass between Everest and Changste; the 'Great *Couloir*', the steep gorge that Edward Norton had first climbed on the 1924 Everest Expedition; the rotten rock of the 'Yellow Band'; the dark cliffs of the Black Band and the impossibly steep Second Step, a rock face at 28,140 ft that no one had ever been able to climb. As Hillary reeled off the names with reverential wonder, Eric thought back to the successes and frustrations of his four previous expeditions to Everest. Part of him was bored with Everest, bored with the bureaucracy and hyperbole that went with a 'British Everest expedition' but another part was still full of wonder and awe.

After a few minutes the clouds parted to reveal the full length of the Western Cwm and the southern slopes leading up towards the summit. To their astonishment, they realised that there was a feasible southern route. The Western Cwm was revealed as a gently angled valley; at its head Shipton could see a way via the western face of Lhotse up to the South Col, the 26,000-ft plateau that lay between Everest and its sister peak, Lhotse. From there a sharp ridge led up to the summit itself. It was first time that anyone had ever had a proper look at the slopes leading to the South Col, a wonderful, exhilarating moment and one that took Eric Shipton by surprise.

Before they got carried away contemplating a new route, there was one large problem: the Khumbu Icefall. They could just make out the tiny ant-like figures of the New Zealander Earle Riddiford and his Sherpa, Pasang, trying to thread their way through the crevasses and *seracs*. Eric Shipton knew that they would have to find a route that could be used many times. It was one thing to force a way through the icefall but for any serious attempt on Everest, they would have to carry thousands of pounds of supplies and equipment into the Western Cwm and set up a series of camps. This would mean multiple trips by heavily-laden Sherpa porters, so the route had to be as safe as possible.

Back at base camp that night, Eric Shipton and Ed Hillary questioned the others. Michael Ward and Tom Bourdillon still looked weak. They hadn't had much success on the flanks of the icefall. Earle Riddiford, on the other hand, was very positive about the central zone. It was dangerous, he said, but not impossible. Although he and Pasang had not reached the top of the icefall, he was convinced that there would be a way.

And so at 8a.m. on 4 October Eric Shipton, Ed Hillary, Earle Riddiford, Ang Tharkay and Pasang trooped from their tents, aiming to become the first men to set foot in the Western Cwm. Tom Bourdillon accompanied them but no one expected him to get very far. With the sun still low in the sky, it was bitterly cold. Ed Hillary and Earle Riddiford were the first to suffer. They had never expected to stay in the Himalayas beyond the monsoon and wore light summer boots. Their feet soon froze and had to be massaged back into life. By late morning the shadows had lifted and the sun blazed down, turning the freezer into a furnace.

There was nowhere to hide from the sun, so they plugged on in shirtsleeves. By mid-afternoon, Tom Bourdillon was too unsteady to continue, so he stopped by a tall snow pinnacle, which became known as 'Tom's *Serac*'. The others moved on, sensing that they would soon get to the top of the icefall.

At around 4p.m. they arrived at the foot of the final obstacle: a huge trough full of icy rubble surmounted by a steep, hundred-foot-high slope that led up to the Western Cwm. It was covered in loose unconsolidated snow and looked distinctly unsafe. There was no alternative: climb it or turn back.

Everyone roped up carefully before they tentatively moved up and across, taking a diagonal path. Pasang was in front, followed by Earle Riddiford and Eric Shipton, with Ed Hillary acting as anchorman at the rear. Everyone was nervous but the Western Cwm felt close and Pasang made steady progress.

Then, without any warning, with a loud crack, the slope began to collapse, breaking up into large blocks that plunged into the crevasse below. With great skill, Pasang leapt above the avalanche line and dug the shaft of his ice axe deep into a patch of firm snow. Eric Shipton somehow managed to dance his way down, skipping from snow block to snow block until he reached the point where Ed Hillary had a good strong hold. Earle Riddiford, however, could not stop himself from being carried down the slope towards the frozen chasm below.

Then the rope suddenly grew taut and, to everyone's enormous relief, held.

Earle Riddiford hung in the air, suspended between Pasang above and Eric Shipton below. He was winded but unhurt and wanted to carry on. Eric Shipton knew that it was far too unsafe, so with only a few hours of daylight left they made a hasty retreat, collecting Tom Bourdillon, who was by then cold and very worried about his friends.

It had been a salutary lesson for everyone. On the north side of Everest, the early stages were relatively straightforward and the mountain became progressively more difficult. Here it was different. The Khumbu Icefall was about as hard a first stage of a climb as you could imagine.

The next few days were spent recovering and planning their next move. Like many new boys to the Himalayas, Michael Ward and Tom Bourdillon were finding it difficult to get used to the high altitude. Eric Shipton decided to split the party: he and Ed Hillary, with a couple of Sherpas, would explore the area to the east of Everest while the others would head north-west to ascend a pass into Tibet. Both parties would return in a fortnight and make a second attempt to reach the Western Cwm. By then Shipton hoped that everyone would be well acclimatised and a lot of the loose snow might have blown away.

For Ed Hillary it was beyond his expectations: two weeks with his hero, solving blanks on the map. They did not climb anything particularly taxing but it was the sort of free-wheeling exploration on which Eric Shipton thrived. He was so pleased with the way things were going that he sent a runner to the British embassy in Kathmandu, carrying a letter asking for a formal application to be put to the Nepalese government for an expedition the next year.

On 19 October Eric Shipton and Ed Hillary were the first to return to the Khumbu Glacier, accompanied by Ang Tharkay and another Sherpa, Utsering. There was no sign of the others so, after re-establishing base camp, they started work on the Khumbu Icefall. Early progress was good but when they reached the centre, they were forced to stop.

Just beyond 'Tom's *Serac*' they were shocked to see a vast new obstacle: a seemingly bottomless chasm that ran from one side of the glacier to the other. They managed to find a way to cross it but were shocked by what lay beyond. The whole area looked as if it had been hit by an earthquake, with deep crevasses at every turn and new, frightening, towers of ice poised to topple at any moment. In *The Times* Eric wrote that it reminded him of 'a bombed out area of London during the war'[10] but the name they gave it was even more dramatic: 'The Atom Bomb Area'.

When Ed Hillary chopped the edge off a *serac* that blocked their way, it fell deep into a crevasse. Moments later, with an ominous rumble, the surface of the glacier started to shudder and wobble. Ang Tharkay and Utsering instinctively threw themselves down; Eric and Ed managed to keep their dignity and stay upright – but only just. Acknowledging that discretion was the best part of valour, they retreated.

That night they discussed the issue that Eric Shipton had broached at the beginning of the month: even if a way could be found through the Atom Bomb area, would the Khumbu Icefall ever be safe enough as a porter route? Seven Sherpas had been killed by an avalanche on the second British Everest expedition in 1922. Ang Tharkay was now distinctly worried by what he had seen.

Eric Shipton's more pressing concern was the fate of Michael Ward and the others. They were several days late and he would soon have to send out search parties. Perhaps it hadn't been such a good idea to split the group.

Fortunately, they turned up on the 26th and admitted they had mixed up the dates. Michael's party had not managed to reach the pass that led into Tibet but as Eric had predicted, everyone was now much better acclimatised and mustard-keen to get into the Western Cwm. Eric told them the bad news about the Atom Bomb Area but they were not prepared to retreat quite yet. Two days later they climbed en masse up the ridge on Pumori to have a look at the Khumbu Icefall. It appeared just as impassable from above but Eric Shipton agreed that a bigger party might be able to get through.

On the morning of 28 October all six climbers, plus Ang Tharkay and two Sherpas, set off from their tents. Within two hours they had reached the Atom Bomb Area and were warily crossing it. After some very tricky climbing, they arrived at the ice-cliff that had avalanched three weeks earlier. Eric split them into three parties to look for a way around it. The first two were unsuccessful but Tom Bourdillon fared better: he found a large spike that had detached itself from the slope. After two hours of hard work, he had chopped a series of steps along it that took him into the Western Cwm itself. Very nervously, the others followed.

Their moment of triumph was short-lived. Barring the way to any further progress was the biggest crevasse that any of them had ever seen; in places it looked almost 50 ft wide.

Tom Bourdillon and Michael Ward wanted to try to cross it but it was clear to Eric that they had neither the time nor the equipment to go any further. It would soon be November and the days were getting shorter and colder. They would have to wait until next year; in the spring there would be less loose snow and more daylight. With a bigger team and better equipment, they might succeed. As Eric Shipton later wrote in *The Times*:

> The dragon guarding the Western Cwm is now in restless mood; it is not unreasonable to expect that in the spring he may be found sleeping.[11]

A few days later, they were back in Namche Bazaar, knocking back *chang* and *rakshi* and making fools of themselves learning the local dance steps. Their return had coincided with festival season in the Solu Khumbu and the Sherpas were determined to carouse the nights away. Eric Shipton, however, had other priorities.

There was still more than a month before they were due back in India for the return voyage and his two weeks of exploration with Ed Hillary had whetted his appetite for more. The prospect of exploring unmapped regions was as exciting as making an attempt on a particular peak, no matter how high or famous it was. Eric was fascinated by topographical puzzles, working out how one glacier fed into another and how mountain ranges fitted together. When he made a first ascent, he would comment on the other mountains he could see from the top, as well as the joy of conquest. He would have agreed with the nineteenth-century traveller, Isabella Bird: 'Everything suggests a beyond.'

Ed Hillary had run out of time, so he said his goodbyes and went directly to Kathmandu, with Earle Riddiford. Shipton split the remaining men into two parties. Tom Bourdillon, Bill Murray and most of the Sherpas headed for the Nangpa La, the high pass used as a trade route between Tibet and Nepal. Eric took Michael Ward and

Sen Tensing to the unexplored area around Gauri Sankar, a mountain once thought to be the highest in the world.

For Michael Ward this type of exploratory mountaineering was something entirely new. He had made his name as a daring rock climber, braving difficult routes in Britain and the Alps but he succumbed to the romance and excitement of travelling through virgin territory, making maps and naming features. Ultimately, however, it was not this party's geographical discoveries that made the headlines in Britain but something very different and totally unexpected.

As they crossed a remote glacier in the Menlung Basin, Eric Shipton spotted some curious tracks. At first they were large and indistinct but further down the glacier, where the snow cover was thinner, their outline was more precise. They were footprints made by creatures with four middle toes and a large big toe that projected perpendicularly. The tracks were just over twelve inches long and in places there were marks where the creatures seemed to have leapt over small crevasses and dug their toes in on the other side. Sen Tensing had no doubt about their origin: they were Yeti tracks!

Michael Ward and Eric Shipton were not totally convinced: there had been many reports of this legendary beast but no one had provided any solid, scientific evidence. Sen Tensing was adamant and claimed to have once seen a Yeti close to the Thyangboche Monastery. According to local legend, there were two types: one that ate humans and another that preyed on yaks. Both stood about five feet six inches tall and had pointed heads, reddish fur and hairless faces. Female Yetis were said to be slower-moving, because of their large, pendulous breasts.

Eric had encountered mysterious footprints previously in the Himalayas but they had never been as well defined as these. He took a series of photographs, with Michael Ward's ice axe and boot acting as a reference for their size. When the images eventually reached Britain, they caused a sensation in the press and prompted an exhibition at the British Museum.

There were some sceptics who insisted that it was a hoax. After all, wasn't Eric Shipton known to be a practical joker? His rather cryptic comment in *The Times* that it was 'a little sad, to note that so far the British Museum appears to have taken the matter more seriously than the Society for Psychical Research' added to their suspicions. However, throughout their lives both he and Michael Ward maintained that the photographs were genuine.[12] There was corroborative evidence: when Tom Bourdillon and Bill Murray followed a couple of days later, they too noticed the strange footprints:

> *The tracks were about 18" apart and staggered, the pads 10" × 8", probably walking on two legs … The Sherpas are used to them apparently. A man was killed by one of them at Lunak last year and one or more were seen at Thyangboche recently. The Sherpas insist that they are not [from a] bear, though since the bear they know is the brown bear of bamboo country, they might not class something like a polar bear as such. But a polar bear in the Himalayas?*[13]

When the party reunited on 12 November, they spent much time discussing the mysterious footprints but it wasn't long before Eric Shipton made an uncomfortable realisation that was much more pressing than the threat of man-eating Yetis. The events of the next few days were as dramatic as any on the expedition but Eric Shipton did not include them in his dispatches for *The Times* or write about them for many years. The reason was simple: they were lost and had inadvertently crossed the border into Tibet.

For centuries Tibet had been considered one of the most inaccessible countries in the world. In the early 1900s a succession of European and American missionaries and travellers had tried, failed and occasionally been killed while attempting to reach Lhasa, its fabled capital. The British Everest expeditions of the 1920s and 1930s had only been permitted because of considerable diplomatic pressure, backed by Britain's status in the East. After the Chinese invasion of October 1950, everyone assumed that Tibet would become even more hostile, to Westerners at least.

The Sherpas didn't quite see it like that. Their very name meant 'people (*pa*) of the East (*Shar*)' because they originally came from Tibet. Nepalese pilgrims and traders regularly went back and forth across the border without undue attention. A party of British climbers, however, was very different. Having recently been expelled from Communist China, Eric was in no mood for a confrontation with either the Tibetan authorities or their new Chinese masters.

They had two choices: turn around and retrace their steps or climb the steep cliffs above and head back along a different route to Namche Bazaar. Ang Tharkay was not keen on either. He told Eric that there was a much quicker and better alternative: press on through the Rongshar valley and cross a bridge back into Nepal before heading on to Kathmandu. He and the other Sherpas, he said, were familiar with this area from previous cross-border smuggling trips; if they travelled at night they would easily be able to get past the Tibetan fort just before the border without anyone noticing.

The fort? The idea of coming anywhere close to a military encampment filled Eric with dread. A decade earlier, when Tibet was independent, they might have been able to bribe their way out of trouble if caught. A newly installed Communist Chinese garrison was unlikely to be so easily corrupted. Ang Tharkay was adamant that Chinese troops had not yet reached the border areas. It would be no trouble, he insisted. The route was straightforward and they could even rest for a few hours at the nearby house of a friend. Eventually Eric gave in but when their camp was spotted by a group of Tibetan women collecting firewood, he began to regret his decision.

Fortunately, there were no further visitors. They waited until dark before descending towards the village next to the fort. In the clear light of a full moon, they saw herds of wild deer far away in the distance but mercifully no one spotted them. The normally ferocious village dogs stayed miraculously quiet as they made their way along the path, past dark houses and their sleeping owners. They silently blessed their new rubber-soled boots, which made no sound.

After passing the village, Eric relaxed a little but insisted they should press on quickly and make good their escape. The Sherpas began to complain about their heavy loads so Eric relented and allowed them to sit down for a short rest and some food. He and Tom Bourdillon woke up two hours later and started to cook but the Sherpas refused to get up, so they too went back to sleep. When they woke for a second time, it was dawn. Eric Shipton hurried everyone out of camp.

The path took them through an immense gorge, with the river on one side and a smooth, almost vertical cliff face on the other. As Tom Bourdillon wrote in his diary, 'it was a most unreal place'. Gradually, the walls became lower and less intimidating but when Tom looked back he saw an extraordinary sight:

> One Tibetan armed with a sword appeared with much shouting. We went on for a while, Ang Tharkay shouting louder, till seven more appeared. Not so good.[14]

The Tibetans carried ancient-looking muskets and huge swords. There were too many of them to ignore. The redoubtable Ang Tharkay, however, kept his cool. He told Eric Shipton and the British climbers to sit down and returned the soldiers' cries with a verbal barrage of his own. For twenty minutes the two sides engaged in a shouting match that seemed to go first one way, then the other. Eric Shipton calculated that he had 1200 rupees of expedition funds left but he doubted that the soldiers could be bought off. After what seemed like an eternity, Ang Tharkay came back with an apologetic smile. The negotiations were over and he had lost. It was not a good moment.

Then Ang Tharkay grinned: it wasn't what they thought. For the last half an hour, Ang Tharkay had been haggling over their price, not pleading for their release. What was more, it would cost a mere seven rupees each for their freedom. Eric Shipton paid up, breathed a huge sigh of relief and moved on quickly before anyone changed their minds. One hour later they crossed a bridge marking the border with Nepal and after two, thankfully less dramatic, weeks they walked down the dusty road into Kathmandu, narrower of waist but infinitely richer in experience.

It had been a wonderful expedition. They had confounded their expectations and succeeded in finding a southern route to Everest. They had crossed many unknown passes and glaciers, stalked a pair of Yetis and to top it off, outwitted the Tibetan army. As they headed towards the luxurious confines of the British embassy, they thought about next spring, when they would return to complete the job and climb Everest.

But when Eric arrived at the compound and greeted the smiling Ambassador, he heard some utterly shocking news. He would not be returning to climb Everest in 1952, because someone else had asked first.

Chapter 2

THE REAL CLIMBERS

On 28 December 1951 Basil Goodfellow boarded an early morning flight to Zurich. He had first visited Switzerland in the 1930s and, unlike most Britons of his era, was a regular flier. An executive at Imperial Chemical Industries, then one of the world's biggest companies, he travelled constantly, although his main patch was India. Basil was a very bright, very talented man whose interests ranged from fast cars to rare plants. His friends said that had he wanted, he could have reached the top of the boardroom. However, Basil's real passion lay outside the world of business. He was the Honorary Secretary of the Alpine Club and the Joint Secretary of the Himalayan Committee; this morning, he was on his way to meet representatives of the Swiss Foundation for Alpine Research, the organisation that had stolen a march on Eric Shipton and obtained permission to go to Everest in 1952. The Nepalese government was willing to allow only one attempt each year, so this meant the end of Britain's monopoly of Everest.

Basil Goodfellow's mission was simple: to cajole, sweet-talk, bully, or somehow persuade the Swiss to abandon their plans or, at the very least, join forces for a combined Anglo-Swiss expedition. In other words, this was a hostile takeover bid on an international rival.

A month earlier, when news of the Swiss expedition had broken in London, it unleashed a storm of letters and cables among the Foreign

Office, British officials in Kathmandu and Delhi, the Alpine Club and the RGS, as everyone tried to work out what was going on. The sense of shock and outrage was palpable. How dared the Swiss trespass on 'our mountain'? How and when had they managed to get permission, and crucially, did they have anything in writing?

The Swiss Foundation for Alpine Research was a small organisation, which had been set up in 1939, by members of the Swiss Alpine Club. It published a journal and raised money from public and private sources to fund overseas expeditions and scientific research into mountaineering-related issues.

In mid-December Basil Goodfellow sent the Foundation a polite but firm letter, enquiring about its intentions and informing the members that the Himalayan Committee had plans to send a British expedition to Everest in April 1952. This did not prompt the desired supine response, so Goodfellow offered to interrupt his Christmas holiday and meet its representatives at the end of December in Zurich.

The moment of truth had arrived.

After the usual pleasantries the hard bargaining began. Basil Goodfellow tried to take the high ground. He said that Britain had the moral right to go to Everest in 1952 because of its long history on the mountain and because British climbers had just completed the first reconnaissance from the south. He pointed out that there had been a recent change of government in Nepal and that whatever agreement the Swiss had with the *old* authorities, the British had now secured permission from the *new* prime minister. With a dramatic flourish, he took a telephone call from the British embassy to confirm this.

The two representatives of the Swiss Foundation for Alpine Research were not easily intimidated. Ernst Feuz was a former Olympic ski jumper, who had represented his country in the 1930s. His colleague, Edouard Wyss-Dunant, was a fifty-four-year-old radiologist, known as a daring climber in his youth. They replied that Britain had no divine right to Everest and pointed out that Swiss climbers had been trying to get permission since 1926. Feuz and Wyss-Dunant sensed that Basil Goodfellow would not risk antagonising the Nepalese government by appearing to be presumptuous or high-handed. They made it clear that their expedition was at an advanced stage; they had plenty of money and had assembled a very strong team of élite Swiss climbers.

Basil Goodfellow then played his second and most important card: Eric Shipton, one of the world's most famous high-altitude climbers, had recently returned from Kathmandu. The Himalayan Committee was prepared, he offered, to consider a joint Anglo-Swiss expedition, with Shipton as leader. His Everest experience was unparalleled and he had brought back detailed photographs and maps of the southern route. The Swiss replied that they had not one but two leaders: Edouard Wyss-Dunant, in overall charge of organisation and René Dittert, a young and powerful climber, who would take over for the final assault on the summit. The Swiss were interested in Shipton, they said, but the most they could offer was joint leadership.

Basil Goodfellow was not happy with this, as he later wrote in a detailed memo:

> *I explained the difficulties: that Shipton was a public figure and it would be difficult to accept the position for him in any party other than of leader, at any rate on the mountain.*[1]

Basil then telephoned Eric, who was at home with his family in Hampshire. He was more accommodating and less worried about his status than Basil Goodfellow. He said he was happy to climb with the Swiss and to be co-leader with Wyss-Dunant. His only condition was that two New Zealanders should be included in the British contingent. Basil Goodfellow persisted: he felt that though the Swiss were happy to talk about 'complete equality', they didn't mean it. He wanted to secure the top position for Eric to ensure that his side did not end up as minor partners. Basil suggested that Wyss-Dunant could be the leader as far as the mountain, then Eric Shipton would take over once the climbing began.

It was a tempting proposal and the Swiss seemed interested but they were not quite ready to sign up. The meeting ended on cordial terms and 'between outings on skis' the two sides determined to meet again in a few days' time to conclude negotiations.

When Goodfellow flew back to London, he convened a special meeting of the Himalayan Committee on New Year's Day, and drafted a communiqué that was released with the approval of the Swiss:

> The suggestion that British and Swiss climbers should combine in an Everest expedition is a very welcome one. The Himalayan Committee therefore sent a representative to Zurich for a general discussion, the results of which show that there are good prospects of being able to combine the two parties.[2]

On 3 January, a day before Ernst Feuz and Edouard Wyss-Dunant were due to arrive in Britain, Basil Goodfellow received a brief telegram. It gave details of Wyss-Dunant and Feuz's travel plans and stated plainly:

> Seeing no possibility of leaving René Dittert out of joint mountain leadership.[3]

The prospects for an Anglo-Swiss expedition did not look quite so rosy.

In London, the British laid on a good show, fêting the Swiss in high style at the Traveller's Club. Over the dinners that punctuated two days of 'tense UN-style negotiations', they got through two bottles of sherry, three bottles of hock, three bottles of Cheval Blanc, three bottles of Krug, two bottles of port and numerous cigars and cigarettes. Basil Goodfellow produced a new draft agreement, which he hoped might clarify the tricky leadership question. He agreed to the sharing of the role on the mountain, with one proviso:

> In case of disagreement, Mr Shipton, by reason of his seniority and extensive Everest experience, shall have the final say.[4]

The Swiss negotiators rejected the proposal. They reiterated that their plans were very advanced and that they were perfectly prepared to go without the British, unless they were guaranteed joint leadership at every stage.

The talks had come to a head. If Basil conceded, his fears that Britain would be pushed into a minor role might come true, especially if Swiss plans really were so advanced. If he refused, it would mean giving up the chance to go to Everest in 1952 and possibly being beaten to the greatest prize in mountaineering.

A day later, the Himalayan Committee's press release signalled the end of the joint expedition:

> Much as both organisations welcome the idea of a joint expedition of this kind, they have come to the conclusion that this year at any rate it is not practicable to combine the two parties. Swiss plans are on a much larger scale than was anticipated and both parties feel that to add a British team at this late stage would produce an expedition too unwieldy, in the opinion of past Everest climbers, to be easily workable.[5]

This was carried in the late editions of several London papers but it was not long before the real story leaked out. The *Daily Herald* of 8 January was forthright:

> The British wanted our leading mountaineer Eric Shipton to have

undisputed command once actual climbing starts. As far as Base Camp,
they conceded leadership of the expedition to the Swiss Dr Wyss-Dunant.

But the Swiss insisted that their man should be in control throughout – by
radio if necessary, since he is not a high climber. Even on the mountain
they said that Mr Shipton must share the remaining power of decision
with a Swiss, Dr Dittert.

'Shipton would not have had a fair deal', a mountaineering authority
told me last night.[6]

The Himalayan Committee put on a brave face and promised to lend
the Swiss team every assistance possible. A few members, including
Basil Goodfellow, admitted that perhaps it wasn't such a bad thing.
History showed that the Swiss were unlikely to reach the summit on
their first attempt and, more importantly, the British were not ready to
stage a major expedition. They did not have the right equipment and
there weren't enough good climbers with high-altitude experience.
The Himalayan Committee came up with a new plan. It would apply
to climb Everest in 1953 and in the interim, in the spring of 1952, Eric
Shipton would lead a large training expedition to a nearby mountain,
Cho Oyu. Its principal aim would be to test new types of oxygen
equipment and introduce some promising new climbers, who might
become part of Everest 1953, to the Himalayas.

Cho Oyu, the 'Turquoise Goddess', is the sixth-highest mountain
in the world. Like Everest, it straddles the border between Nepal and
Tibet but before 1952 it had not been attempted from either side.
As Eric Shipton wrote in *The Times*, it was an 'old acquaintance'
of pre-war mountaineers, who used to watch the sun set behind
it from their camps on the north side of Everest. At the end of the
1951 reconnaissance, Eric Shipton and Michael Ward had taken
stereoscopic photographs of its southern flanks, while Tom Bourdillon

and Bill Murray had examined it from the north. At 26,906 ft, Cho Oyu was considerably lower than Everest but if they succeeded (and the Swiss failed), it would be the highest mountain ever climbed.

Eric Shipton wrote confidently in *The Times*, who once again sponsored the expedition, about the Himalayan Committee's plans but in private he was uncomfortable. He preferred small, lightweight parties; the idea of 'laying siege' to a mountain with a large number of climbers and crates of oxygen was an anathema to his vision of exploration and mountaineering. For Eric it was essential to move lightly and quickly over the landscape, living on local food, rather than arriving with tons of tinned rations and armies of Sherpas. It wasn't only his instinctive asceticism or his love of nature that brought him to this position. He believed that smaller parties were more flexible and more likely to succeed.

The Himalayan Committee saw things differently. Its very existence was predicated on the idea of big, 'national' expeditions. Working parties, subcommittees, reports, memos, press releases, minutes – this was its version of Everest climbing. Some members of the Committee were irked by Eric Shipton's vague manner and obvious lack of interest in matters organisational but, because he had done a good job in 1951 and there were no obvious alternatives available, no one questioned his role as leader.

Eric Shipton kept his misgivings largely to himself and, to his surprise, enjoyed the role of 'Mr Everest'. The thorny question of finding a job and what to do next could be put off: he had a healthy advance for a book about the 1951 reconnaissance, as well as dozens of lucrative speaking engagements. Though modest by nature, he acknowledged the allure of what he called the 'despised limelight'.[7] In early January Eric was invited to meet the royal family at its rural retreat, Sandringham. In a letter to his wife, Diana, he told of the 'quite terrifying' meal that he had had with the King and how he had spent much of the evening talking to the Duke of Edinburgh about religion.

As he lectured his way around the country, Eric was amazed at the level of public interest. Britain in the early 1950s was in the throes of 'Everest mania'. *The Times* sold over 70,000 copies of a special supplement to commemorate the 1951 Everest reconnaissance expedition. In the 1930s there had been so many failed expeditions that the public had grown bored with Everest stories but whether prompted by post-war excitement, or post-war recklessness, adventure was back in fashion. Thor Heyerdahl's book of his daring voyage across the Pacific on the Kon Tiki had sold over 360,000 copies in its first two years. The French mountaineer Maurice Herzog's account of his harrowing ascent of Annapurna in 1950 was easily the best-selling mountaineering book for decades.

News of the forthcoming Swiss expedition led some headline writers to claim that there was an international 'Race for Everest'. Applications were reported from America, France, Japan, Argentina and Ceylon. Though everyone recognised that Cho Oyu was a lesser challenge, there were inevitable comparisons between the British and Swiss expeditions. Even if 'our boys' couldn't get on to 'our mountain' for another year, they could put up a good show on Cho Oyu.

Caught up in the heady rush of international competition, no one worried too much when Eric Shipton backed out of planning and organising Cho Oyu. He was busy and anyway he was just being Eric. Larry Kirwan, the Secretary of the RGS, invited the New Zealander, Earle Riddiford, to take on the organiser's role. Instead of taking the ship home with Ed Hillary, he had returned to England with Michael Ward in December 1951, and stayed to visit friends and relatives. Earle was a competent organiser so he seemed like the ideal candidate – especially when he was willing to work for free. The fact that he did not get on with Eric Shipton was not recognised as an issue. Earle worked hard in the expedition office during the day and spent his evenings regaling his friends with tales of Eric Shipton's casual approach to organisation.

Eric's strongest opinions were on team selection but he was far from systematic. His first choice was Ed Hillary and he enlisted Ed's friend and climbing partner George Lowe solely on recommendation. Michael Ward was not free but Eric agreed to take Tom Bourdillon and, as far as the Solu Khumbu at least, his wife Jennifer. He turned down the Alpine Club's suggestion of Charles Wylie, a soldier and Olympic class athlete with Himalayan experience and insisted on taking his old friend Campbell Secord, even though Secord was visibly unfit. Eric only agreed to take Charles Evans, another notable British mountaineer, after much persuasion. The last two climbers, Alfred Gregory and Ray Colledge, were unknown to him and had never been to the Himalayas.

The most surprising addition to the team was Griffith Pugh, a forty-two-year-old scientist then working for the Medical Research Council's Human Physiology Division in Hampstead. Tall, gangly and with a shock of red hair, Griffith Pugh was the archetypal absent-minded professor.[8] He had climbed in the Alps and was a gifted skier. During the Second World War he taught mountain warfare in the Lebanon. Charming and cantankerous by turn, 'Griff' was famous for his automotive exploits. He drove like a maniac and occasionally, when he forgot where he had parked his car, he took the train home, reported the car stolen and waited for the police to contact him with its whereabouts.

In the early 1950s, Pugh was carrying out research into how the human body adapted to cold weather, occasionally acting as his own guinea pig. When Michael Ward first met him in 1951, he found him in his laboratory, sitting in a bath full of ice cubes, conducting a 'cold immersion test'. A keen sportsman, Pugh was interested in applying his findings to various kinds of athletic performance and had written a famous paper, published in *The Lancet*,[9] about cross-channel swimmers.

When it came to Everest, Griffith Pugh was convinced that the chances of success of British mountaineers could be considerably improved if more was understood about high-altitude physiology. His planned research programme included work on supplementary oxygen, diet, liquid intake, cold-weather clothing and the rather frighteningly titled 'maximum work tests'. The Royal Society offered to cover his costs and the deal was done. Quite what Eric Shipton really thought about all this is difficult to know but he did have the knack of choosing good people, as well as a penchant for mischief. In 1935 when Eric had led his first Everest expedition, he included the surveyor Michael Spender, brother of the poet Stephen Spender and a notoriously unpopular and difficult character, for the sheer fun of finding out how he would fit in. Spender turned out to be an excellent companion and a very good surveyor. Similarly, Griff Pugh was a wild card but at the very least he would be an interesting addition to the team.

After barely six weeks of preparation, on 7 March 1952, Tom and Jennifer Bourdillon and the main party of British climbers left Britain on the *SS Canton*, with most of the equipment. Eric Shipton and Griffith Pugh planned to follow later by aeroplane.

Before he left Eric had one final duty to perform, even if no one else seemed to approve. He drafted a short but sincere telegram to the Swiss:

British Himalayan Committee send very best of wishes for successful ascent of Everest to you and all your team.[10]

Eric Shipton had visited Zurich twice in the previous two months and given the Swiss team maps, photographs and advice. Recently, he had several times spoken out against the growing competitiveness of Himalayan climbing:

If mountaineering has any value, and its value after all is purely philosophical, it lies in the experience rather than in the result. If competition and above all nationalism are allowed to enter into it, it becomes debased and meaningless.[11]

Claude Elliott, the chairman of the Himalayan Committee, did not feel quite so charitable. In February there had been another spat with the Swiss Foundation for Alpine Research after it complained to the Nepalese government that there would not be enough porters available for its Everest team if the British were allowed to go to Cho Oyu. This was resolved when Eric Shipton offered to take a different route through Nepal but it intensified the tone of competition.

On 24 March, the Swiss sent back a complementary telegram, wishing the British team best of luck on Cho Oyu. By the time it reached Britain, Eric Shipton was on his way to India and the first Swiss climbers were arriving in Kathmandu. The race had begun.

Chapter 3

THE TURQUOISE
GODDESS

The Cho Oyu expedition of 1952 has long been one of the black holes in the history of post-war British mountaineering. Unlike the previous year's reconnaissance, there were no books published or commemorative supplements in *The Times*. In his autobiography, *That Untravelled World*, Eric Shipton spent just one paragraph on the events on Cho Oyu. Other British climbers wrote little more. Ed Hillary covered the expedition more thoroughly in his three autobiographies but left out significant details. It is almost as if everyone was so embarrassed that they wanted to forget about the expedition. Only with the publication of *Everest and Beyond*, Peter Steele's biography of Eric Shipton, and the release of Ed Hillary's Cho Oyu diary and several other archival documents can the full story be told.

It began on 30 March when, after various flights and voyages, they assembled at Jaynagar, close to the Nepalese border*. In comparison to 1951, this was a large team, with six British climbers and three New Zealanders, plus Griffith Pugh and Jennifer Bourdillon. Some knew each other already but this was the first time that the whole team had

---

* Though Tom and Jennifer Bourdillon took the same boat to India as the others they travelled through Nepal via a different route and met the main body of the team in the Solu Khumbu.

come together. As in 1951, the British climbers were amused at Ed Hillary and George Lowe's effervescent manner and the enormous size of their ice axes. George Lowe, however, was not quite so effervescent towards his fellow New Zealander, Earle Riddiford. He had never forgiven him for taking what he considered to be his rightful place on the 1951 reconnaissance. For most of the Cho Oyu expedition, George barely spoke to Riddiford.[1]

The first part of the long trek to the mountain took them across the dusty Terai, before they moved into the more familiar forests of Nepal. Once again, Eric Shipton employed Ang Tharkay as his *sirdar* and once again, he had considerable problems in hiring local porters to carry their loads. Nevertheless, according to Eric Shipton's dispatches in *The Times*, the first two weeks were idyllic, with frequent stops to plunge into rivers for cooling dips and more generally to 'ponder on the excellence of life'.

Griffith Pugh took the prize as most unusual figure in the team. He strode ahead of the others, his bright red hair a stark contrast to the pale blue pyjamas that were his preferred marching gear. In one hand he carried an aluminium measure, while the other whirled a hygrometer, to the bemusement of the Sherpas, who mistook it for a prayer wheel. Eric's description in *The Times* poked gentle fun:

> He marched with his rucksack bristling with test tubes and glass retorts and coiled about with lengths of plastic tubing. With tireless application he counted our heartbeats, measured our haemoglobin and recorded our liquid intake, so that no phase of our changing metabolism could escape his notebook.[2]

Griffith Pugh, for his part, was disturbed by Eric Shipton's seeming disregard of basic hygiene precautions. The British team spent their nights in village houses *en route* where they were easy prey for fleas, lice, stomach bugs and chest infections. In contrast, the Swiss Everest team enjoyed a much more orderly approach to the mountain. They flew into Kathmandu at the end of March and set off for Everest with a large group of porters. At night they avoided villages and carefully supervised their Sherpa cooks.

The Swiss were a tightly-knit team who climbed together regularly. Two were professional mountain guides and, unlike the British, they had all climbed regularly throughout the Second World War. Although the Swiss Foundation for Alpine Research was the principal sponsor, most of the climbers came from the Androsace, an élite mountaineering club from Geneva. Ironically, the Androsace had been planning an expedition to Cho Oyu in 1952 before they heard that permission had been obtained for a Swiss attempt on Everest. It had taken little persuasion to change their plans.

Two of their members, André Roch and Raymond Lambert, were highly regarded in British climbing circles. As luck would have it, Roch was nursing a broken rib, sustained in a skiing accident and suffering from mild jaundice. He had almost pulled out, but Everest was too great an opportunity to miss.

Raymond Lambert was in much better form. He was a huge bear of a man: broad and powerful-looking, with a ready smile and an easy-going manner. On close inspection, he had surprisingly small feet and several stubby fingers. In 1938 Raymond Lambert and a small party of friends had endured three days sheltering in a freezing cold crevasse in the Alps amidst fierce storms. When the weather broke Lambert heroically crawled out to raise the alarm; his companions were saved but his actions cost Raymond all his toes and parts of several fingers.

Many climbers would have given up but not Raymond Lambert. Mountaineering was his obsession, his favourite sport and his livelihood. He had special boots made and adapted his technique. When he walked down the steps of the Indian Airlines plane on to the polo field that was now Kathmandu International Airport, he could barely contain his excitement.

However good-natured, the rivalry between the Swiss and the British was real. During the nineteenth century, British climbers had romped through the Alps, bagging first ascents of many Swiss peaks. Now, it was Switzerland's turn to snatch the greatest prize in world mountaineering. As Raymond Lambert was reported to have said, they would show everyone who the 'real mountaineers' were.

In mid-April the British and Swiss parties almost crossed paths at Namche Bazaar, missing each other only by a day. Both enjoyed the usual festivities and offerings of *chang* and hot potatoes before heading off to their respective base camps.

By the time the British team arrived at their chosen spot, a small collection of yak herder's huts at Lunak, to the south-west of Cho Oyu, most of the team was ill, with a variety of stomach and respiratory infections. Charles Evans, a surgeon at a hospital in Liverpool, was the unofficial team doctor. He took temperatures and dispensed pills from a small medical kit. To make matters worse, the weather was unexpectedly bad, with heavy snowstorms on most days. When they unpacked the cold-weather clothing they were supposed to be testing, some items were too big and some too small.

For Alfred Gregory, a Blackpool travel agent new to the Himalayas, it was thrilling to be surrounded by such fabulous mountains. He had done most of his climbing in the Alps. 'Greg' cut a distinctive figure; invariably dapper, even in difficult circumstances, he sported a small moustache and had, as he declared on the clothing request sheet sent out by Earle Riddiford, 'an unusually small waist and unusually long arms'. He had a French wife and a predilection for *saucisson* on mountaineering expeditions. Ray Colledge, the other new boy, was a textile salesman from Coventry, who had made his reputation with a series of daring, guideless climbs on Mont Blanc.

Originally, the Cho Oyu expedition had been billed as a training exercise, its main aim not to make the first ascent but rather to test men and equipment at high altitude. Griff Pugh had drawn up a programme of experiments and physiological tests and brought some experimental oxygen sets. He didn't need the climbers to get all the way to the summit, just high on the mountain. However, as the expedition had taken shape, everyone in London took it as a foregone conclusion that Shipton's team would go all the way to the top, even though Cho Oyu had never been attempted or reconnoitred.

On 24 April, Eric Shipton sent off Charles Evans and Alfred Gregory with five days' worth of supplies to scout the southern approach he planned to use. At the same time Ed Hillary and George Lowe went north to have a look at other options. Everyone else remained in camp, nursing their colds and upset stomachs, or making occasional forays onto nearby peaks.

After just three days Evans and Gregory returned with some bad news. They had climbed a pass close to Cho Oyu and discovered that the southern route was impossible. The photographs taken in the previous year were deceptive. Instead of an easy ridge leading to the summit, huge steep cliffs covered in snow and ice stretched all the way along the southern aspect of the mountain. Cho Oyu looked totally un-climbable from the Nepalese side.

Ed Hillary and George Lowe came back with much more positive news. They had crossed the Nangpa La, a high pass at 18,880 ft, and gone a short way into Tibet. After a difficult start Ed and George had found a ridge that looked like a possible route. High up there were ice-cliffs and difficult-looking rock slabs to contend with but they were hopeful that Cho Oyu could be climbed from the north.

This was exactly what Eric did not want to hear. The British team had permission from Nepal for an attempt from the south but they did not have, and knew that they would never get, permission to enter Tibet. After his close encounter with Tibetan soldiers at the end of last year's expedition, Eric was not at all keen to take the same risk, neither for himself nor any other member of his team.

In early 1952, there had been reports in the European press about a proposed Russian attempt on Everest. A hundred and fifty crack Russian mountaineers were said to be training hard to make an attempt from the northern side, aided by their Chinese allies. Even though Soviet newspapers had in the past dismissed mountaineering as a decadent, bourgeois folly, it was now presented as a new front in the Cold War. Russian climbers had made mass ascents of Mount Garmo in the Pamirs of Central Asia, then known as 'Mount Communism'. According to rumours, they were planning to put a bust of Stalin onto the summit of Everest. No one was quite sure whether or not to take the story seriously but if there really was a Russian expedition in Tibet, there would be many more Chinese troops in the area.

Eric Shipton knew from his recent experience as the British Consul-General in Kunming how hostile the Chinese could be. Bearing in mind that he planned to return in 1953 with an Everest expedition of his own, he did not want to provoke an international incident by crossing the border illegally. During the build-up to Cho Oyu, Eric had been the focus of media attention and regularly denounced as a spy in the Communist press. If caught, he would be a huge prize. Eric had noticed that there were a surprisingly large number of Nepalese and Tibetan pilgrims and traders crossing the Nangpa La; if they relocated their camp to the Tibetan side, news was bound to spread quickly.

This was a strong argument but Eric Shipton invited everyone to have their say. Earle Riddiford, who had spent so much time organising the expedition, declared that he was willing to cross the border into Tibet and take the risk. Ed Hillary and George Lowe agreed; they were confident that they could outrun any Chinese troops. Tom Bourdillon was not so sure; having left his wife, Jennifer, in Namche Bazaar, he did not want to be arrested in Tibet.

After a day of interminable discussion, Eric opted for a

compromise. He would send a couple of Sherpa spies into Tibet, to find out whether there were any Chinese Communist troops in the area. At the same time, Charles Evans would take a small party of climbers and set up camp on the Nepalese side of the Nangpa La. Then, if it were safe to proceed, a small party would cross the border and make a fast, lightweight attempt on Cho Oyu. There was no question of moving everyone over to the Tibetan side; that would be too risky.

This was a sensible plan but it did not end the arguments. Eric Shipton's disparate team needed firm direction but he was not that kind of leader. By nature, Eric was discursive and egalitarian. His most successful expeditions of the 1930s had been partnerships, rather than teams. On Cho Oyu in 1952 this approach did not work. There were too many strong personalities and the range of abilities was too great. The hours of discussion served only to demoralise and the compromise plan had risks of its own. As Ed Hillary commented in *View from the Summit*, it would have been far better if Eric had simply made a decision, rather than letting everyone have their say. In trying to be a democratic leader, Eric sowed the seeds of dissent.

Twelve miles further east the Swiss had the advantage of being able to follow the route that Eric Shipton and the British reconnaissance expedition pioneered in 1951. The Khumbu Icefall, however, was never going to be an easy first stage for a climb. René Dittert shared Eric Shipton's anxieties about getting Sherpas across quickly and safely but opted for a route closer to the west flank of Everest. Eric Shipton had rejected this approach as too exposed to avalanches but the Swiss preferred to take their chances in 'Suicide Passage' rather than the labyrinthine heart of the icefall.

Dittert's hunch paid off and after three days they had a fully-flagged route. An advance party made it unscathed to the crevasse at the head of the Western Cwm that had halted Eric Shipton's reconnaissance party in the autumn of 1951. Six months later it appeared to have narrowed but in places was still 25 ft wide: a formidable obstacle.

Jean-Jacques Asper, the youngest and most daring of the Swiss team, was not easily intimidated. Fifty years later, when I interviewed him in a farmhouse near Geneva, he had a twinkle in his eye as he remembered his attempts to get across the crevasse.

I said, 'Let me try, I'll go down and if I get far enough I'll try jumping across and jamming my ice axe in on the other side. I didn't have time to get nervous. I wanted to get across so badly that I thought "well I'll just have a go"'.[3]

He asked the others to rig up an improvised rope harness and attempted to swing across the gap at the narrowest point. All he got for his efforts were several bruised ribs. On the following day, the Swiss renewed the attack and lowered Asper deeper into the crevasse. Sixty-five feet down, he found a precarious ice bridge that enabled him to cross. Aching with the effort, he slowly climbed his way up the wall of ice on the other side until he eventually clambered over the top and lay panting in the snow. It was a great moment: the Swiss had overcome the obstacle that had halted the British in their tracks. They put up an improvised rope bridge and were soon stockpiling supplies on the other side of the gap. On 3 May René Dittert sent a short but triumphant cable back to Zurich. It began 'Khumbu problem solved'.[4]

The Swiss exuberance was in stark contrast to the continuing low morale of the British team. By late April everyone was more or less ill. Even Eric Shipton, who was famously resilient, had a respiratory infection. He felt so bad that on 30 April he left Base Camp, with Tom Bourdillon, to recuperate in the nearby village of Thami. They were soon joined by Griffith Pugh, another casualty.

Ed Hillary and George Lowe were left in charge of Base Camp. They kept busy climbing nearby peaks but, as Ed Hillary wrote in his diary, he was shocked to find himself becoming 'rather bored'.[5]

This was not the kind of preparation that anyone had expected for the 1953 Everest expedition.

When Eric Shipton failed to return after three days, Earle Riddiford's frustration boiled over. Why not ignore Eric, he suggested, and make a dash over the border to take a crack at Cho Oyu without him? Ed and George were not quite ready for an outright mutiny, especially one led by Earle Riddiford, but with no sign of Eric Shipton, they left Base Camp and headed for a spectacular peak close to the Nangpa La, which they christened 'the Shark's Fin'. Heavy snows frustrated their progress.

On 5 May, as they fought their way through a blizzard high up on the Nangpa La, Ed spotted a line of porters coming across the glacier below. They raced down only to meet Eric Shipton, who told them that he was now on his way to Cho Oyu to make the first attempt. He was so angry with Ed and George for leaving Base Camp that they were not included in the climbing party.

The two New Zealanders were so annoyed and disappointed that Eric relented and asked them to come along too. Then he changed the plan again and decided not to take part in the assault himself. Instead he returned to Base Camp, leaving Charles Evans in charge of the team. Charles agreed but he too felt very ill and, having taken a good look at Cho Oyu from the north, was not at all sure that it could be climbed.

The expedition was becoming distinctly ragged.

With Hillary and Lowe in the lead, the British party plugged their way up Cho Oyu, establishing two high camps. It was hard going and as the weather continued to deteriorate, Charles Evans's sore throat developed into laryngitis. Eventually, he retreated down the mountain, accompanied by Campbell Secord, leaving Hillary and Lowe to plough on with Tom Bourdillon and Alfred Gregory. No one felt particularly enthusiastic, especially with the thought of the Chinese soldiers lingering at the back of their minds.

Finally, on 10 May, they admitted defeat. In his memoir *View from the Summit*, Ed Hillary recalled it as an undignified end:

> *When someone down below shouted, 'Come down you silly bugger', I knew it was time to turn back. We had been a miserable failure and no one said a word as we retreated back to the ridge camp and finally over the Kyetrak Glacier.*[6]

They headed down to the Nangpa La where, much to Hillary's bemusement, they met Eric Shipton and Earle Riddiford, who had come up to assist them. When he heard about their difficult progress, Eric Shipton immediately agreed to call the whole attempt off. The Sherpas were glad to abandon the camps and cross back into Nepal but the irrepressible Ed Hillary and George Lowe still felt frisky. Taking a few days' worth of food, they set off to climb another couple of nameless peaks.

As the expedition imploded, everyone grew fractious and irritable. Earle Riddiford came down with suspected sciatica, which restricted his climbing and further blackened his mood. Tom Bourdillon argued with Ray Colledge over clothing. Even the mild-mannered Charles Evans became irritated with his teammates. In his expedition notebook, Campbell Secord, the Canadian economist and prime mover of the Everest reconnaissance of 1951, began to compile a list of candidates for next year's Everest expedition. The 'discard' pile included himself, Tom Bourdillon, Earle Riddiford ... and Eric Shipton.

This was extraordinary. In June 1951 Campbell Secord had been one of the first people visited by Eric Shipton on his return from China but now he had lost faith in his old friend. If Eric had been more decisive at an earlier stage and taken the testing and training remit more seriously, everyone might have felt good about themselves. Instead, no one was happy.

Earle Riddiford decided to return to New Zealand, after more than a year away from home. His sciatica was the ostensible cause but as Ed Hillary suspected in his diary, Earle's departure was 'also due to loss of interest in the expedition I should think'.[7] It was an unhappy end for someone who had put so much work in but Earle had never quite settled. George Lowe's continuing hostility towards him had also made for a miserable time.

The remainder of the team split into small parties. With Charles Evans and Alfred Gregory, Eric set off to explore an unmapped region to the west of Everest. He sent Ed Hillary and George Lowe to make an attempt on the Nup La, another high pass, which led into Tibet. Griffith Pugh and the remaining men set up a scientific camp on the Menlung La, close to the site of the previous year's Yeti tracks.

One of the principal aims was to conduct systematic research into the use of supplementary oxygen. This had first been tried on Everest in the early 1920s, provoking much debate in mountaineering circles. Purists denounced bottled oxygen as an 'artificial aid' and claimed that to use it was unsporting. Others argued that the oxygen sets then available were so heavy that the costs outweighed the benefits.

Griffith Pugh had no time for debate about sporting ethics. As far as he was concerned, a mountain like Everest was such a challenge that everything possible had to be done to increase the odds of success. He wanted to find out how much supplementary oxygen was needed to make a significant difference at high altitude. Was there an optimum flow rate at which to run an oxygen set, to offset its weight? If the rate was too high, the oxygen was used up too quickly, if it was too low then there seemed to be no benefit. This was pioneering research, the first time that anyone had done such work in the Himalayas. However, like so much else on Cho Oyu, there were problems from the outset.

Pugh and his test subjects – Bourdillon, Secord, and Colledge – had eight lightweight 'assault sets', equipped with a new type of oxygen cylinder made from Dural, an aluminium alloy. Their capacity was lower than steel cylinders but they were almost half the weight and thus offered a substantial advantage. Pugh hoped to test these new sets on the Cho Oyu expedition and if they proved satisfactory, to use them on Everest in 1953. However, before they had a chance to try them an urgent message arrived by runner from the British embassy in Kathmandu warning them not to use the Dural cylinders. A fatal accident involving similar bottles had occurred at the Dunlop Aviation factory in Coventry. Pugh and his test subjects had no alternative but to abandon the assault sets and use the older, heavier cylinders.

This was a considerable disappointment but they carried on, sweating their way up a measured slope while Griffith Pugh collected as much data as he could. His initial observations showed that a flow rate of four litres per minute was a substantial improvement over two (the rate used on most pre-war expeditions). Ten litres per minute was even better but even at that rate the British climbers could not match the work capacity of their Sherpas. After a week of experiments, they packed their equipment away. Ray Colledge and Tom Bourdillon climbed a 22,000-ft peak before returning to Namche Bazaar, where they had arranged to meet Eric Shipton. Griffith Pugh and Campbell Secord went straight back to Kathmandu and then travelled on to London.

In Pugh's expedition report he noted that exposure to high altitude at first reduced 'conversation, gaiety and general activity' but that this expedition had not been notably ill-tempered. Campbell Secord wrote candidly to Eric Shipton that the scientific research was the only element that made the thousands of pounds spent on the Cho Oyu expedition worthwhile.

It was not long before the Swiss team heard the news about their rivals. Unlike the British, they were equipped with radios; on 18 May René Dittert was told by his co-leader, Edouard Wyss-Dunant, that Shipton's team had given up on Cho Oyu and split into small parties.

By then the Swiss were encountering difficulties of their own. After the 'conquest' of the Khumbu Icefall, they had quickly ascended the long valley of the Western Cwm and set up their Advance Base at its head. Their next challenge was the Lhotse Face, the steep slope that led up to the South Col, the high plateau between Everest and Lhotse. As they discovered, while the Western Cwm had been a relatively easy 'snow plod', the Lhotse Face was quite different.

Once again, René Dittert decided to ignore the route that Eric Shipton had suggested after the 1951 reconnaissance. Instead of going up the right-hand side of the Lhotse Glacier and traversing leftwards to the South Col, Dittert opted for a much more direct approach, climbing straight up the icy slope at the end of the Western Cwm to a band of rock which led to the top. The Swiss christened it 'the Geneva Spur'. If they succeeded it would be a much quicker approach than Eric Shipton's but, as they soon realised, there was a problem.

The Geneva Spur was so steep that there was nowhere to put an intermediate camp between the bottom of the Lhotse Face and the South Col at the top. This meant ascending 3600 ft in a single day. In the Alps such a climbing rate was feasible but in the thin air of the Himalayas it was a much tougher proposition. Dittert's men started preparing a route on 14 May but a week later, had not reached the top. The relentless wind and heavy daily snows sapped their energy. On 22 May the Swiss were trapped in their tents by a thirty-six-hour blizzard. René Dittert grew introspective:

> I recalled how Mallory had said, after his first expedition, that a wise man would do well to reflect and tremble, even on the threshold of his supreme attempt; such is Everest's terrifying harshness.[8]

Eventually, the storm abated and on 25 May Raymond Lambert, the strongest of the Swiss climbers, set off for the South Col with two companions, Leon Flory and René Aubert, six Sherpas and their *sirdar*, Tenzing.

Tenzing had been given his first job as an expedition porter in 1935 by Eric Shipton. Like almost everyone Tenzing met, Shipton instantly warmed to his smile. By 1952 Tenzing had been to Everest four times and knew two members of the Swiss team from an expedition in 1947. So far, nothing had been particularly demanding but over the next few days, Tenzing would prove himself an exceptional Sherpa.

For the first hour they climbed slowly and steadily. Then one of the Sherpas, Ajiba, stopped and, despite the intense cold, started to shiver and sweat. Malaria, an old antagonist, had come back at the most inappropriate time. They were close enough to the bottom for Ajiba to descend by himself but it was not long before two more Sherpas were forced to retreat, suffering from altitude sickness.

By the middle of the afternoon Raymond Lambert had lost half his porters. When at 7p.m. they had not reached the South Col, he was forced to change plan. With darkness falling and the temperature dropping rapidly, they hacked out tiny platforms in the ice and made an emergency bivouac. That night was bitterly cold and cruelly long. They managed to put up two very small tents but there was too little space to unroll their sleeping bags. The wind was so ferocious that Raymond Lambert worried that at any moment they might be blown clean off the mountain.

He emerged from his tent at dawn on the following morning exhausted and very, very cold. He tried to warm up with a few exercises but any movement made him breathless and uncomfortable. When the sun finally reached the slope, Lambert and his comrades began the slow climb up to the South Col. Several hours later they arrived.

It could have been another magical moment of triumph but the Swiss were too exhausted to feel anything other than a fierce desire to get their tents put up as quickly as possible.

In its way, the South Col was as intimidating as the Khumbu Icefall. There was no snow, only rock embedded in ice. To one side was a huge drop down the Kangshung Face into Tibet, to the other a slightly shorter but equally fatal drop into the Western Cwm. For the first time, Lambert had a good look at the South-East Ridge, which led to the summit. It was an awe-inspiring sight, almost like finding a new mountain perched at 26,000 ft.

Pitching a tent in a wind tunnel was not easy. It took two hours to erect, then they had to wait for another hour before the Sherpas arrived with their stoves and food. Tenzing seemed to have amazing energy but the other Sherpas were at the point of collapse. Pasang announced that he wanted to die. Phu Tharkay could not walk in a straight line. Da Namgyal curled up with his head in his hands, suffering from a blinding headache. Overnight the wind abated but on the following day all three went down, insisting they could go no further.

Despite everything, Raymond Lambert was not prepared to give up. At 10a.m. on 27 May he and the remaining men set off up the South-East Ridge, aiming to get within striking distance of the summit.

Their attempt was doomed from the beginning.

When they left the South Col, all they carried was a small, one-man tent. For the first time in the expedition they used artificial oxygen to overcome the effect of the altitude but their sets, designed for coal miners, were unsuitable for high-altitude climbing. They were chest-mounted, making movement awkward, and their valves were so unforgiving that oxygen flowed only when the climbers were stationary.

After a few hours Lambert and Tenzing reached a small natural platform, just wide enough to pitch the tent. This, Raymond Lambert decided, would be the final camp from which they would make a dash for the summit on the following day. There was a problem: the tent was barely big enough for two people, never mind four. It was an agonising moment. Aubert and Flory felt strong enough for the final push but Lambert was their leader and had bonded very strongly with Tenzing over the last twenty-four hours. If they turned back now, Aubert and Flory knew they were giving up their chance to reach the top. They were all in tears, overcome by emotion and the effects of altitude. Then Flory and Aubert turned to descend, promising to wait on the South Col for the return of their comrades.

Tenzing and Lambert squeezed into the tiny tent. They had no stove, no sleeping bags and nothing to eat except a few dirty lumps of cheese and sausage they found at the bottom of their pockets. They had barely drunk anything that day and were incredibly thirsty but all they had to melt ice was a tin and a candle. Sleep was out of the question; their only hope was that sheer desire and willpower would somehow propel them to the summit. If they nodded off, they might never wake, so they spent the night thumping each other into consciousness. Tenzing could speak only a smattering of French and Lambert a tiny bit of English but over the previous few days of shared hardship and endeavour an intense comradeship had grown between them, which sustained them that night.

At dawn on the following day, they were in no state to continue but, nevertheless, they strapped on their crampons, loaded their sets with three canisters of oxygen each and carried on. Their starting point was 27,500 ft, just 1500 ft below the summit. Raymond Lambert estimated they had six hours of oxygen to get there and back but their sets continued to malfunction. The two men moved in spurts, taking a few steps, then making a huge effort to inhale and release some precious oxygen. When the slope steepened, they were forced to clamber on all fours. Sometimes the sun came to their aid, warming them and revealing the surrounding mountains but the weather was capricious. Bright spells were followed by flurries of hard icy snow that stung their cheeks. Mists swirled around them, obscuring where they had come from and where they were going.

At around 11a.m., they arrived at a point where they could see the South Summit, the prominent pinnacle 300 ft below the summit. Even if they couldn't climb right to the top, it would be an enormous achievement to reach the South Summit. But their ambition was not matched by their ability. Tenzing was very tired and starting to lose his balance. Lambert felt good – too good. This was a warning; the same deceptive euphoria he had experienced all those years ago in the Alps, on the expedition when he lost all his toes.

Eventually, they came to a stop and silently signalled to each other to turn back. It had taken them five hours to ascend 650 feet. Lambert and Tenzing had climbed about a hundred feet higher on Everest than any of the pre-war British parties and came back claiming a new world altitude record of 28,210 ft.[9] However, it was at least another five hundred vertical feet to the South Summit and a further three hundred to the highest point. On the way down they found that their tent had been torn to pieces by the wind. When they staggered on to the South Col they had to be dragged to safety by Flory and Aubert. Later that day René Dittert was due on the South Col to lead a second attempt. All Raymond Lambert and Tenzing could think about was sleep and escape.

While the Swiss were making their assault on the summit of Everest, the British team was coming to the end of its various excursions to nearby peaks and passes. On 4 June Eric Shipton returned to Namche Bazaar with Alfred Gregory. Hillary and Lowe hadn't returned from their expedition to the Nup La but Ray Colledge and Tom and Jennifer Bourdillon were there, preparing for a holiday in Sri Lanka before the long voyage back to England. One question was on everyone's mind: had the Swiss climbed Everest?

Ed Hillary and George Lowe asked themselves the same question when, three days later, they and their two Sherpas arrived back on the Khumbu Glacier after an epic trek around the base of Everest and on to the East Rongbuk glacier in Tibet. They had visited the sites of the pre-war British Camps I and II and considered climbing Changtse, a 24,700-ft peak on the far north of the Everest massif but realised they did not have the resources. During this very busy fortnight they had neither seen nor heard any Communist soldiers and had enjoyed themselves tremendously, climbing and exploring.

When they found the Swiss Base Camp, it was deserted but the fires were tantalisingly warm. It was too late for Ed and George to carry on that day, so they waited until the next morning before heading down to Namche Bazaar, looking forward to a good meal and news of both their friends and their rivals. The march was so easy that they dispensed with their heavy boots and walked in plimsolls. The sun was out and after their brief visit to the barren wastes of Tibet, Nepal seemed lush and verdant. At the small village of Phelong Karpo, they met an old man and asked for information about the Swiss expedition.

The old man shook his head. He told one of their Sherpas that no fewer than seven Swiss climbers had reached the summit. It was a depressing moment at the end of a depressing expedition but there was something odd. Seven climbers? It seemed an awful lot.

Just after midday they reached the next village, Pangboche, where they were invited into a local house for a large meal of potatoes. As they tucked in, one of Eric Shipton's Sherpas arrived. He carried their post, a ration of sugar and, best of all, some dramatic news. The old man was wrong. The Swiss had got very high on Everest but they hadn't made it all the way to the summit.

A few hours later Eric Shipton appeared and confirmed the story. After Lambert and Tenzing's attempt, René Dittert had gone up to the South Col but his men were so tired and the weather so bad that they had barely managed to leave their tents, let alone climb up to Lambert and Tenzing's camp on the South-East Ridge.

In his excitement, Ed Hillary left George Lowe and Eric Shipton and raced down to Namche Bazaar to sort out some equipment and find out more from the Swiss. They were camped above the village, in typically neat formation with rows of tents surrounding a flagpole and a large mess area. The Swiss climbers were very welcoming and Lambert and Dittert were happy to share their story. Ed Hillary was impressed.

At the British camp, which looked distinctly ramshackle by comparison, Ed listened to Tom Bourdillon and Alfred Gregory talk about their plans for next year, now that the Swiss had failed. They were sure that plenty of money could be raised and were already putting together an ideal team. Ed Hillary played along but he was now convinced that there were much better climbers at home in New Zealand.

The next day, Ed returned to Eric and George at Pangboche. He became even more disenchanted when Eric Shipton told him that he was considering inviting some Swiss climbers to accompany the British team in 1953. Ed Hillary was a huge fan of Eric Shipton. He had grown up reading his books and had been thrilled to be invited on the Cho Oyu expedition but that night he was scathing in his diary:

Eric is keen on a combined Swiss–British party but largely in my opinion to use the Swiss organising powers and equipment; secondly as a sign of a lack of confidence in British climbers and thirdly as a lack of confidence in Eric's ability to make judgements on snow conditions etc. (André Roch). In my opinion Eric is now quite unsuitable as an Everest leader as instead of a powerful combining and shaping factor in the expedition, he disturbs people's confidence, saps their enthusiasm and fills them with doubts entirely, because he has now little or no confidence in his own judgements, so jealous of the positive judgement of others.[10]

If this was what Eric Shipton's friends thought, what would his detractors in London say?

Chapter 4

A VERY BRITISH COUP

The anniversary dinner of the RGS on 23 June 1952 was the usual grandiose affair. While the Fellows and their guests sipped wine at the Hyde Park Hotel, James Wordie, their esteemed president, reviewed the achievements of the previous year and looked forward to the next. As the *Daily Mail* reported, high on his and everyone else's mind was Everest:

> 'While we hope as sportsmen that the Swiss have reached the top,' I must admit to feeling I would be happier if they have not', he said amid laughter. 'If not, there is still a chance for Britain to win the honour of climbing the world's highest mountain when next year's expedition sets out under Mr Eric Shipton.'[1]

The hall rang with applause but for anyone who knew anything about Everest this was a rather strange speech. In the first instance, by 23 June there were strong indications that the Swiss had failed. The first reports appeared in the press at the beginning of the month and had been confirmed by Reuters on 4 June. Second, as James Wordie must surely have known as a member of the Himalayan Committee, the forthcoming British 1953 Everest expedition was in a somewhat chaotic state and its leader, Eric Shipton, was nowhere to be seen.

Only a few hours earlier Lawrence Kirwan, the Secretary of the RGS, had sent a plaintive telegram to the British embassy in Delhi, hoping it would reach Shipton:

> *Owing mischievous press reports about British expedition anxious know your arrival date to make earliest contact please cable*[2]

The simple fact was that no one in Britain had any idea where Eric Shipton was or when he was coming back. There had been no new dispatch in *The Times* for almost a fortnight. When journalists spoke to Diana Shipton on 6 June, she told them that she hadn't heard from her husband since mid-April. Where was Eric? And what was going on?

The answers to those questions were contained in two envelopes in transit between Kathmandu and London.

The first contained Eric Shipton's latest article for *The Times,* in which he confirmed that the British had withdrawn from Cho Oyu. He did not go into detail and made no mention of the Tibetan border issue. Their attempt had failed, he wrote, because of Cho Oyu's ice cliffs, which had proved impossible to climb.

The second item was a long letter to the Himalayan Committee, which had been drafted in early June by Tom Bourdillon, on behalf of the British team. It did not go into any more detail about the Cho Oyu expedition or its aftermath but looked forward to the following year's expedition to Everest. It was a call to arms, which implicitly criticised the Himalayan Committee:

> *To put it bluntly the expeditions have been based on the spare time efforts of people in London, on selling articles to The Times and on Swiss charity and while no disparagement of any of these sources is intended (in fact they are thought to be extremely praiseworthy) they are not an adequate basis for an expedition of this type.*[3]

Tom Bourdillon went on to demand substantially more training for prospective team members, paid full-time organisers and a systematic approach to designing and procuring equipment, particularly oxygen sets. Funding, he argued, should come directly from the government but if they were unwilling, then the Himalayan Committee should abandon *The Times* and sell their story to the highest bidder. A final paragraph, written by Eric Shipton, added that if a radically new approach were not taken, 'it would be useless to send out an expedition'.

Given the memo's strident tone and sense of urgency, the Himalayan Committee might have expected to hear from Eric Shipton soon, in person. Eric had different ideas. Instead of going back with Alfred Gregory to begin preparing for the 1953 expedition, he took Charles Evans, Ed Hillary and George Lowe and headed off to explore the Barun Valley. Eric had what he always really wanted: a small, highly-mobile party, composed of men whose company he enjoyed. Together, they made several first ascents and crossed much new territory. Freed from the responsibilities of leading a 'national' training expedition, Eric was visibly more relaxed. In a letter to his friend, and former lover, Pamela Freston, he described the exploration of the Barun Valley as 'a glorious month, which has made the whole expedition worthwhile'.[4]

However, although everyone could see that he was enjoying himself, Eric was unsettled. His chest infection had not cleared up and, as an alarmed Charles Evans noted, there were days when he ran a very high temperature. Ed Hillary recorded in his diary that Eric appeared 'pretty ill and rather cantankerous'.[5]

He had chosen to go to the Barun Valley but part of him acknowledged that he should be back in London. He talked frequently about the 1953 expedition, endlessly discussing the pros and cons of large and small parties and occasionally admitting that perhaps he had been wrong not to return straight away.

At the end of June the weather broke and ended Eric's soul-searching. Heavy snow made climbing impossible so they packed up and headed out. Eric was in a desperate hurry to get back but Charles Evans, as intrepid as ever, trekked across the hills to Darjeeling with two Sherpas. Hillary and Lowe stayed with Eric and took a more direct route to India, following the Arun River.

When they reached India, instead of taking the first available aeroplane to Britain, Eric Shipton did something inexplicable: he turned round and went to Kathmandu, with Hillary and Lowe in tow. When he arrived Eric told reporters that he planned to lead the 1953 Everest expedition and hoped to have Tenzing, hero of the Swiss expedition, as his *sirdar*. He never explained exactly what he was doing in the capital. Later he told Pamela Freston that he had come to pay his respects to the Nepalese court but this was odd behaviour for the leader of a forthcoming expedition, who a month earlier had called for preparations to get under way immediately.

In his absence, on 4 July, the day after Eric Shipton reached Kathmandu, the Himalayan Committee held a special meeting at the Alpine Club in Mayfair to hear from three members of the Cho Oyu team who had returned to Britain: Alfred Gregory, Campbell Secord and Griffith Pugh. None of the Committee members were impressed by what they heard.

Campbell Secord had written a long report about the ill-fated Cho Oyu expedition. It echoed Tom Bourdillon's letter from Thyangboche but, if anything, its opening paragraph was more strident:

> *The ascent of Everest is in a category by itself and gives our casual sort of approach no solid chance of success by comparison with Swiss experience or French desperation. Either we must take it really seriously or leave it to others. The prestige implications are so considerable that it is the obvious duty of British climbers to do everything in their power to send out a really effective team next year.*[6]

Secord reviewed in detail the equipment supplied in 1952 and made proposals for a rigorous training regime for the following year. Most significantly, he introduced a new question: who should lead the expedition?

He made no direct criticism in writing but, tellingly, he did not assume that Eric Shipton was the automatic choice. In the second paragraph of his memo, he wrote that a leader would soon have to be chosen. Then, he rather cryptically suggested that they needed a *primus inter pares* from within the core of the team. In other words, if they were stuck with Eric Shipton, he would have to take advice from the most experienced members.

No one was willing to place the blame directly on Eric Shipton but it was very obvious to the Committee that Campbell Secord and Griffith Pugh had not been impressed by his leadership. The expedition report that Pugh later produced was a remarkably detailed document, containing numerous observations on everything from the mental health of the party to their preference for Li-lo air mattresses over reindeer skins, as well as a thorough analysis of the oxygen question. Clearly, the expedition had been valuable from his point of view but had Eric Shipton taken the science seriously? Pugh's bosses at the Medical Research Council thought not and wrote letters of complaint to the Himalayan Committee.

As Thomas Blakeney, the official minute-taker of the Himalayan Committee, recorded in a memo many years later, the Cho Oyu expedition was regarded by many as having been 'a flop':

> The considerable success achieved by the Swiss on Everest was felt to contrast heavily with the British failure to achieve anything on Cho Oyu and though Shipton's party managed a number of climbs in the Barun Valley, the general feeling was that the British expedition had been rather a humiliating failure.[7]

For the first time, the Himalayan Committee started to think the unthinkable: Everest without 'Mr Everest'.

For the previous six months the Himalayan Committee had been in regular contact with the French Alpine Club, which was due to mount a French expedition in 1954.[8] They had succeeded on Annapurna and were likely to put forward a very strong team. The 1953 expedition was looking more and more like Britain's last chance to win the 'Race for Everest'. It was vital to choose the right leader.

Eric Shipton had achieved great things in the past but was he the right man for the job? His reputation among the press and the general public was very high. Only a few months earlier, a week before leaving for Cho Oyu, he had been awarded the Scottish RGS's supreme accolade, the Livingstone Medal. His book on the 1951 reconnaissance expedition was eagerly anticipated. However, the reports coming back from Cho Oyu seemed to confirm what some members suspected already: Eric Shipton was past his prime. He was too disorganised, too soft and he clearly didn't have any enthusiasm for a 'national' expedition.

However, there was a problem: who else could take his place? During the 1940s there had been precious little British mountaineering, either in the Himalayas or anywhere else. There was simply no one available with Shipton's experience, other than, perhaps, Bill Tilman, his former partner. Tilman, however, was regarded as another maverick and was known to be a poor acclimatiser, so he was never really in the running.

It was not surprising, considering that it contained several former military men, that the Committee turned its thoughts to the Army. Two Ghurkha officers immediately came to mind: Major Charles Wylie and Major Jimmy Roberts. Both knew the Himalayas, spoke the local languages and had decent climbing records. Neither, however, was personally known to anyone in the room.

One name aroused more interest: Colonel John Hunt, a

distinguished soldier with a DSO and a CBE, then serving with the 1st British Corps in Germany. He had lived abroad for most of his life, so was not well known in the British climbing world but he had a good record in the Himalayas and the Alps. In 1951, he had met Basil Goodfellow, the Honorary Secretary of the Alpine Club, in Switzerland and had spent several days climbing with him. Could John Hunt be the man to bolster the team – or even replace Eric Shipton? Basil Goodfellow thought so. Hunt was a 'tiger', he said, the kind of determined leader that the 1953 Everest expedition needed. There was no guarantee that the Army would release either him or any of the other soldiers but there was a long history of military men taking part in British Everest expeditions, so the odds were good.

The events of the following three months are some of the most contentious in the history of British mountaineering. Even now, the arguments continue as to what occurred and why. For many years, key documents lay hidden in private files. Today, it is possible to piece together what happened, although some mysteries remain.

According to the Himalayan Committee's official minutes of the 4 July meeting, it was agreed that until Eric Shipton returned 'no further progress could be made' but it is obvious from letters in the RGS's archives that the Himalayan Committee was splitting into two factions, each led by the men who were most active in the day-to-day organisation of the expedition.

Lawrence Kirwan, the urbane Secretary of the RGS, was Eric Shipton's most important ally. Although he frequently found him exasperating, Lawrence had a great fondness and respect for Eric Shipton, a man who he referred to as 'the greatest-ever British traveller'. His approach was to try and bolster Eric's leadership by appointing an organising secretary from within the current team to help prepare the 1953 expedition. A few days later he sent telegrams to Alfred Gregory and Charles Evans to ask if either of them were interested in the position.

Basil Goodfellow, by contrast, had now got to the point where he wanted to replace Shipton altogether, if a good candidate could be found. He didn't think that there was anyone suitable within Shipton's Cho Oyu team, so he wrote to John Hunt on 10 July to sound him out either as a potential new leader or deputy to Shipton. He invoked the memory of General Bruce, the legendary British soldier who led the 1922 and 1924 Everest expeditions:

> EES [Eric Earle Shipton] has been very unfit on Cho Oyu and it is thought he may not wish to go to Everest except perhaps as an advisor and not as assault leader. Other names are being actively considered including naturally yourself. I hope I do not raise false hopes. But most of us are certain that we need another General Bruce in 1953 and your name stands out.[9]

At the end of the page Basil Goodfellow added a caveat, warning Hunt that at forty-two, his age might be a problem; some members believed that a younger team was needed. It was an extraordinary opening letter. A few months earlier Basil Goodfellow had been negotiating hard with the Swiss, arguing that Eric Shipton was the only man who could lead the proposed Anglo-Swiss expedition. Now, he too shared the feeling of embarrassment at the British failure on Cho Oyu and was worried that the same thing might happen again on Everest in 1953.

One week later, on 17 July, Eric Shipton arrived at London Airport. He gave an impromptu press conference but made no mention of international races or great causes. Eric said he wanted a compact team of six men for 1953 and that his priority was to develop a new type of oxygen set. He carried on to London, where he had a brief meeting with Basil Goodfellow, before returning to his family in Hampshire.

This prompted another very candid letter from Goodfellow to Hunt, just before Basil left for his annual climbing holiday in the Alps:

For private reasons he [Eric Shipton] may fall out altogether; if he comes he is unlikely to go really high. In the former case we need a new leader and you know your name stands really high in the list. In the latter case it will not be easy to define his position both in the expedition as a whole and in the assault proper. But his deputy and climbing leader might then have to be a much younger man. This will probably be settled within 10 days and to my great regret during my absence. So we shall see what comes for you. Don't raise your hopes too high. I wish you were with us in Courmayeur.[10]

Basil never explained quite what these mysterious 'private reasons' were but it is obvious that he thought that Shipton was unfit.

Prompted by Basil Goodfellow's letters, on 23 July John Hunt wrote to Claude Elliott, the Himalayan Committee's elderly chairman:

I hope that you will forgive this letter, which comes from my heart, to tell you that should I be called on, I would be overjoyed to serve the great cause in any capacity and would spare no effort to encourage and assist in getting a British pair to the top.[11]

Eric Shipton could never have written this letter – the idea of Everest as a 'great cause' would have been completely alien to his way of thinking. It was, however, perfectly in tune with the mood of the Himalayan Committee. With the failure of the Swiss expedition, the war-drums of a great national expedition were beating increasingly loudly. On 28 July they reached a crescendo when Eric Shipton took a train up to London for a much-anticipated meeting with the Himalayan Committee.

Tension was high. Would he redeem himself and charm them back on to his side or would this be the moment when Eric Shipton resigned or was asked to stand down? Several members of the Committee were out of the country but six were present: Lawrence Kirwan, the Secretary of the RGS, R.W. Lloyd, the Committee treasurer, Sir Claremont Skrine, the sixty-four year old former British consul to Kashgar, Harry Tobin, a seventy-three- year-old former soldier and founder of the Himalayan Club, Colonel D.G. Lowndes, a former soldier and plant collector, and Claude Elliott, the Committee chairman and current provost of Eton. They were an august group who took themselves seriously and apart from Lawrence Kirwan, none were known to be fans of Eric Shipton. In the event, something quite extraordinary happened.

After a brief discussion of Cho Oyu, attention turned to Everest and the question of who should lead the expedition. To everyone's surprise, Eric Shipton declared that perhaps he was not the right man. He reaffirmed his aversion to large parties, acknowledged he was getting older and reiterated his dislike of the nationalistic element in mountaineering. He implied that he was slightly bored with Everest and that perhaps new thinking was needed. As he wrote in his autobiography, *That Untravelled World*:

> Long involvement with an unsolved problem can easily produce rigidity
> of outlook, a slow response to new ideas and it is often the case that a man
> with fewer inhibitions is better equipped to tackle it than one with greater
> experience.[12]

Eric was very ambivalent about Everest. He was not interested in big 'trophy' peaks and the idea of an international 'race for Everest' ran contrary to his belief that mountaineering should be above such petty rivalries. He had previously shared his doubts with both Christopher Summerhayes, the British ambassador to Nepal, and Basil Goodfellow. On the other hand, Everest had been so important to him for so long that it was part of his identity.

That day, Eric Shipton's characteristically honest self-criticism either spiked the guns of his detractors or perplexed them to such an extent that they ended up talking him into taking on the job.

This was an extraordinary turn of events, which ran against the tide of the previous two weeks. It would have been one thing for Eric to turn up at the meeting and win everyone over with a stirring speech and a healthy portion of humble pie but instead he was unsettlingly candid. Claude Elliott did suggest appointing an 'assault leader' who would take over for the final stages of the climb but Eric Shipton was unsure about this and Elliott did not press the point. Instead, Eric nominated Charles Evans as his deputy leader and asked if he could also be made the official organiser. The discussion then moved on to selection of team members and the important question of oxygen equipment before the meeting broke up and they said goodbye for the summer.

The 28 July meeting was one of those occasions when everyone came away with a slightly different idea of what had been agreed. Even though he had deferred to Eric Shipton on the day, the Committee's chairman, Claude Elliott, immediately wrote to John Hunt, offering him the role of expedition organiser and reiterating that Eric Shipton would not be in sole charge:

> *We decided to offer him [Eric Shipton] the leadership on the understanding that that there would be a deputy leader who would take over when Shipton had gone as high as he thought right or could and who would probably lead or direct the final assault. Shipton accepted the leadership on those terms.*[13]

Eric Shipton, on the other hand, left the meeting believing that he had been reconfirmed as leader and would choose his own deputy. A letter went to Charles Evans, still in India, offering him the organising secretary's role. In case he was unavailable, Charles Wylie and

Alfred Gregory were also sounded out. Within a few days Eric had written to Ed Hillary, George Lowe and Harry Ayres, (another New Zealander, highly recommended by Ed Hillary), inviting them to join the expedition. Lawrence Kirwan compiled a long memo listing the practical issues that had to be addressed. Soon there were committees for everything from oxygen to high-altitude diet.

However, the story was not quite over yet.

When Basil Goodfellow returned from the Alps in early August, he was amazed to hear Eric Shipton had been appointed leader. Having heard Eric's doubts in July, Basil assumed he would have resigned the leadership or that at the very least the Himalayan Committee would have delayed its decision. On 12 August, he sent John Hunt an eight-page letter and, ignoring the other offers that had been recently been made, invited him to become organising secretary. He made it very clear that he thought John Hunt should be appointed deputy leader, regardless of Eric Shipton's desire to have Charles Evans.

Basil Goodfellow's letter was long and rather rambling but it was undoubtedly heartfelt. He began by stating that Shipton was the right leader but it was obvious that he didn't really believe this, as he revealed a few pages in:

> Shipton is altogether too gentle, far too vague in matters of organisation
> in detail for us to believe that without an infusion of fresh blood, Everest
> '53 not be another damp squib.[14]

Peter Lloyd, one of Basil Goodfellow's allies on the Himalayan Committee and another admirer of John Hunt, wrote to him in even more candid terms:

> I'm very much hoping that you're going to take on Everest next year as it
> seems to me that you're the obvious choice for it. Eric, I'm sure, has been
> to Everest too often and has grown sick of it; the Cho Oyu fiasco makes it
> necessary to face these things and to put our house in order.[15]

No one criticised Eric Shipton in public; after all, his appointment as leader had appeared in the press but behind the scenes it was very different. Basil Goodfellow had too much respect for Eric to stage an outright coup but he invited John Hunt to come over from Germany for a meeting at the RGS. It transpired that Charles Evans could not be released from his hospital to work as expedition organiser, so the role was open. In Goodfellow's ideal world, John Hunt would win Shipton over and become both his organiser in London and his deputy on Everest. It did not work out that way.

The two men met at the Everest Office in the RGS on the morning of 22 August. Eric Shipton had not been privy to any of the letters between Goodfellow and Hunt and thought that he was talking to a potential organiser who might also become an expedition member but never his deputy leader. John Hunt thought that this was his chance to impress and admitted in his biography, *Life is Meeting*, that he appeared far too eager.

Shipton showed Hunt some photographs and maps of Everest and discussed potential routes through the Khumbu Icefall but it quickly became obvious that their temperaments were very different. Instinctively, Eric Shipton was drawn to quiet men and repelled by anyone known as a 'tiger' or a 'thruster'. Inevitably, the meeting ended unhappily; John Hunt promised to write to Eric with his thoughts but he left Britain disappointed, convinced that he would not be taking part in the 1953 expedition. A few days later Major Charles Wylie was appointed official organising secretary.

As Eric prepared to leave for a family holiday in Cornwall, everything seemed to be on track. Charles Wylie had a preliminary list of things to do; Alfred Gregory, a veteran of the Cho Oyu expedition, was preparing to take a party of Everest hopefuls to the Alps in early September and work had started on new oxygen sets. The Swiss announced they were going back to Everest in the autumn of 1952 to make a second attempt but no one had ever made a real success of a post-monsoon expedition to the Himalayas, so the odds of reaching the summit were low. The crisis over Eric's leadership, however, was far from finished.

Throughout the summer there had been small but continual reminders of Eric Shipton's casual attitude to organisation. In the middle of August a huge pile of gear from the Cho Oyu expedition arrived at the RGS in unlabelled bags. Inside, personal items were jumbled up with delicate scientific equipment. On August 18, Lawrence Kirwan sent Eric Shipton an angry letter complaining that some pieces of surveying equipment had arrived 'in a disgraceful state ... they were packed in kitbags which were unlabelled together with crampons and similar gear. The result is that the glasses have been smashed.' This was not Eric Shipton's fault; he was the expedition leader, not the chief packer, but it was not the only problem. The Himalayan Committee had also received a demand for £600 from the War Office in lieu of lost and damaged equipment from the 1951 reconnaissance expedition and in addition, a demand from the Bombay Customs Office for excise duty on a set of pressure gauges. They had been imported into India for experiments on Cho Oyu but had not been documented as having left the country. It transpired that they had been abandoned on the mountain.

Some of the expedition's most important supporters were also grumbling. In July, Basil Goodfellow lunched with Ralph Deakin, one of the foreign editors of *The Times*. Deakin had made it plain that his bosses were unhappy that Eric Shipton had provided so few dispatches from Cho Oyu and were particularly annoyed with him for giving an interview to Reuters news agency just before he returned to England. Deakin, a sometimes spiky and difficult man, added that the news value of Everest had diminished because the Swiss had done so well in 1952. He warned Goodfellow that *The Times* would probably only offer

£5000, half the amount it had originally proposed, for the rights to the 1953 expedition.

The Medical Research Council also continued to have doubts. When Lawrence Kirwan wrote to them to ask for assistance in developing oxygen sets for the 1953 expedition, Sir Harold Himsworth, the Secretary of the MRC, warned him that they might not be willing to take part, because of the conduct of the Cho Oyu expedition. After several letters and meetings Sir Harold was assuaged but it was embarrassing to receive such criticism from an organisation that everyone hoped would play an important role in the preparations.

None of these were major crises but cumulatively they added to the feeling of chaos surrounding Eric Shipton. Much more seriously, at the end of August several members of the Himalayan Committee began arguing in private that the leadership question should be revisited. The fact that Eric and John Hunt's meeting in late August had gone so badly did not stop Basil Goodfellow from contacting the army to check if Hunt might be released for the expedition. He continued writing to him in very bullish tones:

> I find that feeling is running very high on the question of leadership. Most individual members of the Committee wish to see you appointed deputy leader and some would be glad to see EES [Eric Shipton] resign and you appointed leader in his place.[16]

The final act in the drama began on 28 August with a memo from Basil Goodfellow:

> To all members of the Himalayan Committee:
>
> Urgent matters concerning Everest 1953 demand that a meeting of the Himalayan Committee be held as soon as possible after Mr Shipton's return from holiday on September 8th.[17]

Basil suggested 11 September and drew up an agenda. The first item was a call for a written report on the Cho Oyu expedition; the second was a discussion of the deputy leadership.

When Eric Shipton came back from holiday, he was given no indication of the conversations that had gone on behind the scenes. He installed himself in the RGS and wrote letters to expedition members and sponsors. He even found time to test a new design of tent, pitching it on the lawn at the back of the building.

Just after 10a.m. on Thursday 11, Eric Shipton and Charles Wylie took a taxi to the Alpine Club on South Audley Street. Compared to the Queen Anne splendour of the RGS, the Alpine Club's premises were distinctly low-key, a small, not particularly convivial ground floor of a town house in Mayfair. Its main attraction was a large lecture hall; otherwise there wasn't much else than a famously echoey toilet and a few offices.

The meeting began with the approval of the previous set of minutes. Then Eric Shipton was asked to produce a series of reports on the performance of individual members of the Cho Oyu expedition, as well as notes on equipment. After a formal announcement that Charles Evans, Eric Shipton's preferred choice for deputy leader, would not be available to work in London, Eric and Charles Wylie were asked to leave the room while the Committee discussed alternative deputies.

Both men thought that this was a bit odd. Why was Eric asked to leave the room? Did he not have a say in choosing his deputy? He and Charles Wylie sat outside for almost an hour, wondering what was going on.

Inside the room, one by one, the Committee members proceeded to damn Eric's reputation in no uncertain terms. Colonel Harry Tobin asserted that the expedition needed a 'more forceful and dynamic personality'[18] if it were to succeed and live up to its responsibility to the nation and the Commonwealth. Next came Colonel D.G. George

Lowndes. He criticised Shipton's diffidence at the previous meeting and reminded everyone that they had a responsibility to their financial backers to put on a serious attempt and not simply to give members 'a holiday in the Himalayas'. James Wordie, the venerable President of the RGS, who had proclaimed Eric Shipton's leadership at the end of June, said that he had never thought Eric Shipton should be the leader and that John Hunt should be appointed instead. In deference to Shipton's 'feelings', he suggested appointing him 'adviser' to the expedition. Sir Claremont Skrine, like Shipton a former British Consul-General in Kashgar, seconded Harry Tobin's comments and suggested that Shipton should be retained as overall leader because of his skill at writing and his good relationship with the Sherpas, but that the leadership on the mountain should be in other hands. R.W. Lloyd, the Committee's treasurer, called for Hunt to be given full power. George Finch, a distinguished climber and chemist, who was standing in for Peter Lloyd, argued against the idea of joint leadership, preferring to designate Eric Shipton as the expedition 'adviser'. None of these comments subsequently appeared in the official minute book, although they were recorded in detail in a memo.

No one fought for Eric Shipton. His two most ardent supporters, Lawrence Kirwan and Lawrence Wager, a respected climber and geologist who had reached 28,000 ft on the fourth British Everest expedition, in 1933, were both out of the country and unable to attend.

Claude Elliott, the Himalayan Committee's chairman, vacillated. He wanted to find a compromise that might include Shipton. He reminded everyone that at the previous meeting they had offered Eric the job and continued to pursue the idea of joint leadership along the lines of the Swiss expedition. A statement was drafted to present to Eric:

That the Committee felt that as it was now necessary to recognise that the expedition was of national importance, the party should be strengthened by the association of a man of dynamic personality with the leader. Two men were considered, Dr Evans and Col Hunt. The Committee felt that the man chosen must be available in London as soon as possible, in order to take charge of the organisation. The Committee also felt that he should be in sole command after the base camp. They therefore wished to suggest to Mr Shipton that he should accept Col Hunt as co-leader, to be sole leader from the base camp and to be given spheres of responsibility elsewhere which would be defined.[19]

Eric Shipton was invited back but most of the committee withdrew, leaving Elliott, Goodfellow and Wordie to put forward the proposition.

Eric was utterly shocked. He thought that the Himalayan Committee's behaviour was a little odd but no one had given him any indication that his leadership was under threat. When they talked about deputy leader and 'co-leader', it was now clear that they really meant John Hunt would take over the expedition and that he would play a supporting role. If he accepted their proposal, he would take a secondary role during the organisational phase in London and on the expedition itself, once it reached Base Camp. What were they really offering him – responsibility for the boat trip to Nepal and the walk to Namche Bazaar? It was impossible for him to agree to those terms.

As a concession to the Committee, Eric Shipton agreed to invite John Hunt to join the team and become a second organising secretary but he drew the line at appointing him deputy. If, however, the Committee felt that it would be best for the expedition, Eric declared that he would stand down as leader. Furthermore he added that if Hunt were appointed in his place, he would resign from the expedition altogether.

Eric left the room and re-joined Charles Wylie. Wylie, the most gentlemanly of English gentlemen, had spent much of the Second

World War in a Japanese prisoner-of-war camp. He was not someone prone to melodramatics. However, this day was so inscribed on his memory that fifty years later he remembered it vividly:

Eric was in there for a couple of minutes and he came out again and said:

'I've been offered dual leadership of the expedition. What do you think of that?'

And I said:

'I don't think anything of it at all. You can't have two leaders. That's asking for trouble.'[20]

Inside the committee room Claude Elliott informed the other members of Shipton's response. They agreed to accept his resignation and appoint John Hunt as the expedition leader. Claude Elliott was an instinctive compromiser and felt deeply uncomfortable about what they had done, even though he was as convinced as everyone else that John Hunt would do a better job than Eric. He tried to revisit the idea of taking on John Hunt as 'deputy' leader but D.G. Lowndes would have none of it. He reminded Elliott that the Committee had decided to offer the leadership to John Hunt. Half an hour later, Eric Shipton was invited back for a second time.

It was not Claude Elliott's finest moment. In a memo written years later, the official minute-taker, Tom Blakeney, remembered that Claude Elliott was so flustered he couldn't quite bring himself to tell Shipton what they had decided. He dithered for so long that Eric had to put the question himself:

'Am I to understand that Hunt is to be offered the leadership?'[21]

Claude Elliott finally said 'yes' and Eric asked for more time to consider his position. The meeting broke up.

On the taxi ride back to the Everest Office at the RGS, Eric Shipton and Charles Wylie sat in stunned silence. Intentionally or not, Eric had been utterly humiliated. Why this sudden change of heart and why had no one discussed this with him earlier? He had been very candid about his doubts at the meeting on 28 July; why had the Committee not reciprocated?

On 12 September Basil Goodfellow sent a telegram to John Hunt to offer him the leadership. He immediately said yes. Four days later, Eric wrote a very dignified letter to Claude Elliott, resigning from the team. The drama wasn't quite over.

As the news of Shipton's replacement leaked out, there was widespread amazement and anger amongst his supporters on the team and in the British climbing world. Who was John Hunt and what had he ever done? Why had the team not been consulted by the Committee?

When Lawrence Kirwan and Lawrence Wager came back in mid-September, both were outraged. Kirwan suspected that the 11 September meeting had been scheduled deliberately to coincide with their absence. Another meeting was called for 24 September, to reconsider the issue.

This was an even more tense affair. Tom Bourdillon appeared in person to call for the return of Eric Shipton. Lawrence Wager conveyed a message on behalf of Charles Evans and several other members of the 1951 and 1952 expeditions, also calling for Eric Shipton to be reinstated. Lawrence Wager and Lawrence Kirwan made their own protests and refused to endorse the decision made at the previous meeting. The Committee wobbled a little but ultimately stood firm. D.G. Lowndes pointedly remarked that if they changed their minds yet again, they might as well all resign immediately and admit that they weren't up to managing anything. When it came to the vote, Kirwan and Wager were defeated six to two.

In the weeks that followed John Hunt wrote several letters to Eric Shipton, commiserating and trying to persuade him to re-join the team. Claude Elliott even offered Eric Shipton a seat on the Himalayan Committee but unsurprisingly he said no to both Hunt's and Elliott's suggestions. Eric's first priority was to find a job that would support his family but he continued to lecture in public about Everest. Although most people remarked how well he took everything, he was deeply hurt and angered by what had happened.

In November 1952 Eric Shipton wrote to James Wordie:

> That the Committee on maturer consideration of what I had said at the first meeting, or of other factors unknown to me, should wish to reverse their decision is understandable and would have my full sympathy. To do so without consulting me, without keeping me informed of the trend of shifting opinion or of the private discussions which must have preceded their volte-face, without, even in the event, informing me of their reasons for it, to do so without troubling to ascertain the views of several absent members of the Committee or of those of my colleagues on the recent expedition, many of whom, with the Committee's approval, I had invited to join the next expedition, was an action that cannot escape censure.[22]

It was a dignified and damning letter. Only time would tell if the Committee had made the correct decision but few people doubted that the members had treated Eric Shipton badly. To invite him to become the leader despite his reservations and then barely a month later to change their minds was hardly cricket. Even if it was the right outcome, as many maintained, it had been done in the wrong way.

The controversy haunted Britain's mountaineering establishment for many years. When Eric Shipton published his autobiography, *That Untravelled World*, in 1969, he pulled his punches after his friends advised him to tone down his criticism. However, when Charles Evans reviewed Eric's book for *The Alpine Journal*, he wrote that Eric had been removed from the leadership by an 'unworthy device'. This prompted a bout of soul-searching. The Himalayan Committee's former chairman, Claude Elliott, wrote a long memo in which he attempted to justify his actions. Naturally, continuing in the great tradition of secrecy which characterised the whole affair, it was buried in the archives, marked 'Very Private'.[23]

Looking back almost sixty years later, it is clear that the leadership controversy was a crucial moment in the 1953 expedition. Ironically, the talk in Tom Bourdillon's letter of early June, about doing things properly and taking Everest seriously, had rebounded on Eric Shipton and his supporters. The Himalayan Committee had behaved ruthlessly and, some might argue, shabbily, but they genuinely believed that if British climbers were going to seize the day in 1953, they would have to learn the lessons of the Cho Oyu expedition and that meant a change of leadership.

The sad fact for Eric and his supporters was that this was not a battle between two opposing candidates, as it is sometimes presented. John Hunt was never interviewed by the Himalayan Committee and was only really known to two of its members. It was all about Eric Shipton and the fact that so many had lost faith in him. Even his old friends, such as Campbell Secord, had turned against him. Eric had a fantastic climbing record in the 1930s and had skilfully led the 1951 Everest reconnaissance expedition but the Cho Oyu expedition had been so shambolic at times that it almost looked as if he were deliberately trying to sabotage his leadership credentials.

Eric was profoundly and utterly out of sympathy with the 'Everest establishment'. He had no time for committees, subcommittees or the paraphernalia of a 'national' expedition. The Himalayan Committee wanted someone utterly focused on winning the race, someone who shared their sense of ownership of Everest and who was demonstrably well organised. This wasn't Eric Shipton but it was a good description of Colonel John Hunt.

In September 1952 Hunt found himself in the invidious position of becoming leader after a scandal and inheriting a team whose strongest members were loyal to his predecessor. In five months time he had to travel to Nepal, climb a mountain that he had only glimpsed in the distance and all with the eyes of the world upon him. Some of those eyes expected, indeed hoped, that he would fail. He might have wondered if this was the opportunity of a lifetime or a poisoned chalice.

Chapter 5

A PAPER MOUNTAIN

On 8 October 1952 Charles Wylie looked down from his window on the first floor of the RGS. A large shooting brake, laden with skis, pulled into the car park below. A few moments later, Colonel John Hunt emerged. He had just arrived from Germany and looked forward to a week packed with meetings and conferences. With the exception of Charles Wylie, a career soldier from a military family, who had no fear of military officers the others involved in Everest were wary. As Basil Goodfellow wrote to John Hunt in late-September:

> There is some nervousness that the expedition will become a military operation, not in the British mountaineering tradition.[1]

Even the Foreign Office and the British ambassador to Nepal, Christopher Summerhayes, were concerned that Hunt's military rank should be downplayed in any contacts with the Nepalese government. It was clear to Charles Wylie, from the letters and telegrams he had already received, that John Hunt was going to be very different to Eric Shipton but would he turn out to be the martinet that some feared?

John Hunt was born in 1910 in the Indian hill town of Simla. His was a military family. Like Eric Shipton, he had lost his father at an early age, a casualty of the First World War, and was brought up by a strong but rather distant mother. After that the similarities ended. John Hunt was an archetypal high achiever. He graduated from Sandhurst military academy at the top of his year, winning a gold medal and an ornamental sword. He had then returned to India as an officer in the British Army.

During the Second World War he was appointed Chief Instructor of the Commando Mountain and Snow Warfare School in Wales, before seeing active service in Europe. He won his DSO in the bitter fighting of the Italian campaign and his CBE in Greece, where he spent several very tense months keeping the peace after the country was liberated. By 1952 he had reached the rank of Colonel. However, behind his impressive record and military background was a rather surprising person. He was a distant relative of Sir Richard Burton, the distinctly unconventional nineteenth-century explorer and translator of the *Kama Sutra*. At first, like Burton, John Hunt had not felt entirely comfortable in the army. He gained a reputation as a poor mixer and 'difficult chap', who preferred to play rugby with the lower ranks rather than polo with his fellow officers.

During his time off duty, he indulged his two great passions: skiing and mountaineering. After learning to climb on family holidays to the Alps, in 1935 he took part in his first 'proper' expedition, to Peak 36, now known as Saltoro Kangri, in the Karakoram Mountains. It was a small-scale, loosely organised affair, but tremendously fulfilling. He and his friends did not succeed in reaching the summit but, despite terrible weather, they made a determined effort. Their adventures were reported in the Indian papers and even mentioned in *The Times*.

In the same year, at the age of twenty-five, John Hunt was elected to the Alpine Club and the RGS. To his amazement, he was invited for a trial in the Alps for the 1936 British Everest expedition. He met its leader, Hugh Ruttledge, and the famous British climber, Frank Smythe, but just when everything seemed to be going well, he was 'ploughed' (deselected) by the expedition's medical committee. They had detected a heart murmur and warned him that, never mind Everest, he should take care when climbing the stairs.

For someone so used to success this was a bitter blow which made no sense considering his climbing record. He took it very badly and never forgot his rejection by the doctors. His depression lifted only in the following year when he married Joy Mowbray-Green, a Wimbledon-standard tennis player. Soon she too was converted to mountaineering and they spent their holidays climbing in the Himalayas.

After the war John Hunt was stationed in France and Germany. His skills as a linguist and a mountaineer won him membership of the *Groupe de Haute Montagne*, an élite French climbing club. In the early 1950s, John Hunt was probably better known in French climbing circles than in British; he numbered the famous mountaineers Gaston Rébuffat and Maurice Herzog among his friends. When Basil Goodfellow contacted him about the Everest expedition, the offer came totally out of the blue. Ironically, when he was dropped from the 1936 Everest expedition, Eric Shipton had been very kind to him. Both John and his wife, Joy, found the leadership controversy very difficult.

However, that morning, as he climbed the stairs to the Everest Office, he was very firmly focused on the future not the past. His approach could not have been more different to Eric Shipton's. Unlike his predecessor, who adhered to the 'less is more' school of planning, John Hunt was determined to climb Everest on paper long before he set foot in the Himalayas. His arrival at the RGS was preceded by a blizzard of letters and memos which continued for the next six months. One of his first moves would have caused Eric Shipton to fall out of his chair: he asked the Himalayan Committee for a written directive regarding the aims and objectives of the forthcoming expedition. Eric had no time for the bureaucracy of a big expedition but John Hunt was totally at ease.

By the end of October he had received his directive and used it as the foundation of a long document, the *Basis for Planning*, which formed the template for both the Everest preparations and the climb itself. John Hunt was at pains to point out that it was only meant to set the general strategy, rather than literally dictate their tactics on the mountain, but in the event it was remarkable how closely it was followed. The first paragraph was utterly unambiguous:

> *The ultimate aim of the Expedition, as defined by the Sponsoring Authority, is the ascent of Everest during 1953 by a member or members of the party. This aim may appear self-evident but it is of vital importance that it should be borne constantly in mind, both during the preparatory phase and, later, in the field. All planning and preparation must lead us methodically towards the achievement of that aim.*[2]

This expedition would have one goal and one goal only. It would not be a reconnaissance; its purpose was not to fill in blanks on the map or map new peaks and passes. Everything, man and machine, would be geared towards winning the race to Everest. Years later, in the dedication page of his first autobiography, Ed Hillary summed up the difference between John Hunt and Eric Shipton perfectly:

> *To*
> ERIC SHIPTON
> *for his inspiration and unquenchable spirit*
> *To*
> JOHN HUNT
> *for his courage and singleness of purpose*[3]

This absolute single-mindedness was the hallmark of Hunt's leadership and exactly what most members of the Himalayan Committee wanted.

During his first few weeks in Britain there were plenty of hands to shake, meetings to chair and documents to be read. Top of John Hunt's priority list was selecting and confirming his team. This was never going to be easy. Basil Goodfellow wrote several times during September to warn him that much ill-feeling remained over the Shipton affair. Eric had given formal invitations to three New Zealanders – Ed Hillary, George Lowe and Harry Ayres – and made informal commitments to Tom Bourdillon and Charles Evans. However, there was serious doubt that any of them would come. Tom Bourdillon sent the Himalayan Committee a letter of resignation and Charles Evans was thought to be very close to Eric. Basil Goodfellow warned that the New Zealanders would be very difficult to win over, because they too were very loyal.

It might have been easier to start from scratch but John Hunt knew that he had to take several of Eric Shipton's men. There weren't enough other British climbers with good Himalayan experience. It was obvious from their climbing records that Shipton's core team contained the best mountaineers from the British expeditions of 1951 and 1952. In a letter written on 30 September Hunt acknowledged Basil Goodfellow's concerns but remained confident that he would be able to bring the doubters back on board:

> I shall work on the assumption that our attempt on Everest is far too big a matter for personal jealousies to intervene; I cannot believe that any of the personalities whom you have mentioned in your letter are so small-minded, as to withdraw their services to the cause, unless they have very much stronger reasons than I know of.[4]

Hunt wrote several times to Eric Shipton, seeking advice and, more crucially, asking him to intercede personally with the doubters on the Everest team.

There is a persistent myth that John Hunt had to be talked into taking Hillary and Lowe – Ed Hillary was one of the first people he contacted, in a letter of 16 October:

> *I believe that Eric Shipton has written to tell you about the change in the leadership of the 1953 Everest expedition; you may, in any case, have seen press reports. I expect that you must be feeling puzzled and disappointed that this should have come to pass; it is most unfortunate that it should have happened in this way and very bad luck on Eric Shipton.*
>
> *However, you will, I am sure, agree with me that there is only one way of looking at it – we must go ahead with the planning with a firm determination to get to the top.*[5]

Hunt withdrew Eric Shipton's invitation to the third New Zealander, Harry Ayres, on the grounds that, unlike his compatriots Hillary and Lowe, he was a professional mountain guide. As Hunt insisted many times over the coming year, and repeated for the rest of his life, this was a team of equals, both in their love of mountaineering and their amateur status. Despite Ed Hillary's admiration of Eric Shipton, before long he was corresponding regularly and flatteringly with his new leader.

About a week after he wrote to Ed Hillary, John Hunt went to Liverpool for lunch with two of the other Shipton loyalists, Charles Evans and Alfred Gregory. Hunt came through this test with flying colours. Both men agreed to sign up, though Alfred Gregory was taken aback by the suggestion that at thirty-nine, he might be too old to take part. On the following day Alfred sent Hunt a very humble letter saying that he had been profoundly shaken by the comment and insisting that he had been one of the best acclimatisers in the Cho Oyu party.

Bringing Tom Bourdillon back proved to be a tougher proposition but Hunt recognised from the beginning that he was vital to the team, both for his climbing ability and his technical expertise. Even though he had resigned from the team, Bourdillon continued working on a new design of oxygen set, which he hoped would be much more powerful than the traditional model. The Himalayan Committee's oxygen controller, Peter Lloyd, wasn't sure that it would be ready in time but John Hunt was happy to let the work continue. Scrawled on the back of a press release written in early October 1952, stored in the Everest archives of the RGS, is an intriguing hand-written note from John Hunt to Peter Lloyd:

I am very keen that Bourdillon should be kept sweet i.e. by continuing his present work but answering to the Himalayan Committee through you.[6]

John Hunt seems to have hoped that if Tom Bourdillon carried on working on the oxygen equipment, eventually he would be tempted back to the expedition. He may have been right but it took several interventions by Eric Shipton to convince Tom to take part.

Once he had secured Shipton's core group, John Hunt began casting about for new members. Whereas Eric Shipton had wanted a team of six, John Hunt and the Himalayan Committee believed a much larger party was needed, ideally ten or eleven climbers.

John Hunt's principal selection criteria were age, mountaineering record and availability. He received several letters from European hopefuls, all of whom he turned down. As the rejection letter stated, 'the policy is that our party should be an entirely British one'. This was not just for nationalistic reasons. John Hunt believed that his team should spend as much time as possible together before the expedition and that was obviously much easier if they were all British. He was prepared to make an exception for Ed Hillary and George Lowe because they already knew so many members of the team. Basil Goodfellow sent circulars to British mountaineering clubs and received dozens of applications and letters of recommendation for the remaining places. This trawl produced the team's two youngest climbers: George Band and Mike Westmacott.

At twenty-three, George Band was two years below Hunt's age requirement and was still a student at Cambridge University. Luckily for him, he met John Hunt shortly after completing an unusually long and successful season in the Alps. John Hunt was impressed, especially when George informed him that he had treated the whole thing like a 'military appreciation' or planning exercise. In a letter to Ed Hillary John Hunt wrote that George Band was 'an experiment' but he had high hopes.

Mike Westmacott was a twenty-seven-year-old statistician who worked at the Rothamsted agricultural research centre in Hertfordshire. He had written to Eric Shipton in the summer of 1952 but was called to interview by John Hunt. Like George Band, he had recently returned from a very good season in the Alps and had the added advantage that he spoke Urdu, having served as a sapper in India during the Second World War. Obviously, this would be an advantage for dealing with porters and Sherpas but as Mike wrote in the Alpine Journal's Everest 40th Anniversary edition in 1993, he didn't tell John Hunt, for typically modest reasons:

> I felt that this would hardly be fair to other aspirants, friends of mine who had not had the luck to serve in India. When with John Hunt, one bends over backwards to be fair.[7]

Mike Westmacott was on and off John Hunt's selection list for several weeks until his place was confirmed in early November.

Wilfrid Noyce, the third new member, was a schoolmaster and well-known mountaineering writer. He was the only climber already personally acquainted with John Hunt. They had both worked at the Mountain Warfare School in Wales during the war and later climbed together in the Lake District. The final member of the team was Charles Wylie, who had been working tirelessly as the expedition's organising secretary for the previous two months. Five candidates who didn't make the final selection were designated as official reserves.[8]

Like Eric Shipton before him, John Hunt was concerned not to let the tail become too large but was much more positive about the scientific aspects of the expedition. He committed himself to taking Griffith Pugh again, and promised to get him as high he could to conduct further physiological experiments. Hunt balked at the Medical Research Council's request that two physiologists should accompany the expedition but as a compromise agreed that the team doctor could act as Pugh's assistant.

Initially, the position was offered to Charles Evans but he said no. Fortunately, the other candidate, Michael Ward, the instigator of the 1951 Everest reconnaissance, was more amenable. Although he also wished to play a role in the climbing team, he was very interested in high-altitude medicine and Griffith Pugh's work.

Before the final letters of invitation were sent out, Pugh advised the Himalayan Committee that the proposed climbers for 1953 would need a thorough medical examination. Remembering his unhappy experience in 1935, John Hunt reluctantly agreed. This time, he left the RAF out and persuaded the Queen's physician, Lord Horder, to carry out the examinations. John Hunt asked Horder to look for 'the Excelsior Spirit' rather than hidden heart complaints.

By early November the team was in place and preparations began in earnest. Those who worried that John Hunt might be a sergeant major figure were proved wrong. John Hunt's twenty years in the army had turned him into a very effective leader. Instead of barking orders, he displayed an easy manner and a well-practised charm. George Band, who quickly became known as the team wit, jokingly compared him to Dale Carnegie, the well-known American management guru. 'He had all the techniques', George remembered, 'and you almost, at times, doubted if he was really being sincere and yet he was.' Hunt's particular obsession was team-building; he organised as many occasions as possible for everyone to come together, with regular meetings at the RGS as well as longer field tests in Snowdonia. Each member of the team was assigned a particular area of responsibility to share the workload and to make everyone feel involved.

George Band and Griffith Pugh were put in charge of expedition food. While Pugh reviewed the scientific evidence from previous expeditions and the dietary research he had carried out on Cho Oyu in 1952, George sent questionnaires about dietary preferences and called for suggestions for the 'luxuries' box. Looking at those questionnaires now, it is striking how some climbers were very specific and detailed about what they liked and disliked, while others seemed completely uninterested. Mike Westmacott claimed he had no dietary preferences at all, while Ed Hillary and George Lowe gave long lists of their likes – tinned fruit, salmon, dehydrated soup, dried fruit, chocolate, fresh stew, honey; and dislikes – pemmican, Grape-Nuts, service biscuits. George Band made one rather unhappy mistake over expedition sweets: in his first memo he told everyone that they would get five ounces each per day during the assault phase, only to later admit that he had meant five sweets per day.

If Ed Hillary thought the eleven thousand miles that separated Auckland from London might get him out of expedition chores, he was wrong. Hunt put him in charge of bedding and cooking equipment. Ed found a New Zealand supplier who offered a much better deal on down sleeping bags than the Canadian company used for Cho Oyu. He also offered to provide Hillary Honey, harvested on the family farm.

As the various members busied themselves in mid-November, researching their particular field, two major headaches remained for John Hunt and the Himalayan Committee. The first and most important was what the Swiss were doing. A second Swiss team had gone out in early September to make a post-Monsoon attempt on

Everest. They had a large, well-equipped party and much-improved oxygen equipment, with which they hoped to make a rapid dash for the top before the winter set in. To John Hunt's great frustration, there were few reports about them in the press and no one seemed quite sure how they were getting on. The second, linked, problem was money. The Himalayan Committee assumed that a large proportion of expedition funds would come from selling the newspaper and book rights but *The Times* refused to hand over any money until it was sure how the Swiss had fared.

This made life very difficult for the Himalayan Committee. If the Swiss succeeded in the autumn of 1952, it was not at all certain that the 1953 British Everest Expedition could go ahead. John Hunt suggested they should look for a Plan B, his favourite being Kanchengjunga, the third-highest mountain in the world. However, it was doubtful that another mountain would be as attractive to *The Times* or other potential sponsors.

John Hunt did not have time to sit and wait. He pressed hard to purchase and procure equipment and that meant spending money sooner, rather than later. Claude Elliott, the chairman of the Himalayan Committee, was much more circumspect, especially when he was informed that he and the other members of the Committee were personally liable for any debts incurred. He turned to R.W. Lloyd, the treasurer, for advice.

Robert Wylie Lloyd was an extraordinary figure. He was eighty-four years old, a confirmed bachelor who had risen from childhood poverty to become a successful businessman and the chairman of Christie's, the fine art auctioneers. Lloyd was a famous 'collector of collections', interested in everything from Turner paintings to Samurai swords. He wore an orchid in his lapel and owned a country house as well as chambers in London. However, his most famous characteristic was his meanness, which drove climbers to distraction.

After the 1951 reconnaissance expedition Lloyd tussled with

the Scottish climber Bill Murray over the repair of an umbrella that had been damaged in the field. Other members of the team had purchased umbrellas in Nepal, using expedition funds, so Bill Murray thought it reasonable that he should be allowed to put in an expenses claim to have his trusty umbrella refurbished, particularly when the expedition's costs were well within budget. Lloyd didn't see it like that and the two entered into a lengthy correspondence. Their battle climaxed with a familiar refrain from Robert Wylie Lloyd, guaranteed to annoy:

> *I am sure, when you think it over, you will feel with me that this was a holiday at the Himalayan Committee's expense.*[9]

Bill Murray's reply was succinct and to the point:

> *Trying to climb Everest is not enjoyable. It is unpleasant in the extreme.*[10]

When Ed Hillary submitted his expenses for the 1951 expedition, which included numerous receipts from Nepalese and Indian tea-houses, Lloyd was just as feisty and tight-fisted. 'Gentlemen', he admonished Hillary, 'pay for their own cups of tea.' To which Hillary replied, 'We're New Zealanders, not gentlemen.'

In spite of his meanness over small sums of the Himalayan Committee's money, Lloyd could be generous with his own. He offered the Himalayan Committee a bridging loan from his personal account and gave a substantial donation to the 1953 expedition. He also began a funding drive to solicit donations from the City of London as well as large British firms and sent a letter to the expedition's equipment suppliers asking for financial assistance:

> *The Himalayan Committee are finding the expenses very considerable and as this endeavour to climb Everest has become really a matter of national prestige (and we need something to raise our prestige in the*

East), I wonder if you could see your way to give us this amount as a donation towards the cost of the Expedition.[11]

This appeal met with limited success. Some companies offered their goods for free or at a substantial discount but others wrote back to say that they couldn't afford to. Big business was similarly reticent but gradually the money started to come in.

ICI were one of the first companies to make a large donation. With a significant overseas operation and a notable presence in India, they were just the kind of company to which R.W. Lloyd's invocation of British 'prestige in the East' was designed to appeal. The fact that Basil Goodfellow, Honorary Secretary of the Himalayan Committee, worked for ICI undoubtedly helped loosen its purse strings.

The Swiss expeditions of 1952 had been backed by the Swiss Foundation for Alpine Research but Hunt was able to draw upon a much bigger British military–industrial infrastructure that had developed during the Second World War and was still largely in place. The Royal Air Force had done a lot of work on masks and oxygen delivery systems and the Korean War had prompted the British and American armies to make improvements in cold-weather clothing. The Himalayan Committee was well connected in the British establishment and was able to secure direct funding for the salaries of Hunt, Wylie and Bourdillon and persuade the Medical Research Council and the RAF to provide their expertise and facilities for next to nothing.

During the Second World War, Britain's scientists had affectionately been mocked as 'boffins' but no one questioned their value. Men like Alan Turing, who helped decode the German High Command's 'Enigma' code and Barnes Wallis, the inventor of the bouncing bomb, made significant contributions to the war effort. Griffith Pugh, the Everest team's resident scientific adviser, was once memorably described to the Duke of Edinburgh as 'a boffin but nice'. Although he was not always taken as seriously as he would have liked, there was no doubt about the importance of Griffith Pugh's contribution, or that of the other 'backroom boys'.

In late September Pugh travelled to Switzerland to meet representatives of the Swiss Foundation for Alpine Research. He came back with equipment lists and detailed notes on the performance of the both the Swiss climbers and the Sherpas. He was convinced that insufficient time to acclimatise had played a significant part in their failure on Everest. Poor diet and low intake of liquids had also contributed. At the climax of the expedition, when they should have been at peak fitness, they showed clear signs of exhaustion. The fact that they were drinking so little that they were clinically dehydrated compounded their problems.

Considerable effort went into developing the best possible oxygen equipment for the British team. Peter Lloyd, a member of the Himalayan Committee, was the expedition's 'oxygen controller'. Lloyd (no relation to the treasurer R.W. Lloyd) was a gifted engineer, who had worked on a ground-breaking jet engine project during the Second World War. He was a powerful mountaineer, who had been on British expeditions to Nanda Devi and Everest before the Second World War. As a mountaineer, Peter Lloyd once said, he would prefer Everest to be climbed without supplementary oxygen but as a scientist and engineer he was sure it was needed. In 1938, he had tested oxygen on Everest and come back convinced of its benefits.

In autumn 1952, while Griffith Pugh analysed the results of his research on Cho Oyu, Peter Lloyd set to work on the practical details of getting the sets designed and manufactured. His principal assistant was Alf Bridge, a rock climber by inclination and gas engineer by trade. Alf worked tirelessly to liaise between the many different private firms and official bodies involved, clocking up so many miles that R.W. Lloyd, the Himalayan Committee's treasurer, complained about his petrol expenses.

Dr John Cotes, a specialist in respiratory medicine, was drafted to adapt RAF masks for use on the mountain. He invited the team to the Institute of Aviation Medicine at Farnborough to experience the perils of high altitude in a decompression chamber. George Band and Griffith Pugh were among the guinea pigs.

George Band sat on a bench in the chamber, holding a clipboard, as the air was gradually pumped out and the pressure reduced, to simulate conditions on the summit of Everest. Then his oxygen mask was removed and he was repeatedly asked to sign his name on the clipboard. It seemed like an easy task, until he slipped into unconsciousness. When his mask was put back on and he was revived with a blast of oxygen, he was unaware that anything had happened. George was shocked to discover that, to everyone's amusement, while he was unconscious the RAF doctor had removed his wristwatch and tie.

When Griffith Pugh's mask was removed, his lips turned blue and he twitched uncontrollably before falling to the floor. When the RAF doctor tried to re-fit his mask, Pugh fought him off. For the benefit of posterity, and cinema audiences to come, the episode was immortalised by Tom Stobart, the cameraman (who shot the official film of the expedition). It was all good clean fun but demonstrated the insidious danger of oxygen starvation at high altitude, an invisible killer which affected both mental and physical abilities.

Many private British companies were involved in designing specialist clothing and footwear. The expedition benefitted from two new designs of climbing boot, one for the early stages and one for the assault on the summit. Wartime research had shown that 1 lb on the foot was the equivalent of 4 lb on the shoulders, so it was important that footwear should be light as well as warm. In 1952, the Swiss team used reindeer-skin boots, the traditional cold-weather footwear of Finnish Lapps, but the British team took a much more modern approach. Their low-altitude boots weighed just 3 lb 12 oz and were insulated with possum fur sandwiched between two layers of leather. The higher-altitude model was a more radical design, with a kid leather exterior wrapped around an inch-thick insulating layer of kapok fibres and an inner sweat-resistant lining. The soles were made from a new type of microcellular rubber. The combined efforts of no fewer than thirty-five British firms were needed to manufacture one pair. Under Griffith Pugh's supervision, boots were tested both in the field and in cold chambers, where unlucky guinea pigs sat for hours, monitoring the state of their toes.

Given the publicity that the expedition received, there were no end of madcap suggestions from around the world. An Israeli inventor sent plans for a harpoon with a rope at one end and an incendiary bomb at the other. On impact, it was intended to sink into the ice on a slope which would then refreeze, giving the climbers a firm anchoring point to haul their way up. Another designed a helium balloon to assist the climbers on their ascent. Its only snag was that to make any impact, it had to be enormous. Solutions offered to the oxygen problem ranged from laying a rubber pipeline from the South Col to the summit, to providing each man with a small set of bellows attached to their leg, which would compress the atmospheric air and allow them to breathe a higher proportion of oxygen. Needless to say, none of these ideas were taken up but John Hunt entertained some slightly less bizarre, though ultimately equally fruitless, suggestions.

One was a type of catapult that was intended to fire a grapnel hook and a trailing rope over crevasses. British commandos had considered this device and Hunt went so far as to stage an experiment in the garden of the RGS. With Hunt and Wylie holding opposite sides of the elasticated rope, the catapult was drawn back and the grapnel launched. John Hunt watched in horror as it flew through the air at high speed, towards the busy highway of Kensington Gore. If it hadn't been for a large tree at the end of the lawn, the spiky grapnel might have sailed happily over the wall and embedded itself in a passing taxi. Unsurprisingly, the catapult was abandoned as being too unpredictable.

Another of John Hunt's innovations was taken up, though it provoked a long-running and rather comical stream of correspondence. The idea was to take a small two-inch mortar along as an avalanche gun to clear the Lhotse Face of unstable snow. The idea was first mooted as a PS to a letter sent in late November to Colonel Proud, the splendidly-named military liaison officer at the British embassy in Kathmandu. It was followed by letters to the British War Office, which was asked to provide the mortar and the bombs from their stocks.

All seemed to be proceeding smoothly until Colonel Proud wrote to Charles Wylie in January 1953 to warn him that the Nepalese government was having second thoughts. Officials were worried about antagonising both the Chinese government and their own people, some of whom believed that a severe earthquake in 1934 had been caused by a British flight over Everest. The idea of bringing a mortar to fire at the mountains dubbed 'the abode of the gods' sounded distinctly irreverent and likely to provoke their anger. Several letters later Hunt was given permission, only for the expedition's shipping firm, P&O, to refuse to carry any bombs. Instead, they had to be procured from the Indian Army. When, a few weeks later, Charles Wylie asked for permission to take two hunting rifles, there were inevitable jokes that the expedition was cover for a military coup.

If there was a real weakness in John Hunt's planning, it was one that he shared with the Himalayan Committee: how to deal with the press. On the day he arrived in Britain John Hunt had found himself in the middle of a minor press furore over his appointment. No one had informed the British newspapers that the leadership had changed; only when Eric Shipton went to Norway for a series of lectures did the story come out in the Oslo papers. The Himalayan Committee was forced to issue a hurried press statement, in which they claimed that the transition from Shipton to Hunt had been completely amicable and that there had been, as the *Manchester Guardian* reported on 9 October, 'no behind the scenes quarrel'.

The *News Chronicle*, the popular newspaper whose offer of sponsorship had been rebuffed by the Himalayan Committee in 1951, looked as if it was going to create a fuss. It pointedly reported that John Hunt had never been to Everest, whereas Eric Shipton was a veteran of no fewer than twelve Himalayan expeditions. However, Eric Shipton's sacking did not develop into a running story.

The bigger issue that the Himalayan Committee failed to understand was that if it were to promote Everest 1953 as a 'national' expedition, it would inevitably garner a lot of press attention. This would make any exclusive deal with *The Times* a source of irritation to other British newspapers, which might naturally claim that they too should be part of this great patriotic story. In the event, dozens of journalists, from both the British and the world's press, were sent to cover the expedition but because of the *Times* deal, all the Himalayan Committee could offer were a few crumbs from *The Times's* table. The unsustainability of this position became more and more apparent as the months went on.

For the moment, John Hunt had more pressing issues to think about. At the beginning of December 1952 he flew to Switzerland with Charles Wylie, Alfred Gregory, Griffith Pugh and a huge pile of equipment they hoped to test. Their chosen outdoor laboratory was the Jungfraujoch, in the Bernese Alps. They arrived on 3 December in the middle of a snowstorm and had a real battle to put their tents up. It was −20°C and the nearby mountains were wreathed in cloud. Over the following days they had two further bad weather days and another two when the sun shone; an ideal, if uncomfortable, variety of weather in which to test their gear.

On their last evening Alfred Gregory and Griffith Pugh slipped off to a nearby hotel for a well-earned beer. John Hunt and Charles Wylie stayed behind in camp. As soon as they reached the bar, Alfred

Gregory heard some great news (for the British expedition): the second Swiss attempt had failed.

This expedition had been a rushed affair. The Swiss went into the field too late in the autumn and even though they had more advanced equipment, including much better oxygen sets than had been available in the spring, they laboured under two major disadvantages: colder weather and shorter days. From the very beginning, there were serious problems. Two porters died of cold on the way in and the expedition leader, Gabriel Chevalley, one of the two veterans of the spring attempt, came down with a dose of fever caused by an infected leech bite.

When they reached the top of the Khumbu Icefall, the Swiss climbers were amazed to find that the rope bridge that they had set up during the spring expedition was still in place. They made rapid progress and reached the Lhotse Face in late October, only for Chevalley to make a very strange mistake. Despite having declared in several newspaper articles, written over the summer, that he intended to take the longer and less direct approach, climbing up the Lhotse Glacier before traversing left towards the Geneva Spur and the South Col, he opted to head straight up to the rocks of the Geneva Spur. Once again, this meant having no intermediate camps on the Lhotse Face. It was an incomprehensible decision, only reversed after a fatal accident. On 31 October, a huge block of ice flew down the Lhotse Face, hit one Sherpa, Mingma Dorji, and caused three others to fall off. Mingma Dorji died soon afterwards from a perforated lung and the others were so badly hurt that they were unable to play any further role. Gabriel Chevalley decided to change route but it was too late.

On 19 November, Raymond Lambert, Ernst Reiss, Tenzing and seven Sherpas finally reached the South Col. It was so cold and windy that they could barely summon the energy to erect their tents. Their food was frozen and it was very hard to boil water. On 20 November, they made a brave but unsuccessful attempt to re-establish their old high camp at 27,265 ft on the South-East Ridge. On the way up they passed the remains of an eagle, flattened against the snow. It was a bad omen. After just 700 ft, battling against the bitter cold and the wind, they gave up and turned back. They abandoned almost all their equipment before retreating down the Lhotse Face, feeling lucky to escape with their lives. As Gabriel Chevalley wrote in *Forerunners to Everest*, they had been 'purged from Everest'.

The Swiss failure was a huge fillip for the British team. John Hunt could stop worrying about finding a Plan B and organise in earnest for the spring. As soon as John Hunt heard the news he wrote to the Foundation for Alpine Research to request a meeting with the Swiss team when they returned from Nepal, to discuss what had gone right and what had gone wrong.

As the New Year came, the pace of preparations increased. Packing started at a shipping agency in Wapping. While the men pored over endless boxes, Joy Hunt and all available 'expedition wives' were drafted in to sew name tags onto clothing and paint names onto tin mugs.

In mid-January they held an oxygen test in Wales, before John Hunt and Charles Evans flew to Zurich for a meeting with Raymond Lambert and other members of the Swiss team. The meeting went very well, aided considerably by John Hunt's fluency in French. Despite the rivalry and the undoubted sense of national competition, in 1952 and 1953 the British and Swiss teams were very helpful to each other. John Hunt left with a map showing where the Swiss had cached supplies and equipment, and contact details for Draeger, the company that had supplied most of the Swiss oxygen cylinders. Draeger provided design details that enabled the British team to make special adaptors which allowed them to use the Draeger bottles abandoned on the mountain. Raymond Lambert, however, had a rather pessimistic parting message for John Hunt: '*Mon Colonel, vous aurez des gros problèmes'* (Colonel, you will have big problems). These were prophetic words, but not quite in the way Lambert intended.

In early February, just after the final expedition conference and barely a week before he was due to sail from Tilbury with the main party, everything fell apart for John Hunt. What started as a minor cold developed into severe catarrh, not in any sense life-threatening but terrible news for someone planning to go to very high altitude. When doctors examined him, they discovered that both his nasal antra, the large cavities behind the nose, were blocked and there was significant damage to one nostril from an old injury. It looked like it might be 1935 all over again, with the doctors denying him his chance on Everest.

However, John Hunt took a brave step and elected to have an operation. On 8 February, he wrote to Charles Wylie to tell him that everyone had been close to despair, because it seemed to have gone badly. A few days later, showing a resilience that would become the hallmark of his leadership, he sent another note saying that things had improved considerably and he would soon return home.

There was one positive aspect to the delay. With the expedition now on a more certain footing, the Himalayan Committee's treasurer, R.W. Lloyd, achieved a major coup by persuading Prince Philip, the Duke of Edinburgh, to become the expedition's patron. A week after Wylie and the others set sail for Bombay, Lloyd and John Hunt went to Buckingham Palace. Afterwards Lloyd wrote a memo noting that the Duke had asked 'exceedingly intelligent questions'. More importantly, he quickly arranged for the Duke's name to be added to the expedition letterhead, to help with the funding appeals.

Securing the Duke of Edinburgh's patronage was particularly significant in 1953. As the date of the coronation of Queen Elizabeth II grew closer, Britain enjoyed a new mood of optimism. The popular writer Philip Gibbs published *The New Elizabethans,* comparing the Britain of the 1950s to the England of Elizabeth I. In the press, there was much talk of a 'New Elizabethan Age' and it did not go unnoticed that the next Everest expedition would take place in coronation year. Would John Hunt and his men come back with a suitable gift for the new queen and revive the great British tradition of exploration and adventure?

On 28 February 1953, when John Hunt boarded a plane for India with Tom Bourdillon, he was keenly aware of the enormous weight of expectations on his shoulders. However, at that moment, his thoughts were on more mundane things. After months of planning, the preparations were over and they were on their way. The meetings, the equipment trials, the letter writing, the hand-shaking and the interviews were over. From now on all he had to think about was mountaineering.

If only life were so easy. Kathmandu was to bring more stress and unexpected complications.

Chapter 6

THE KATHMANDU COLD SHOULDER

On the morning of 3 March John Hunt and Tom Bourdillon arrived in Delhi after a long, uncomfortable flight. Unlike today, when it is possible to take a direct flight from Britain to India, they had made several stops and endured a twenty-six-hour delay at Basra in Iraq. For John Hunt, who was recovering from the operation on his nose, the take-offs and landings were particularly uncomfortable. Nor was he looking forward to the final series of flights to Kathmandu.

At Delhi Airport they were warmly greeted by Arthur Hutchinson, the first of two reporters that *The Times* had assigned to cover the Everest story. Hutchinson had worked in India and the Middle East since 1950 and was responsible for *The Times*'s coverage of the Swiss expeditions. In a few weeks he planned to move from his home in Delhi to Kathmandu to act as the contact man for a second reporter who would accompany the team.

John Hunt was as cordial as ever but he was exhausted and a little depressed. He'd missed his wife, Joy's, fortieth birthday and felt guilty. Tom Bourdillon was equally homesick; he had left Jennifer ill with typhoid. To make matters worse, she had picked it up when she had accompanied him to Nepal for the Cho Oyu expedition a year earlier. Both men wanted to get to Kathmandu as quickly as possible and get a good night's sleep.

As they sat in the lounge making small talk, a tall, thin man with greased-back hair and a weather-beaten face watched them. After a few minutes he came over, and with a smile for his old pal 'Hutch' Hutchinson, introduced himself: Ralph Izzard, special correspondent of the *Daily Mail*.

Ralph was a been-everywhere-done-everything reporter, Fleet Street through and through. His father, a legendary correspondent for the *Daily Mail*, was said to have been the model for one of the characters in Evelyn Waugh's *Scoop*. Following in his footsteps, Ralph was the *Daily Mail*'s Berlin correspondent in the late 1930s before serving with British Naval Intelligence for most of the war. When he returned to journalism, he spent much of his time covering conflicts in Korea and the Middle East. His current assignment was safe by Ralph's usual standards but it would not be easy. He had been sent to break *The Times*'s monopoly on Everest.

When Arthur Hutchinson saw his rival bearing down on him at Delhi Airport, he was reassured by John Hunt's response. As Ralph Izzard recounted in his book, *The Innocent on Everest*, John Hunt leant on his ice axe and read him the Riot Act:

> We might as well get this straight at the start. We can't take you along with us; we are not equipped for that sort of thing; all our kit and provisions have been worked out exactly. Also, there is nothing to prevent you reporting facts but you must understand that as part of our agreement with The Times, I am forbidden to tell you anything and that applies as well to all members of the expedition.[1]

Every member of the Everest team had signed a contract that included a detailed clause forbidding them to talk to the press without the permission of the Himalayan Committee. A parallel clause in the expedition's agreement with *The Times* gave them exclusive rights to all official press coverage until the final dispatches were published. This also applied to members of the Committee, to Griffith Pugh and Tom Stobart, and even the expedition's secretaries. John Hunt was made a special correspondent for *The Times* to make it easier for him to turn down interview requests from other newspapers.

From the Committee's point of view, the deal with *The Times*, their traditional partner, kept everything simple. They received £10,000 and a percentage of future profits if the story took off and were assured that the expedition would be treated with due discretion. *The Times*, for its part, sold its exclusive coverage to several newspapers around the world, thus making it even more protective of its rights. Griffith Pugh had been told off in January when comments he made at a lecture were reproduced in the *Manchester Guardian*. As Charles Wylie reminded John Hunt, *The Times* took contractual breaches very seriously. In 1938, they had fined a previous Everest expedition £500, after one member of the team had gone for a drink with a Reuter's correspondent and given away a lot of expedition news.

In 1953 maintaining exclusivity was not going to be easy. *The Times* deal was an open challenge to other British newspapers and especially to competitive journalists such as Ralph Izzard. Round one at Delhi Airport was a victory to *The Times* but as John Hunt ruefully commented, Ralph Izzard was a 'persistent type' who didn't give up easily.

On the flight from Delhi to Allahabad, John Hunt and Tom Bourdillon slept for most of the journey. When they stopped at Lucknow, Izzard approached Hunt again, to try to get something out of him about every British newspaper's second-favourite Himalayan story: the Yeti, or as British papers called it, 'the abominable snowman'. Ralph reminded Hunt that in 1937 he had apparently seen Yeti tracks in Sikkim; did he think that they might encounter more on this expedition? Hunt's brief reply gave Ralph enough material for an article a few days later. When they stopped at the small airport in Patna, in India, John Hunt managed to give Izzard the slip, disappearing into the lounge with some Jesuit missionaries.

Several stops later, they touched down in the late afternoon in Kathmandu. John Hunt and Tom Bourdillon went to the British embassy with the Ambassador, Christopher Summerhayes, leaving Ralph Izzard to tussle with Nepalese customs over the two bottles of whisky that he carried for 'medicinal purposes'.

In 1953 Nepal, like Britain, was at a transitional point in its history. For most of the previous century it had been ruled by one family, the all-powerful Rana clan. They had maintained Nepal's ancient Gorkha monarchy but kept power for themselves, distributing the prime ministership and the important government jobs among family members. Fearful of outside influence, the Ranas pursued a policy of isolation, fiercely protecting their borders. There had been no tourists, no missionaries and no European merchants; any Ghurkha soldiers or traders returning to Nepal after a period abroad were required to purify themselves and pay a special tax.

In 1950 King Tribhuvan, the latest puppet monarch, unexpectedly fled from the royal palace at Kathmandu and sought sanctuary in the Indian embassy. Backed by the Indian government, he deposed the Ranas and proclaimed a revolutionary plan to turn Nepal into a modern democracy.

Over the following three years there were changes of government, attempted coups, rent strikes, police mutinies and endless conspiracies. The British government, which was happy to deal with the Ranas, at first opposed King Tribhuvan's revolution. Its long-term priority was to maintain Nepal as a stable country from which it could recruit Ghurkha soldiers, who were then much in demand to fight Britain's colonial wars in South Asia and Africa. The British government came to accept the new status quo but, as everyone knew, Nepal was far from stable. Basil Goodfellow and the Himalayan Committee were so concerned about the possibility of a coup or a Communist insurrection that they had taken out an expensive insurance policy in case the expedition had to be cancelled due to civil unrest.

The British embassy in Kathmandu was a large, rather brutal, neo-classical building set amid lush gardens and well-tended lawns. It was a potent image of British civility and for the last few years had been a home from home for parties of British climbers. The explorer and mountaineer Bill Tilman was the first to visit, in 1949; Eric Shipton stayed there in 1951 and 1952. The building was due to be handed over to India in 1954 but for the moment, the Union Jack flew high.

The Ambassador, Christopher Summerhayes, had proven himself a very important ally of British mountaineers. In reports to the Foreign Office, he argued that climbing expeditions were good for British prestige but he clearly also took a personal interest. Tall and gaunt, with a thin moustache and a taste for Tyrolean overcoats, Christopher Summerhayes was a keen walker and outdoorsman, who worked tirelessly to secure expedition permits and lobby for British teams. He even carried out some low-level espionage, sending John Hunt notes on the Swiss team's tentage and oxygen equipment after meeting them in 1952. When, that summer, Christopher Summerhayes discovered that the Swiss had substantially changed their team for the second Everest attempt in the autumn, contradicting an assurance given to the Nepalese government, he contacted the Foreign Office and the British embassy in Switzerland to ask whether an unofficial protest should be lodged. As he wrote in August 1952:

> It [Everest] is a race that our men have striven hard to win and all decent races keep to some rules or should do so. I am of course particularly concerned with this one.[2]

Christopher Summerhayes had been surprised to hear of Eric Shipton's replacement but he was quickly won over by John Hunt's passion and professionalism.

In early March the British team converged on the Kathmandu embassy in piecemeal fashion. Charles Evans and Alfred Gregory were the first to arrive, as an advance party sent to organise porters and provisions. Next came Charles Wylie and the expedition cameraman, Tom Stobart, who hoped to get some scene-setting shots before it got too busy. On 3 March, when Hunt and Bourdillon arrived, the main body of the team was working its way across Nepal by foot and lorry, along with the expedition's seven and a half tons of equipment and supplies. No one was quite sure when it would appear but on 4 March another major element of the expedition arrived: twenty Sherpas, their girlfriends and wives and most important of all, their *sirdar*, Tenzing. Tenzing had by then replaced Eric Shipton's favourite, Ang Tharkay, as the most famous Sherpa in the Himalayas. Although no one in the press could agree on his name – Tensing, Tenzing, Tenzing Bhotia, Tenzing Norgay, Tensing Norkey, Tenzing Sherpa or, Dan Shin, as one Indian academic suggested – everyone agreed there was something special about Tenzing.

Over the last couple of months John Hunt had spent a lot of time thinking about the Sherpas, as he poured over his plans and diagrams. He realised that the Swiss had failed in the previous spring because of their logistical management. Everest could only be climbed by a team that got enough food, equipment and oxygen up to the South Col. If the British wanted to succeed where the Swiss had failed, it would require both John Hunt's own organisational and planning skills and the strong shoulders of a willing group of Sherpas. A good *sirdar* would play a vital role, so Hunt had appointed Tenzing, who had done so well on the Swiss expeditions of 1952.

In some respects, Tenzing's background was typical, almost archetypal, of the high-altitude porters who had been a feature of

British Everest expeditions since the early 1920s. He was born in Tibet around 1914, the son of a yak herder. A few years later his family crossed the border into Nepal's Solu Khumbu, to join the community of recent Tibetan migrants, Bhotias, as they were called. They lived side by side with the Sherpas, an older, more established group of immigrants, who had likewise migrated from Tibet some years earlier. To the British, there was no real distinction between the two groups but in the émigré community Bhotias were definitely of lower status than Sherpas. They were regarded as loose cannons, proud and easy to offend, quicker with their knives than their mouths. Tenzing was never violent but several British climbers noticed how sensitive he could be. In later life he kept quiet about his Tibetan roots and was invariably referred to as a Sherpa; only after his death did the truth about his birthplace in Tibet emerge.[3]

Like many others, Tenzing moved from the Solu Khumbu to Darjeeling, in India, to look for work. In the 1930s Darjeeling was both an important trading centre and a hill station for the British colonial community, where they could escape the heat and dust of the Calcutta summer. Darjeeling boasted a polo club, an occasional cinema and even an ice-rink. For the Sherpas and Bhotias who flocked to its shanty-towns, life was by no means easy but many found work as rickshaw men and porters for local merchants and colonial officials.

There was also a more glamorous, though not necessarily much better paid, occupation on offer: expedition porter. As European mountaineers quickly discovered, the terrain was so difficult and pack animals so scarce, most equipment had to be carried in by hand. Over the decades the Sherpas and Bhotias of Darjeeling proved themselves to be strong and reliable, and raised their status above the level of the ordinary Nepalese and Tibetan coolies, the less skilled day labourers and porters. A typical Himalayan expedition might hire hundreds of men and women to carry its gear to its Base Camp but after that, the more skilled high-altitude work was invariably done by Sherpas and Bhotias. Those capable of getting really high were given the accolade of 'Tiger' and were able to demand more pay.

Although the term 'Sherpa' properly describes an ethnic group, today it has come to be synonymous with 'high-altitude porter'. Like Hoovers and Biros, Sherpas have turned themselves into such a powerful brand that other Nepalis claim to be Sherpas, regardless of their true ethnic background.

When in later life, he was asked what inspired him to take up mountaineering, Tenzing told how as a boy he was impressed by the stories he heard about Everest. He described how he had once paid for the privilege of trying on the heavy climbing boots of a Sherpa recently returned from a British expedition. He got his first portering job in 1935 and gradually worked his way up the hierarchy to become a *sirdar*. The first sign that there was something special about him came in 1947, on a Swiss expedition to the Garhwal Mountains, in India. When the original *sirdar* was hurt in a fall, Tenzing took over and impressed his clients. They included André Roch and René Dittert, who were instrumental in offering him the *sirdar*'s job on the Swiss 1952 Everest expedition. Tenzing was distinguished both by his skill as a climber and his enthusiasm to get to the top. Other Sherpas might be as technically proficient but very few seemed to think of mountaineering as anything more than a job.

Like the French and Swiss peasants who had worked as guides for British climbers in the Alps during the nineteenth century, in the early days most Sherpas had no real empathy for the Westerners who came to the Himalayas to climb their high peaks. They saw mountaineering as essentially a strange, risky leisure activity for wealthy foreigners. As in the Alps, local legends about the spirits who lived on the high summits were often accompanied by warnings and injunctions not to climb them. These prohibitions were powerful in Nepal and Tibet where, according to religious teaching, the high mountains of the Himalayas were 'the abode of the gods'. The Sherpas were both devout and pragmatic, so despite their reservations, they were prepared to work in the mountains.

Being employed as a high-altitude porter had a certain macho glamour but foreign climbers were frequently surprised and slightly disappointed that their Sherpas seemed to show so little genuine enthusiasm. When the French alpinists Maurice Herzog and Louis Lachenal climbed Annapurna in 1950, their *sirdar*, Ang Tharkay, opted not to accompany them on the final climb to the summit, saying that he didn't feel up to it. In retrospect it was a wise move, for both Frenchmen suffered severe frostbite but at the time Herzog was surprised by Ang Tharkay's attitude.

Tenzing was different. He *wanted* to climb mountains and was unhappy when foreign climbers *didn't* let him accompany them to the summit. By the end of the 1940s he had been to Everest four times and had reached the summit of the famously remote Indian mountain, Nanda Devi, with a French team. However, nothing in his previous experience compared to the two Swiss Everest expeditions of 1952. These were life-changing events for him. Tenzing's passion for climbing flowered under the Swiss, who treated him with respect and real warmth. He formed a particularly strong bond with the Swiss climber Raymond Lambert, with whom he seemed to have an instinctive rapport.

The first expedition, in spring 1952, garnered him international fame when he and Lambert got so close to the summit. The second expedition, in the autumn, increased Tenzing's renown and won him a medal from the King of Nepal but he ended the year ill, exhausted and twenty pounds lighter. On the walk from Everest he twisted his leg, his first serious accident on a mountaineering expedition, and was forced to hobble back on improvised crutches. When the expedition broke up in December, the other Sherpas returned to Darjeeling but the Swiss took Tenzing, suffering from an attack of fever, to the hospital in Patna in India. He did not return home until early January and was far from well when Jill Henderson came knocking on his door, hoping to hire him for the 1953 British expedition.

Jill Henderson, the wife of a tea-planter, was the local Honorary Secretary of the Himalayan Club, set up by British mountaineering enthusiasts during the colonial era to organise and regulate the hiring of Sherpas. It kept records, tried to set rates of pay and liaised between foreign teams and their porters. With her friendly smile and maternal manner, she was a much-loved figure among the Sherpas.

Tenzing was worried about his fitness and his wife, Ang Lahmu, did not want him to go back to Everest, fearing that he might never return. Furthermore, he wasn't sure if he wanted to join a British expedition. Tenzing had worked for the British on many occasions and found them to be much more reserved and distant than other Europeans. When, six months earlier, he was first approached to take part in the 1953 expedition, he refused to commit himself. Now, at the end of the year, he felt even more uncertain.

Jill Henderson was confident that she could change his mind. It was to be a busy year in the Himalayas, with a Japanese expedition to Manaslu, a German expedition to Nanga Parbat, an American expedition to K2 and a couple of smaller Indian expeditions. However, by far the biggest and most prestigious event would undoubtedly be the British Mount Everest expedition. How could an ambitious Sherpa like Tenzing say no? Did he really want Ang Tharkay or Pasang Lama to take his place? What would he do instead?

On 2 January 1953 Jill Henderson telegraphed John Hunt:

> *Tenzing prepared to go but not to climb beyond Camp 3 unless fit. Complications likely unless he goes. Team will be chosen Monday letter will follow immediately.*[4]

A few days later she sent a follow-up letter to Hunt, confirming Tenzing's agreement but adding:

He is looking extremely pulled down at the moment but with good food
and rest he should be his old self before long.[5]

The question of Tenzing's fitness lingered over the next few
months but his health gradually improved. With characteristic self-
discipline and energy, he embarked on a training programme that
involved carrying a rucksack full of stones on long walks around
Darjeeling.

It is important to realise that although by the end of the expedition
he was referred to as a member of the climbing team, initially Tenzing's
role was that of *sirdar*. This was made clear in a letter from John Hunt,
written on 20 January 1953:

I am writing to tell you how delighted I am that, despite your great efforts
last year with the Swiss, you have decided to go with us to Everest this
year as Head Porter. With you at the head of our porter team, I am most
confident of success this time.[6]

The distinction between being head porter and being a fully-fledged
member of the climbing team was slightly artificial. Many Sherpas
had climbed to great heights on previous Himalayan expeditions and
clearly played a much wider role than that of porter but it mattered
to Tenzing that the Swiss had made him an honorary member of the
Swiss Alpine Club and referred to him as both the *sirdar* and a member
of the climbing team. The British did neither. Perhaps John Hunt was
genuinely unsure whether he would get beyond Base Camp but from
the beginning the British fundamentally underestimated Tenzing and
his motivations.

Tenzing did not see himself as just an employee. Not only did
he want to climb Everest, he shared the sense of ownership with the
British. Everest was his mountain and he wanted to be the first to the
top, ideally with his Swiss friends, when they returned in 1955 or 1956.

Tenzing shared his doubts with his friend and mentor, Rabindranath Mitra, a Bengali tea planter and social activist. When I interviewed him in 2002 he was old and frail but when he talked of Tenzing his eyes lit up:

He was a truly great man ... He wanted an assurance from me in case of his death, who will look after his family. I gave him that assurance. 'Well Tenzing, if I get a morsel of food for me, then you rest assured that your children and your family won't die of starvation.'[7]

When Tenzing left Darjeeling for Kathmandu on 1 March 1953, his friends and family were in no doubt about his intentions: this time he would triumph on Everest or die trying.

Three days later Tenzing and his team of Sherpas reached the British embassy on the afternoon of 4 March. The British climber Charles Evans, a trained doctor, was shocked to see Tenzing looking so pale and ill. John Hunt was delighted to meet the Sherpa that he had heard so much about. He arranged to see Tenzing later that evening for a proper discussion. Before that could happen, Tenzing was whisked off in a jeep by two Indian journalists and an English reporter recently arrived from Cairo: a certain Ralph Izzard of the *Daily Mail*.

Since Tenzing had not been taken on as a full member of the team, he had not signed the same contract as the British and New Zealand climbers and was perfectly at liberty to talk to any journalists. The two Indians were Roy of the Press Trust of India, a large news agency, and Harish Srivashtava of *The Statesman*, one of India's most respected newspapers, based in Calcutta. Ralph Izzard had not met either previously but in accordance with what he later called the freemasonry of the press, particularly of the embattled kind, they agreed to join forces in their mutual struggle to break *The Times*'s monopoly of Everest news.

Despite his exhaustion, Tenzing was keen to talk and spent an hour with the three copy-hungry pressmen. This year, he said, he was determined to succeed; if the weather held, nothing would stop him going all the way to the top. It did not take him long to get on to his favourite subjects: how much he had enjoyed the Swiss expeditions and his continuing friendship with Raymond Lambert. After an hour Tenzing left for his meeting with John Hunt but he promised to finish the interview when he got a chance.

From the beginning of the 1953 expedition Tenzing was lionised by the Indian and Nepalese press. They wrote about him for two reasons: first because he was already a local hero with a public profile and second because he was the only important member of the team who was willing to speak to them.

Shortly after the end of the Swiss expedition of 1952, from which the local press were also excluded, *The Times* correspondent Arthur Hutchinson contacted his bosses in London, warning them that such behaviour had bred ill feeling:

> *Local journalists are likely to try and exercise a good deal of political pressure in an effort to break our news monopoly on the forthcoming [Everest] expedition. The line of argument they propose to adopt is, apparently: why should no news of a major event taking place in Nepal be allowed to reach the Nepalese press and people and be confined to the readers of a foreign paper – and not even an Indian paper at that?*[8]

From the beginning there was antagonism between the British team, viewed as haughty outsiders, and local journalists. Tenzing bridged the gap – he was both within the British team and outside it – and the local press played up his position as a consequence. Arthur Hutchinson's suggestion that *The Times* should be a little more generous and a little less exclusive was not taken up.

By 8 March the British party was complete and the equipment

had arrived. For the New Zealander Ed Hillary, several members of the British team were old friends but he had never met John Hunt. Despite exchanging several cordial letters, Ed was rather nervous. John Hunt was well aware of the potential for awkwardness and recognised the importance of a good first meeting. As soon as he saw Ed Hillary, he strode across the embassy lawn, shook his hand warmly and immediately invited him into his confidence. Within a few minutes John Hunt told Hillary that he was feeling very positive about the whole thing, intended to lead from the front and wanted Ed to join his 'executive committee' of core climbers. Like everyone else, Ed recognised the professionalism of Hunt's leadership style but he also quickly saw that Hunt was both organised and genuinely passionate about Everest.

In an early letter home to his wife, Joy, John Hunt described Ed Hillary as a 'rough dominion type' but as the expedition progressed he came to realise that Hillary was both a very accomplished climber and a very driven character. In many ways he was as much of a 'thruster' as John Hunt. Charles Evans, the third member of Hunt's executive committee, was really a mountaineer-explorer in the mould of Eric Shipton but Ed Hillary was a fiercely determined peak-bagger, who wanted to get to the top of Everest and was willing to take the necessary risks.

One of the first things that Hillary did when the equipment arrived on 8 March was to try on his all-important high-altitude boots. He was impressed with their design and fit; in contrast to the chaos of Cho Oyu, this seemed to be a well-organised expedition. He wrote to his friend Jim Rose at the New Zealand Alpine Club, with characteristic frankness:

> *John Hunt has impressed me considerably. I've had some long talks with Hunt and have been through his large file on the expedition and I must admit that for the first time I'm really starting to feel that we could get to*

*the top. The party seems to be a very decent bunch indeed and with a good
deal of ability – none of the deadbeats we had on the last trip.*[9]

Over the next few days their equipment and supplies were transferred
to a nearby military parade ground and organised into porter loads.
Between the work there were cocktail parties at the British and Indian
embassies and meetings with officials and members of the Nepalese
royal family.

One lunch time John Hunt gave a talk about the expedition for
local dignitaries, on the by-now-familiar theme of 'Why we climb
Everest'. When the Indian press corps heard, they packed the room
and attempted to hijack the question and answer session until Colonel
Proud, the embassy's military liaison officer, cut the session short and
whisked John Hunt off the stage.

Early March 1953 was a busy time for news desks around the
world. As well as the war in Korea, there were disturbances in Berlin,
the Middle East and Kenya. The death of Josef Stalin on 5 March
dominated the front pages of most British and Indian newspapers
for several days. Nevertheless, the British Everest expedition
received considerable coverage, especially in India. The first stories
concentrated on Hunt's plans and the comings and goings of the
British team but Indian newspapers also gave a lot of prominence to
Tenzing and the interviews that he had given on 4 and 5 March. *The
Statesman* reported that the British party 'would be led by Tenzing the
Sherpa'. The esteemed *The Times of India* included an article in which
it announced that Tiger Tenzing 'is planning to lead an expedition
to the world's highest peak' and reported his complaints about the
foreign teams making attempts on Everest while India remained
indifferent:

*'Someone should finance an Indian expedition, it is bound to meet with
luck', he said.*[10]

The article that really stirred things up came from Ralph Izzard. It was first published in the *Daily Mail* on 6 March and then syndicated to a number of Indian newspapers. Under the headline 'The Tiger is picked for Everest' Izzard repeated Tenzing's assertion that if the weather held nothing could stop him from getting to the summit. It added that John Hunt had already agreed to include Tenzing in the final assault party and given him permission to carry on to the top of Everest alone, if a partner couldn't continue. The third paragraph, subtitled 'So Critical', focused on Tenzing's opinion of British teams:

> *Tenzing prefers climbing with Swiss and French to previous British teams he has been with. He says: 'The Swiss and French treat their Sherpas on a footing of full equality regarding food, clothing and equipment generally. This has not been so with the British.*
>
> *'Consequently the British generally have to encourage us and boost our morale. Last year with the Swiss because of our treatment we were in such good condition that it was finally we Sherpas who were encouraging the climbers.'*[11]

When John Hunt read this, he was furious. The expedition had suffered a shaky start in London with the Shipton controversy; the last thing he wanted was an argument with his head Sherpa.

It seemed unfair. Tenzing undoubtedly preferred Swiss expeditions to British but the other statements were dubious. John Hunt and Griffith Pugh had been in touch with the Swiss team regularly over the last four months, discussing everything from equipment to their experiences on the mountain. They knew that there had been problems on the spring expedition precisely because the Swiss had not provided their Sherpas with the same clothing and equipment as the climbing team. Far from encouraging the Swiss climbers, few Sherpas had reached the South Col in the spring, even though they had been offered substantial bonuses.[12]

It was also untrue that Tenzing had already been offered a place on the summit team. John Hunt had not made any decisions about who would or would not be chosen for the final stage. According to his expedition bible, *Basis for Planning*, Sherpas would play only a supporting role and would not be included in the summit attempt. As for the more general implication that British mountaineers were cold and aloof, this was certainly not the attitude of Eric Shipton and Bill Tilman, the most recent and active British mountaineers in the Himalayas.

The traditional British attitude to the Sherpas was a complicated mixture of paternalism, genuine respect, a vestigial conviction of racial superiority and simple affection. Sherpas were paid employees, who were both porters and manservants – climbers usually had a personal Sherpa for the march in to the mountain, to look after their kit and do the cooking. Their fundamental job on the mountain was to carry the equipment and supplies while the *sahibs* did most of the lead climbing. In practice it was never as simple as this. The most skilled Sherpas often did some lead climbing and some British mountaineers, such as Bill Tilman, habitually carried very heavy loads, because they did not like to be seen as any less tough and hard-working than their Sherpas.

The relationship was inevitably complicated by cultural ideas inherited from the days of the British Empire. Though Nepal had never been ruled by the British, many of the mountaineering Sherpas lived in Darjeeling, which before the Second World War was very much an outpost of the Empire; an empire that frequently characterised its native subjects as uncivilised. They were, to quote the British writer, Rudyard Kipling, 'the white man's burden' – even when, in the case of the Sherpas, the natives were expected to do most of the carrying. Simultaneously, the Sherpas were idealised by some climbers as a hard-working, unsophisticated race who might have been better off if they hadn't come into contact with decadent Westerners and their cash. Bill Tilman and Eric Shipton preferred Sherpas with pigtails and saw short European-style haircuts as a sign that a Sherpa had been 'spoilt' by contact with Europeans.

In a similar vein, one of Charles Wylie's first letters to John Hunt in September 1952 discussed the issue of who would play the role of *sirdar* on the expedition. He noted that Shipton had already asked for Tenzing but added a caveat:

> *The Swiss have rather glorified Tensing by giving him the status of a European climber and making him a member of the SAC [Swiss Alpine Club]. However, Sherpas are the last people in the world to become spoilt, so this should not worry us.*[13]

This fear of spoiling the Sherpas reflected both a paternalistic sense that the West could corrupt and destroy a people that had got on perfectly well by themselves, and the familiar patronising idea of 'childlike' natives. On a less high-flown and more selfish level, the Himalayan Committee and the Himalayan Club also wanted to keep costs down. In the build-up to 1953 there were frequent complaints from the British that the Swiss had paid too much for both men and merchandise and therefore increased costs for everyone who followed.

A few days after the *Daily Mail* article was published, Ralph Izzard bumped into John Hunt at the cable station next to the embassy. He found him in a foul mood. Hunt did not mince his words and refuted almost everything that he had read in the article. Ralph Izzard was 'duly contrite' but pointed out that part of the problem was the expedition's attitude to the press. Ralph explained that many of the quotations used in the article had come from the second interview that Harish Srivashtava and Roy had conducted with Tenzing, at which he had not been present. If John Hunt refused to talk to journalists, how could he possibly check his articles?

John Hunt was not mollified but realised that at this stage of the expedition there was nothing he could do to stop anyone talking to either Tenzing or the other Sherpas, other than politely asking the Sherpas not to do so. As he wrote to Gerald Norman at *The Times*, on 10 March:

> *You must expect it [unauthorised interviews] to continue, at any rate as far as the Sherpas are concerned. I cannot muzzle them, though I have asked Tenzing not to speak to Pressmen, he has a complete right to do so.*[14]

The bigger point that no one seemed to have considered was that any British attempt on Everest in the early 1950s would be treated differently to one made by a Swiss or French team, especially if it were billed as a 'national' expedition. The very fact that the mountain was named after a British Surveyor-General was a reminder of the days of empire. However warm and friendly they might be as individuals, no British expedition could entirely shake off its historical baggage. The lionisation of Tenzing and the criticism of the British team also reflected wider antagonism towards Britain in post-colonial Asia.

Oddly, there was one story that neither Izzard nor the Indian journalists discovered that was precisely about status. When they arrived at the embassy, the British team either slept in the main building or were billeted with members of the embassy staff in their quarters. This meant camp beds in corridors and shared rooms, rather than four-star luxury, but nevertheless it was far superior to the stable block-cum-garage to which Tenzing and the Sherpas were allocated. This did not have a toilet; when, in protest, a few Sherpas used the road outside as a latrine, the embassy staff reacted furiously. At the time, it was a minor incident, which Tenzing didn't mention either to Ralph Izzard or the Indian journalists but when the story came out at the end of the expedition it was presented further as proof of the British team's residual imperial attitudes.

To an extent this was unfair. British teams had slept in far worse buildings on previous expeditions and it had been the embassy's decision to put the Sherpas in a garage, not John Hunt's. On the other hand, this was not a good way to start the expedition. As Ralph Izzard wrote in his memoir, *The Innocent on Everest*, by 1953 the more experienced Sherpas had come to see themselves as an élite corps who expected to be treated far better than the average day labourer or coolie. Tenzing might live in a one-room house in Darjeeling with no running water but only a few months earlier he had been presented with a medal by the King of Nepal. He was a famous man and had brought most of the top Sherpas with him. The act of urinating in front of one of the embassy buildings was, in its own way, shockingly provocative and at the very least, an indication that the British were no longer held in awe.

For John Hunt, these were minor irritations but a few days before their departure from Kathmandu, he certainly did not need extra work. On Monday 9 March he was delayed at the cable station for three hours, waiting for a long-distance telephone call from Britain. He assumed that it was the Himalayan Committee wanting to talk about Ralph Izzard's article and was distinctly unamused when it turned out to the *Daily Express* fishing for a story.

Back in Britain, *The Times*'s British rivals were proving that they could be just as inventive as the Indian press. Several newspapers ran stories that Hunt had already chosen George Band, the youngest member of the expedition, to be the other member of the summit team with Tenzing. Despite the fact that George was only twenty-three and had never climbed outside the Alps, according to the *Daily Herald*, John Hunt regarded him as 'Britain's finest present day mountaineer'. The story was pure fabrication, credited to 'sources close to the expedition' but it was so widely reported that George Band's father, a retired Presbyterian minister, was prompted to write to *The Times* to ask if he was permitted to talk to other newspapers:

If the expedition is successful and my son is among those who reach the summit, there will probably be a great rush for his life story together with pictures of his boyhood, schooldays and previous mountaineering experiences. What should I do?[15]

Francis Matthews of *The Times* promptly wrote to warn him that any news based on letters that George might send home was embargoed by *The Times* contract. A few weeks later Emlyn Jones, one of the reserve climbers, who was acting as the expedition secretary in London, composed a letter to the families of the expedition members on behalf of the Himalayan Committee, warning them to keep any letters from their loved ones on Everest to themselves.

Given the bother of the press coverage and the squabbles with the Sherpas, it is not surprising that John Hunt was keen to get out of Kathmandu. The expedition was so big that he decided to split it in two parties. The first group, which included most of the climbers, left on Tuesday 10 March. Their departure made for a grand spectacle: 162 porters carried 9720 lb of equipment made up into 60-lb loads. Before setting off, Tenzing's Sherpas came forward with great ceremony to receive their advance of thirty rupees, signing the expedition receipt book with an inky thumbprint. At 11.30a.m. they set off, Charles Evans striding out in front and Tenzing at the rear.

As they marched past the tall arches and ancient buildings of Bhadgaon, the former capital of Nepal, Ralph Izzard and the Indian reporters rushed ahead to take photographs. Ed Hillary had developed a dislike for 'that ratbag reporter' Ralph Izzard, so he did everything he could not to appear in shot. John Hunt, in a slightly more conciliatory mood, posed for a personal portrait after Izzard agreed not to take a group photograph of the team. Once he had seen everyone off, John Hunt returned to Kathmandu for a few hours' rest before another evening of official functions.

On the following day, he left with the second group of 200 porters and the remaining 7000 lb of gear. Charles Wylie was in charge of this particular convoy, assisted by Michael Ward and Griffith Pugh, whose large coffin-like box of scientific equipment was a source of much interest to the Sherpas. John Hunt stayed with them for most of the day but when they stopped to make camp, he carried on to catch up with the main party.

The next fortnight was a thankfully relaxing time for everyone; John Hunt's troubles in Kathmandu were largely forgotten. He deliberately avoided forcing the pace; he wanted everyone to acclimatise to the increasing altitude slowly and gradually and also to continue the all-important process of team building.

It was an easy-going group. The British members of the team were remarkably, or perhaps predictably, homogenous. There were two Georges (Lowe and Band), two Charles (Wylie and Evans), two Michaels (Ward and Westmacott), and two Toms (Bourdillon and Stobart). Three members – John Hunt, Michael Ward and Charles Wylie – had been to the same public school, Marlborough, several had been to university in either Oxford or Cambridge and almost all had been in the army at some stage. Compared to the New Zealanders, the British were quiet, low-key characters, who by George Band's admission were 'backward in pushing themselves forward'. Several were keen bird-spotters and John Hunt and Mike Westmacott were amateur lepidopterists. Ed Hillary was amazed when one day they produced butterfly nets and chased rare Himalayan specimens.

For those of a more aggressive disposition, like Ed and Tom Bourdillon, there was more fun to be had with the pair of .22 rifles that had been brought to shoot game. Tenzing warned John Hunt that it might bring bad luck if they started taking pot-shots at local animals but there was nothing to stop them peppering tin cans and makeshift targets. Wilfrid Noyce, the expedition's resident poet, eschewed the rifle range and preferred to entertain himself with more literary pastimes. In his rucksack he carried both volumes of Dostoevsky's

The Brothers Karamazov, Dante's *Il Purgatorio* and six other equally worthy books. No wonder it weighed 27 lb.

For the most part, the trekking was easy, with no particular challenges. There was a lot of ascending and descending but it was a much easier route than Shipton had taken in 1951. The most uncomfortable part of the day was when they donned their oxygen masks for familiarisation sessions. They had been warned that they would need to get used to the close fit but their masks were unpleasant to wear on hot days. John Hunt in particular found them very uncomfortable. This did not stop him from setting a good example.

Occasionally, there was some friendly competition; John Hunt seemed to need to prove himself against the younger men. In a letter to Joy Hunt, written on 14 March, he reported with glee: 'I'm very fit and at least up with the swiftest of us!', Ed Hillary's diary for 17 March told a slightly different story. He recorded how he and George Lowe had raced John Hunt up a 2000-ft hill and beaten him to the top by five minutes. A few days later, however, John Hunt won the return match, climbing a 4000-ft hill in a very creditable one hour and forty-five minutes.

As he took stock, John Hunt was pleased with how the men were bonding. In another letter home, he ran through their individual characteristics. Tom Bourdillon and Wilfrid Noyce were the quiet men of the team; George Band was the expedition wit, 'intelligent and amusing'; Mike Westmacott 'an authority on pigs and butterflies' and the two New Zealanders the readiest to laugh. Like Eric Shipton, he was impressed by Charles Evans, regarding him as a very able deputy who could take over if anything happened to him. His only regret was that because they were travelling in two groups he could not get to know Michael Ward, the expedition doctor and reserve climber. One of Hunt's most memorable and triumphant moments came when Tom Bourdillon approached him one night and remarked what a happy group they were. Considering that Tom had resigned a few months earlier, Hunt regarded this as a major achievement. Charles Evans, another erstwhile member of Eric Shipton's team, was equally impressed with Hunt. After the discord of the Cho Oyu expedition in 1952 this felt like an harmonious expedition, principally because of John Hunt's management.[16]

The second caravan, led by Charles Wylie, had a somewhat less harmonious time. One night a panther prowled through their camp and there were repeated problems with drunken porters. Michael Ward had to get out his medical kit one day after a knife fight between a local porter and a Sherpa. The wounds were not serious and they carried on without delay.

On 25 March, John Hunt's party arrived at Namche Bazaar, the largest Sherpa village in the Solu Khumbu and was greeted with the customary bowls of *chang* and hot potatoes, which as Tom Stobart noted, were kept warm in their hosts' armpits. This time, following Griffith Pugh's warning about catching flu and other unpleasant conditions in Sherpa houses, they stayed just one night. First thing the next morning, they left for Thyangboche, and set up camp close to the monastery. As with most visitors, John Hunt was enraptured by the scenery. Ed Hillary wrote in his diary how his leader was 'visibly overwhelmed and said that it was the most marvellous spot that he had ever visited'. In his diary, John Hunt commented on the amazing view of Ama Dablam, a striking nearby peak known as 'the Matterhorn of the Himalayas'. It looked, he wrote, like 'the most inaccessible mountain' he had ever seen.

The biggest surprise for everyone was the presence of an Indian police radio station at Namche Bazaar, recently set up to monitor traffic crossing the border between Tibet and Nepal. It was ruled over by Mr Tiwari, a burly policeman who constantly complained about the mountainous terrain and the unremitting cold. Ed Hillary commented drily in his diary:

Namche has lost all interest for me with the onrush of civilisation.[17]

Once Wylie and the second party had arrived, they spent three days reorganising their equipment. For the first time, all the tents were erected in their full splendour. With typical independence, Tenzing attached a Swiss Alpine Club pennant to his tent. It was somewhat overshadowed by the large Union Jack that flew over the camp. Everyone busied themselves with their own particular department, whether it was rations, equipment or clothing and a festive atmosphere prevailed. When Griffith Pugh weighed the team, he discovered that almost everyone had put on a few pounds. On the first day the Sherpas bought a sheep. As Buddhists, they were not keen to kill it but George Lowe, whose father had once worked as a butcher, had no such compunction. George Band unpacked their large radio receiver, which allowed them to listen to Radio Ceylon and hear the thrilling news that the Cambridge team had won the annual Boat Race against Oxford University by eight lengths.

The calm of the beautiful campsite was ruptured by two crises, both with the potential to derail the expedition. The first came when they distributed clothes and climbing gear to the Sherpas. No one complained about its quality but when the recipients were warned to look after everything carefully, because they would have to hand it back at the end of the expedition, the Sherpas grew mutinous. They were used to keeping their expedition clothes. It was not an absolute rule but they considered it an important perk and source of future income. However, mindful of the possibility of a second expedition in the autumn if the first one failed, Hunt had been told by the Himalayan Committee to keep as much as he could. He didn't believe that this would be possible but hatched a plan to give the high-altitude clothing to the Sherpas at the end of the expedition, as a reward for good service, rather than as an automatic right. However, the Swiss clothing that Tenzing habitually wore was visible evidence of his predecessors' generosity. Not wanting another round of arguments, Hunt backed down without much of a fight when he saw the Sherpas' strength of feeling.

The second, more serious crisis came when Tom Bourdillon unpacked the oxygen crates to discover that fifteen out of forty-eight bottles were completely empty and several others were far from full. John Hunt immediately sent a message to Kathmandu, via the Indian police radio station, asking for the main consignment of oxygen, which was travelling separately, to be unpacked and checked. This presented Hunt with a dilemma: on the one hand the team needed to practise with the oxygen sets on the training climbs; on the other hand, if there were problems with the main batch of canisters, it would be awful to have squandered precious gas unnecessarily. Tom Bourdillon reassured him that it was worth carrying on: the first consignment of oxygen cylinders were an old-fashioned RAF type, whereas the next batch would be made up of lighter and better-designed aluminium alloy bottles. It would be very bad luck if both sorts leaked.

Hunt could do nothing but wait to hear from Kathmandu and hope that Tom Bourdillon was right. In the mean time he went ahead with acclimatisation expeditions to local peaks. Their purpose was two-fold: first to introduce the British climbers gradually to the thin air of the Himalayas and second to train some of the Sherpas in the use of oxygen sets. Although there was no pressure to climb anything in particular, the acclimatisation expeditions were an integral part of the plan. In 1953 very little was known about high-altitude physiology but Griffith Pugh was emphatic about the need for an acclimatisation period before the start of the expedition proper and John Hunt concurred. The trick was to do just enough to be ready to take on the main objective but not so much that high-altitude deterioration set in. Hunt split the team into three groups, led by himself, Charles Evans and Ed Hillary. Already there was a definite hierarchy on the expedition but Hunt was careful to make everyone feel valued by continually emphasising each person's specific technical role.

As in 1951 and 1952, Ed Hillary fell ill early; he developed a sore throat and a high fever and had to languish in camp while the others in his party headed off on their first excursion. It was a frustrating way to begin, particularly for someone as competitive as Ed Hillary. Fortunately he recovered quickly and within a few days was able to join and then lead his party.

On 6 April the three training parties reunited at Thyangboche, pleased with what they had achieved. Everyone was well, other than John Hunt, who developed the first of a series of coughs and sore throats that was to plague him throughout the expedition. Michael Ward was concerned but time and again on the expedition, John Hunt displayed amazing powers of recovery. Before long, according to Tom Stobart, Hunt was 'working, planning and worrying in a dedicated way I have never seen in any other man'.

There was good news about the second consignment of oxygen cylinders: they had been checked and none were found to be leaking. The earlier difficulties with some of the Sherpas, however, had not gone away. One man in particular, Pasang Phutar, nicknamed 'The Jockey' because of his second career at the Darjeeling race-track, grumbled continuously. On 8 April his complaints came to a climax when he declared that he had had enough of the British team. It was a depressing moment but, paradoxically, John Hunt could not believe his luck. Although Pasang Phutar had been good friends with Tenzing, he was awkward and had a reputation for causing trouble on other expeditions. John Hunt was scathing about him in his diary:

> I had been expecting trouble from Pasang Phutar. He had been constantly difficult from the start and was a shirker, unfriendly and lazy ... We had discussed getting rid of him before and this was a clear opportunity.[18]

After consulting with Tenzing, John Hunt accepted Pasang Phutar's resignation, took back his gear and paid him off with thirty rupees. He hoped that this would put an end to his Sherpa troubles but on the following day Ang Dawa, a much more popular figure, also resigned.

Ang Dawa's specific complaint was that the Sherpas were being asked to carry excessive loads. John Hunt agreed to reduce the average weight to 50 lb but Ang Dawa wasn't satisfied and followed Pasang Phutar back to Darjeeling. In his diary Hunt was surprisingly phlegmatic, noting that 'things have been very smooth indeed so far'. In a couple of days two replacements were recruited and shortly afterwards the three parties set off again for a second bout of acclimatisation climbs and oxygen training.

Tenzing had never been comfortable mediating between the British team and the Sherpas. He enjoyed the status, and the pay, of being *sirdar* but as several climbers remarked, he did not have the natural authority of Ang Tharkay. However, he had something that was ultimately more important to the outcome of the expedition: a passion for mountaineering and a real ability. By early April the fears about Tenzing's health and fitness had been dispelled. As George Lowe wrote to his sister Betty:

> *He's very fit, a beautiful mover and very used to high altitudes. As well, he's an unspoiled character after the publicity of his climbing. He's the ideal companion with an infectious sense of humour and the desire to yodel and whoop like hell when he's happy (most unusual in a Tibetan). He speaks a little English and is teaching me Hindustani and a bit of Tibetan. He's everybody's favourite.*[19]

Charles Evans and John Hunt were equally impressed. As Evans wrote to Christopher Summerhayes, they expected 'big things' of Tenzing in the weeks to come.

The first stage of their Nepal venture had been much more troublesome than Hunt had anticipated but finally they were hundreds of miles from the nearest journalist, they had got rid of their most disruptive Sherpa and within a few days the Ghurkha Officer and mountaineer Jimmy Roberts would arrive with their main consignment of oxygen and hopefully, plenty of mail. So far, the weather was holding and the plan was working but the next phase would be much more challenging for everyone. Within six weeks, by Hunt's calculations, they had to be within striking distance of the summit. If not, like all the expeditions of the 1930s, they risked being defeated by the monsoon.

Before he could start thinking about summit attempts, one small hurdle remained: the Khumbu Icefall.

Chapter 7

THE ICEFALL

The Khumbu Icefall, the huge broken glacier that guards the entrance to the south-west face of Everest, is not the biggest icefall in the world but it is undoubtedly the most famous. It is one of the most dangerous places on the mountain, claiming many lives over the last fifty years. In 1970 eight people died in the Khumbu Icefall and in some respects it is as dangerous as the infamous 'death zone', the final 3000 ft below the summit. Today, before the climbing season starts, a team of Sherpa 'ice-doctors' try to make it as safe as possible, rigging numerous ladders and rope handrails but it remains an intimidating introduction to Everest.

In the spring of 1953 the dangers were there but the safety equipment was not. Save a few old Swiss marker flags, twisted at strange angles, it was a vast, empty white labyrinth of tottering towers of ice and bottomless crevasses. Eric Shipton's restless dragon, waited for the next group of heroes with which to do battle.

John Hunt nominated Ed Hillary to lead the charge. A veteran of the 1951 reconnaissance, he was the obvious choice and quietly relished the opportunity to impress his leader. When he set off on 9 April he was accompanied by George Band and Mike Westmacott, the two youngest members of the expedition and, at his special request, the other New Zealander, George Lowe. Ed and George were a powerful and pushy partnership but both realised that John Hunt was not going to let them take over the expedition. It had required some arm twisting just to get George Lowe along on this trip. It turned out to be one of the few times they climbed together during their two months on Everest. Ed Hillary's large party also included Tom Stobart, Griffith Pugh, five of the expedition's high-altitude Sherpas and a small army of thirty-nine villagers from Namche Bazaar, hired to carry the first batch of supplies to Base Camp.

They started in good weather but as they headed up the Khumbu Valley, the skies grew more and more threatening. When they pitched camp for the night, at roughly 14,500 ft, the first flurries were falling. By the following morning everything was covered in a thick layer of snow. It was picturesque but for Ed Hillary this was a real problem. The climbers and the Sherpas were equipped with snow goggles but the local porters had nothing. If they carried on, those without protection risked painful snow-blindness but if they stayed put, Ed would lose at least one day. Encouraged by the Sherpas, who laughed off his worries, he decided to press on.

Some porters resorted to the traditional Tibetan method of holding their pigtails in front of their eyes. It was better than nothing but only just. The following morning most had streaming, swollen eyes. Four were so badly affected that they were paid off and sent back. Ed Hillary was in equal measures guilt ridden and frustrated: what should he do? Their intended Base Camp was over a day's march away but could he justify losing more people? Luckily, Tom Stobart had an idea.

Tall and thin, with a big smile and an uncontrollable mop of blond hair, Tom Stobart had quickly become popular among the climbers. Having travelled the world with his camera, he had an endless fund of anecdotes and unlikely stories. The expedition was very lucky to have him. His previous filming trip had taken him to Australia to film crocodiles. He got the shots but he also picked up a liver infection that laid him low for several months. When the Everest invitation arrived, Tom was recovering in a London hospital. His doctors were not happy but Tom was determined to go and the production company responsible for the expedition film, Countryman Films, was willing to take the risk.

An experienced Arctic traveller, Tom Stobart was no stranger to sore eyes and blinding snow. He asked everyone if they had any spare lenses for their goggles and then delved into his camera bag, bringing out a roll of black photographic tape, a ball of string, some visors and a pair of scissors. Within a few hours he had rustled up dozens of pairs of hand-made snow goggles. It saved the day and gave Tom a warm glow of satisfaction.

The weather improved, the goggles did the trick and two days later they reached their temporary home for the next month: the Khumbu Glacier. The chosen spot was little more than a series of icy humps in the middle of a forest of ice-towers but it was the flattest area available. At 17,590 ft they were almost 2000 ft higher than the summit of Mont Blanc, the highest mountain in the European Alps. The Swiss had chosen the same site a year earlier; close by the British team found a large heap of firewood. Less welcome were the dumps of human waste scattered around the edges of the camp.

Once the local porters were paid off, the high-altitude Sherpas began putting up tents and organising the site. Ed Hillary loped off towards the Khumbu Icefall. It was just a few hundred feet away but the terrain was so tortuous that it took an hour to reach. Ed was shocked by what he saw. 'It was a thousand times worse than in 1951 and really looked quite hopeless',[1] he wrote to Jim Rose of the New Zealand Alpine Club.

The next morning George Lowe woke up with the first case of 'base camp-itis' – a particularly unpleasant combination of sore throat and diarrhoea that would plague the team for much of the expedition. Ed Hillary sympathised but he only had twelve days to find a good route before John Hunt was due to come up, so he set off with George Band and Mike Westmacott, leaving a rather miserable climbing partner behind.

By April 1953 the Khumbu Icefall had been ascended several times but for George Band and Mike Westmacott, who were both new to the Himalayas, it was an exhilarating challenge. This year, Westmacott was the first person to have a feature named after him: 'Mike's Horror', an ice-wall above a deep crevasse. He reached its top after cutting a series of precarious steps around a high and very dangerous corner. George Band didn't get his name on the map but he never forgot his first encounters with the icefall:

You had these great seracs, towers of ice and pinnacles and great lumps and strips the size of a row of cottages that could slump down at any moment. You could only go as far as you could jump, unless you could descend down one side, which you usually couldn't, and climb another. But then you would cast around to see if there was a natural snow bridge and you would go across very gingerly.[2]

As Ed Hillary's party worked its way up through the freezing labyrinth, at Base Camp Tom Stobart and Griffith took it easy, acclimatising to the thin air of high altitude and thinking about the filming opportunities and experiments to come. George Lowe's diarrhoea continued throughout the day, forcing him to make frequent sorties from their tent.

On one of those trips, in the late afternoon, he was watched by the expedition's old friend – the *Daily Mail*'s temporary correspondent in Kathmandu, Ralph Izzard. George Lowe didn't notice him but when Griffith Pugh emerged a few minutes later, Ralph Izzard introduced himself. It was a surreal moment: Ralph, the great showman, had taken the trouble to shave and neatly comb his hair that morning and was sporting a silk cravat, a golfing jacket and a pair of plimsolls.

Map 2 The Khumbu Icefall

For several days he had been on the trail of the expedition. At last he was face to face with one of its members. How would he react? Would Izzard get the Kathmandu cold shoulder? Or would Pugh be amenable and maybe even impressed by his efforts?

Griffith Pugh was more shocked than hostile. At first he couldn't quite believe that an untrained, under-equipped journalist could get all the way up to Everest Base Camp with little preparation and minimal support. Surely he should be suffering from some form of altitude sickness by now? The questions continued inside the tent as Tom Stobart and Griffith Pugh served tea. Ralph explained that although he had received no help from John Hunt and only the most grudging assistance from the British embassy, he had put together his own expedition, spurred on by rumours that Reuters also intended to send a correspondent. He and his small party of Sherpas had arrived at Thyangboche Monastery a few days earlier, just after the British team had left for their second series of acclimatisation climbs. Ralph admitted that there had been several moments when he had been tempted to give up but although he didn't know whether it would be worth the effort, he had persevered.

Unfortunately for him, Ralph didn't get much more than a cup of tea. None of the three team members were willing to be photographed; George Lowe made a few comments on the state of the snow and that was all. In the distance Ralph could see Ed Hillary and the others high up on the icefall but, perhaps mindful of Hillary's hostility in Kathmandu, decided not to wait for their return. Before leaving he asked if he could have some medicine, for one of his Sherpas who had a fever. However, Griffith Pugh couldn't oblige; he had left his medical kit at Thyangboche. With the light fading quickly, Ralph Izzard took a few photographs of a strangely empty campsite and headed down. Although George Lowe appeared brusque, he was impressed by Ralph Izzard's efforts. He wrote to his sister Betty about Ralph's 'commendable enterprise' both in getting permission to enter Nepal and in managing to reach Base Camp with so little gear.

Ralph Izzard's bizarre game of high-altitude hide-and-seek continued for the next few days. He met Charles Evans and Charles Wylie in the small village of Dingboche, finding them to be even less hospitable and even more camera-shy than Lowe and Stobart. They banished him to the perimeter of their camp with barely a word, leaving him with no alternative other than to attach a long lens and take yet more photographs of British tents. The two Charleses were a little friendlier when Ralph met them again a few days later at Thyangboche; although they remained tight-lipped, they did at least give him some medicine.

His last, and strangest, encounter took place just below the village of Namche Bazaar where he chanced upon a solitary young Englishman leading a rather motley convoy of porters carrying a consignment of oxygen cylinders. Ralph didn't recognise the latest member of the team but he invited him to sit down for tea and biscuits. As they drank cup after cup, Ralph found his guest to be surprisingly loquacious and both interested in Ralph's mission and willing to talk about John Hunt. Could he be so new to Everest that he hadn't signed a formal contract? As they were getting on so well, Ralph took a chance and asked the young man if he could take a couple of portrait shots. To Ralph's great amazement, the stranger agreed, on condition that he too could take a few snaps of his charming host, the famous reporter.

Suddenly Ralph's new friend burst out laughing. He had to come clean: he wasn't a climber but another of Fleet Street's finest! He was James Morris,[3] the twenty-six-year-old assistant foreign editor of *The Times*, assigned to the expedition as its official correspondent. As James Morris reminded Ralph, they had met a year earlier, in Egypt. Ralph Izzard took it all in good grace and they were soon swapping gossip. Izzard was deeply envious of James Morris's access to the British team but also knew that however threadbare, he had a story that the *Daily Mail* would be happy to run. His priority was to get his reports back to England before James Morris had a chance to write something. After a final cup of tea, they said their goodbyes and Ralph raced down the track. Three weeks later the dramatic tale of his expedition appeared in the *Daily Mail*, garnished with attention-grabbing headlines: '*Nightmare March on Slopes of Everest, Blind Man's Bluff on a Glacier*'. For the next few months, Ralph Izzard spent most of his time in Kathmandu, but James Morris lived in perpetual fear that one day he would return to steal the rest of his story.

By 20 April the entire team had reached the Khumbu Glacier. Base Camp was re-established on a new site a little further down the glacier, away from what the team doctor, Michael Ward, prosaically called 'all the Swiss shit'. Even after they moved, the expedition was plagued by 'base camp-itis'. Despite far greater attention to hygiene, it was impossible to keep everyone healthy.

John Hunt managed to avoid diarrhoea but he had other worries. He had never quite forgotten his rejection from the 1936 Everest expedition on medical grounds, although he had proved the doctors wrong on many occasions. He was strong and very proud of his fitness but he was also the oldest member of the team by three years and was deeply concerned about letting himself and the others down. As James Morris remarked in a television interview many years later, the British climbers were driven as much by the fear of shame as they were by the lure of fame and glory.[4]

Hunt's problems began in early April, with a sore throat and difficulty in breathing. A few days on 'the dope' helped temporarily. During one of the acclimatisation climbs his breathing difficulties became much worse. As he wrote to his wife, Joy, on 14 April:

> *I was going awfully badly having had somewhat a breathless night ... This was rather tantalising as you can imagine but there could be no doubt I wasn't up to it. Mike has run me over with the stethoscope and given various drugs – he suspects pleurisy but thinks he's checked it.*[5]

With characteristic optimism he added: 'Anyway, I'm feeling much better already'. However, John Hunt was rattled and so was Michael Ward. He prescribed antibiotics and ordered Hunt down to a lower altitude until it improved. Hunt had swallowed his medicine but he was only willing to take the minimum amount of time off. Although he insisted that everyone else should periodically descend to a rest camp down the valley, John Hunt never stopped working, preferring to be at the heart of things. His hard work did not go unnoticed by the other climbers. George Lowe called him the 'most conscientious man that ever led an expedition'[6] and before long all the Shiptonites were won over to the great cause.

Base Camp's most prominent feature was a large dome-shaped mess tent where meetings were held and meals eaten. Griffith Pugh had thought to bring a portable chair but the others spent most of their time reclining on the floor in their sleeping bags. The expedition cook, Thondup, received mixed reviews: his food occasionally tasted of the paraffin that fuelled his stove but sometimes it could be very good. The rations brought from England were supplemented by fresh mutton and yak meat but most of the nearby villages were so poor that there were very few surplus animals available to buy, although fresh eggs were relatively plentiful and a welcome treat.

Some of the men liked to sleep in the dome tent but others preferred more private accommodation in their own tents. Tom Stobart dug an ice cave in one of the larger *seracs* to store his film stock and camera gear. He grew so fond of it that it became his bedroom. Unlike the thin-walled tents, which could go from oven one minute to deep-freeze the next, depending on the sun, the ice cave had a near-constant temperature of –6 °C. At first Tom was very happy with his bespoke accommodation but in late April, after a few days filming, he started coughing up blood. It was pneumonia, the legacy of his previous filming trip, exacerbated by the privations of an Everest expedition. Michael Ward ordered him to descend to the rest camp to recuperate; it was several days before he was well enough to come back up to Base Camp and many weeks before he felt really fit again.

Griffith Pugh fared better in terms of health but found the expedition frustrating for other reasons. Other than Michael Ward, no one was terribly enthusiastic about his experiments and he invariably had to use himself as a test subject. In Britain he had a played crucial role in the preparations but on Everest he sometimes felt marginalised. On one occasion Pugh slogged up the Khumbu Icefall to conduct some work on oxygen starvation, only to find when he reached Camp 3 that his equipment box was full of chutney jars. There were plenty of laughs at Pugh's expense but no one owned up.[7]

At the end of the expedition Pugh was the only member of the team to complain on record about the official film. He wrote to the production company, Countryman Films, objecting to the commentary over a shot of one of his Work Capacity Tests. In sardonic tones, the narrator said that Pugh's experiments were unpopular with the climbers, particularly at the end of a hard day. In his angry but rather plaintive letter, Pugh revealed that only towards the end of the expedition, when they had very little to do other that wait in Advance Base, did any of the climbers take part in such a test. Being an expedition physiologist was a somewhat thankless task. Pugh complained to John Hunt at the time but, as one himself, he was realistic about the inevitable tensions between sportsmen and scientists. In a television interview twenty-five years later,[8] Griffith Pugh ruefully acknowledged his agenda was 'different to the climbers'. He wanted to make life easier for them, to use his scientific understanding to enhance their performance, but they frequently preferred to do things the hard way. What he called 'the cult of toughness' had no place in his worldview but as he discovered it was alive and well on Everest in 1953.

The other non-climbing member of the team, James Morris, had no previous experience of big expeditions but he was young and fit and impressed everyone with his stamina and good humour. Other than occasional forays into the icefall and up to Advance Base, he spent most of his time at Base Camp, writing dispatches based on his observations and on notes from the climbers. He handed these dispatches to runners, who sped to Kathmandu, where the other *Times* correspondent, Arthur Hutchinson, was stationed. It could take anything from five to ten days to reach the capital and up to two more weeks for the dispatches to appear in *The Times*.

His Sherpa runners were well paid. They received a basic fee of £10 for the journey to Kathmandu, with an extra £5 if they managed it in eight days and £10 if they made it in seven. The top bonus, £20, was reserved for anyone who could reach the capital in six days. This was such a demanding feat and such an expensive one, even for *The Times*, that it was only called for at the very end of the expedition. James Morris's first report, billed anonymously as from 'Our Special Correspondent', appeared on 7 April.

By the end of the month Morris had plenty to write about. Work had begun in earnest on the icefall. Hillary's pioneering party had been followed by others, whose job was to mark the route with flags, put up ropes and generally make it as easy as possible for the Sherpas with their heavy loads. The names they gave to the other sections of the icefall – 'The Ghastly Crevasse', 'The Nutcracker' and 'Hell Fire Alley' – told their own story. Hunt's aim was to get three tons of supplies and equipment from Base Camp into the Western Cwm. One final obstacle remained to be overcome: the huge crevasse at the end of the Khumbu Icefall that had stopped Shipton's party in its tracks. In 1952 the Swiss had traversed it using an ad hoc rope bridge but it was uncomfortable and nerve-wracking to use.

After considering the problem for six months, Charles Wylie had come up with a simple and ingenious solution: aluminium builders' ladders. Lightweight and relatively indestructible, they came in six-foot lengths that could be bolted together. The only problem was getting them through the Khumbu Icefall without covering their porters in too many bruises. Some Sherpas balanced them on their heads and others carried them on their backs but no one found a perfect solution.

Wylie's big moment came on 25 April. John Hunt watched as three lengths were bolted together and gingerly pushed across the huge crevasse. Ed Hillary crawled over, carefully roped up to George Lowe. Tenzing and Charles Wylie stood by, in case one of the ladders gave way. Fortunately, they held and Ed Hillary proudly stepped into the Western Cwm. In a typically brash moment, he suggested that he and George Lowe should press on to establish the next camp, because of their great experience on snow and ice. John Hunt immediately pointed out that he too was very experienced. Ed realised it was not a good idea to press the point, and graciously allowed John Hunt to take the lead.

As they had anticipated, the Western Cwm was a lot easier to ascend than the Khumbu Icefall, although it was slightly steeper than they had expected. After a couple of hours of exploration, as the light began to fail, John Hunt and the others turned back, aiming to return the next day with a larger party. Close to the edge of the great crevasse, Hillary and Tenzing were thrilled to uncover a large cache of Swiss food. However, to Ed's great disgust, it turned out to consist principally of tins of pemmican, a mixture of ground meat and fat, which he loathed. Further up the Cwm were richer pickings, including bacon, porridge and jam. After several weeks of British army rations, everyone was delighted to crunch into Vita-Weat biscuits and delicious Swiss cheese.

Once they had decided on a site for Advance Base, the icefall ferries got under way in earnest. The pattern was simple: teams of less-experienced Sherpas carried the loads from Base Camp to an intermediate camp on the edge of the great crevasse. There, the more experienced men ferried the loads up the Western Cwm, before returning to start again. It was monotonous work and very hazardous. Although the route across the icefall was marked by flags and fixed ropes, the Sherpas were always escorted by members of the British team. In London the Himalayan Committee had conscientiously insured the lives and limbs of the high-altitude porters. Each man was entitled to 150 rupees if they lost a finger or a toe. The families of married men would receive 2500 rupees if they died; the families of single men 1500. This was significantly more than the amount for which the Swiss had insured their Sherpas. The Committee's generosity did not extend to the climbers. They were left to take out their own policies; some chose not to because the premiums were so high.

Fortunately, the Sherpas had no serious accidents in the Khumbu Icefall, although several came close to falling into crevasses, much to the amusement of their friends, who preferred to laugh rather than worry in the face of adversity. As well as the small number of aluminium ladders brought by the British team, the Sherpas had carried tree trunks all the way up the Khumbu Valley from Thyangboche to act as makeshift bridges over crevasses that could not be circumvented or jumped. At first they crawled or shuffled across, legs akimbo but after a few weeks, they sauntered across the icy logs in their crampons. The *sahibs* too managed to avoid accidents but surprisingly it was Ed Hillary, the great 'snow and ice' man, who came closest to injury.

By late April Ed had decided that John Hunt was very unlikely to pair him with George Lowe for one of the summit attempts. Honorary 'Brits' or not, John Hunt would not want Everest 1953 to become an all-New Zealand triumph. So, Ed gravitated towards Tenzing, who was clearly a very strong climber. On 26 April he and Tenzing partnered for the first time, for a trip from Base Camp, at the foot of the Khumbu Icefall, to Advance Base in the Western Cwm. It was a demanding exercise but they accomplished it in fine style, moving much more quickly than John Hunt and Charles Wylie, who accompanied them.

After a few hours at Advance Base Ed and Tenzing went back, leaving the others to stay the night. On the way down they encountered George Lowe and a party of heavily-laden Sherpas. They chatted for a few minutes before Ed and Tenzing moved on, promising to continue the conversation during the nightly radio conference. To do this, he and Tenzing would have to get through the icefall in less than an hour, a record speed.

All went well until they reached the infamous Atom Bomb Area. Ed led in typically exuberant fashion, leaping over crevasses and weaving past dangerous *seracs*. Just before the end he took one jump too many. When he came down on the far side of the final crevasse, its outer edge gave way, sending him hurtling into the depths below. As he arced through the air, Ed realised that he could easily find himself wedged between the frozen walls of the crevasse and the large lump of ice that had come off with him. He jammed his crampons into one side of the crevasse and his shoulder into the other. At the same moment, he felt the rope go taut. Tenzing had reacted quickly and made a firm belay. After a few minutes to get his breath back, Ed hauled himself out and they continued. They even managed to make the radio conference. That night, in his diary, Ed was full of praise for Tenzing, who he declared an 'admirable companion'. It was a minor incident, the kind of slip that happens on many expeditions but it would come back to haunt Ed at the end of the expedition.

For the next few days, Ed rested at Base Camp. As he recorded laconically in his diary on 27 April he found himself 'doing nothing and eating much'. John Hunt was far busier. Once the Khumbu Icefall had been flagged and the Western Cwm broached, his next target was the Lhotse Face. This, he realised, was the critical phase of the expedition. In spring 1952 the Swiss had got through the icefall with relative ease but their attempt had foundered at the second stage. They had not managed to get sufficient supplies up the Lhotse Face to the South Col to make a serious attempt on the summit.

He was determined not to commit the same error but, as he admitted to his diary on 29 April, he was increasingly tense:

I'm holding on alright – but some cracks, pretty strongly sometimes,
Joy and the children are seldom away from my thoughts – the really

important part of life. I hope this mountain won't keep us waiting after 15th May. Certainly this thing we are doing is a great test of faith on the part of myself, the team and all those who believe in the outcome of what we are endeavouring to do.[9]

James Morris once described John Hunt as 'authority and responsibility incarnate'[10] but Hunt's Everest diaries and letters reveal him to have been a much more emotional figure than his public persona suggested. A few days after the diary entry of 29 April he received a batch of letters from his wife and a tiny present from his mother-in-law. His response took him by surprise:

I'm afraid some little things reduce me to tears, such as the thought of family putting flowers by my photo and your mother sending me a little fluffy black cat – I couldn't bear it any more and just broke down. Foolish of course. What is there about what we are doing which stirs people so?[11]

At the beginning of May Hunt accompanied Charles Evans and Tom Bourdillon on a preliminary reconnaissance of the Lhotse Face. It had two principal aims: to get as high as possible, and to test Tom's experimental 'closed-circuit' oxygen sets.

At the bottom of the Lhotse Face, at 22,000 ft, it is difficult to breathe. At the top, 4000 ft higher, it is even harder, especially during exertion. The leader of the Swiss expedition, Edouard Wyss-Dunant, memorably called it the *zone fatale*: the death zone. In the short term it is just possible to cope but a prolonged stay at high altitude is very dangerous. As well as hypoxia (oxygen starvation) and acute mountain sickness, climbers become increasingly prone to cerebral and pulmonary œdema, in which liquid collects on the brain or lungs. Essentially, above 26,000 ft climbers live on borrowed time.

Although the oxygen equipment the British team carried was an enormous improvement on anything that had been used in the past, it was crude by modern standards. On the insistence of Peter Lloyd, the Everest team's oxygen controller, most of the sets were of the traditional open-circuit type: basically a bottle of oxygen connected by a tube to a face-mask, with a regulator in between to adjust the flow of gas. When a climber breathed in, he inhaled a mixture of bottled oxygen and atmospheric air; when he exhaled, his breath went straight into the atmosphere. The higher the oxygen flow rate, the better it felt, until the bottle ran out.

Tom Bourdillon also brought a number of experimental closed-circuit sets, which worked on a different principle. In these sets, the oxygen mask was much more tight-fitting. When a climber breathed in, he inhaled pure oxygen, with no atmospheric air. When he breathed out, the exhaled air was directed into a canister filled with soda lime which removed the carbon dioxide and recycled the rest of the gas, to be breathed again. Closed-circuit sets had two big advantages: first, they delivered oxygen at a far higher pressure and second, because of the recycling, they were much more economical, enabling a climber to go further and faster. The downside was that they were heavier and more complicated, with more to go wrong.

A malfunctioning set was a real danger, especially for someone in the middle of a difficult pitch. If a valve iced up or an oxygen bottle ran out, the unlucky mountaineer was left terribly exposed. As a consequence, some of the climbers were wary of their oxygen sets, resenting the feeling of dependency they inevitably engendered. As Charles Evans quipped to Wilfrid Noyce, the question was not whether it was possible to get up Everest *without* oxygen but whether you could get up *with* it. The Lhotse Face reconnaissance was the perfect opportunity to find out.

There had been some optimistic talk about climbing all the way to the South Col but by the time they set off no one really thought this was possible. If they could get high, and if the closed-circuit sets proved as effective as Tom Bourdillon hoped, this would have a significant effect on John Hunt's plans for the final 'assault' phase. It might also ensure Tom Bourdillon's place on one of the summit teams. His dreams of glory were somewhat punctured when John Hunt told him that, because he was going on the Lhotse Face reconnaissance, he would probably not be chosen for one of the assault teams but Tom refused to become downhearted. As he confided to his diary on 29 April:

Things don't always work according to plan.[12]

On 1 May, Tom Bourdillon and Charles Evans left camp, with several Sherpas and John Hunt in support. The Sherpas climbed unassisted but the three British climbers wore closed-circuit sets.

It was a hot, almost windless morning. As they slogged up the Western Cwm, they found themselves sweating profusely and growing very tired. A closed-circuit set loaded with two oxygen cylinders weighed roughly 45 lb; in addition they carried personal gear and sleeping bags. When they reached Advance Base and took their sets off, they suddenly felt exhausted and light-headed. Another downside of the closed-circuit system was that because it delivered oxygen at such a high pressure, when a climber took his set off he was effectively transported from sea-level to his current height in a very sudden jump, producing a feeling of lassitude and breathlessness. Ironically, open-circuit sets did not have quite the same problem because they were less efficient and operated at a lower pressure.

The next morning began well but quickly deteriorated. At the foot of the Lhotse Face, Tom Bourdillon found the site of another Swiss camp and dug up more welcome supplies of food but by the time they reached the first set of ice-cliffs, at around 23,000 ft, it was unbearably hot. To add to their discomfort, the closed-circuit sets made things worse. When the exhaled carbon dioxide passed through the soda lime canister, it warmed up, sending the recycled gas back at a higher temperature. This could be an advantage at high altitude, where it tended to be colder but on a hot day with the sun streaming down, it was distinctly unpleasant. Then the weather changed and it began to snow heavily. Having climbed just 600 vertical feet in one and a half hours, the three men turned and descended. When their oxygen bottles ran out, John Hunt and Charles Evans were only too glad to abandon them in the snow, along with the equally heavy soda lime canisters.

As the designer and main advocate of the closed-circuit system, Tom Bourdillon was acutely embarrassed, especially when he arrived at Advance Base only to find Hillary and Tenzing full of life after an impromptu oxygen test of their own. That morning they had come all the way up from Base Camp in just over five hours, using the old-fashioned open-circuit sets. It was a prodigious feat, designed rather shamelessly by Ed Hillary to keep him at the front of John Hunt's thoughts as he planned the summit attempts.

The following morning was once again very hot. When they set off, Tom Bourdillon adjusted their sets to open-circuit mode for the first few hours, avoiding the soda lime canister altogether. This was a pragmatic decision, and also an admission of defeat. Ably assisted by Charles Wylie, who had come up to replace John Hunt, they managed to reach the site of the Swiss team's sixth camp, about a third of the way up the Lhotse Face. There they found yet more culinary delicacies and several abandoned Draeger oxygen bottles, which were as welcome as the food. Charles Wylie helped them pitch a tent before he retreated, leaving Tom Bourdillon and Charles Evans to brew tea and work on their diaries until it was dark.

Their final day, 5 May, was infinitely more successful. They left at 10a.m. and climbed far above their camp, reaching 24,000 ft before they turned round and headed back to Base Camp. After the poor start three days earlier, when they had almost given up on Tom's experimental sets, they returned to Base Camp with glowing reviews. At lower altitudes the closed-circuit sets did not seem to improve performance significantly but higher up, the increased oxygen pressure made a big difference and their tendency to overheat did not matter so much.

It was now almost a month since Ed Hillary and his party had started on the icefall. The date that John Hunt had set for the first possible summit attempt, 15 May, was approaching rapidly. At Base Camp there was definite tension in the air. Though the climbers had developed a very strong team spirit, they were all very ambitious. Everyone wanted to play a significant role in the final stages and, if possible, get to the summit.

According to John Hunt's *Basis for Planning*, there would be up to three attempts on the summit, each party consisting of two climbers and two Sherpas. The first two attempts would happen in quick succession but there might be a pause for regrouping before the third, if it proved necessary.

As John Hunt reviewed his options, he had plenty to think about. Most of the climbers had suffered a touch of 'base camp-itis' but they seemed to have recovered. The two youngest men, Mike Westmacott and George Band, had shown themselves to be very able. Wilfrid Noyce and Alfred Gregory were climbing well and Charles Wylie, the Ghurkha officer, was proving to be a vital link to the Sherpas, as well as an impressive climber.

The two New Zealanders, Ed Hillary in particular, were very strong. At first Tenzing had spent much of his time organising but had recently begun to form a powerful partnership with Hillary. As John Hunt knew, the closer they got to the summit, the more Tenzing's experience and knowledge of the terrain would count. In a letter to his wife, Joy, John Hunt wrote that Tenzing and Hillary were 'well above the rest of us in performance so far'.

John Hunt had his personal ambitions to consider and battle with. He liked to be at the front and had harboured hopes of getting to the summit himself. As he wrote to Edwin Herbert in February 1953:

I have always been determined to lead and not push the party up.[13]

However, he recognised that as expedition leader it might be better if he were at the heart of the action, rather than at its head. Although completely recovered and feeling very fit, he still had a troubling cough. At the back of his mind lay the ever-present fear of what he called high-altitude 'deterioration'.

On the morning of 7 May he invited James Morris to witness his deliberations with the two other members of his 'inner core': Charles Evans and Ed Hillary. At the planning stage Hunt had stated his intention to launch all the summit attempts from a high camp on the South-East Ridge. In the field, it had become increasingly apparent that this would not be possible. They simply did not have the manpower to get a sufficient amount of equipment high enough to support more than one of the climbers. So what was the solution?

After a long discussion, at 11.30a.m. John Hunt called the team into the mess tent. The two Georges, Lowe and Band, were high up in the Khumbu Icefall but everyone else was there, waiting expectantly. Some lay in the familiar 'Everest position' – on the groundsheet in their sleeping bags – while others leant against packing cases. Outside it was warm and unusually still.

John Hunt began by confirming that the first attempts would take place on, or soon after, 15 May. This would require everyone other than a few Sherpas to move up to Advance Base for the remainder of the expedition. The Lhotse Face reconnaissance had shown how tough the next stage would be and everyone would have to work very hard over the coming weeks. They would break into small teams: some consolidating Advance Base, others preparing a route up the Lhotse Face to the South Col. Only then could they strike out for the summit itself.

When John Hunt finally announced the names of the men chosen for the final assaults, James Morris registered a snap in the tension.

There were no great surprises. John Hunt's two confidants were to be in the vanguard: first, Charles Evans and Tom Bourdillon would make an attempt from a camp at 25,890 ft on the South Col using the experimental closed-circuit oxygen sets. If they failed, next up would be Hillary and Tenzing, using the traditional open-circuit sets. They would have the advantage of starting from a final camp placed 1500 ft higher on the South-East Ridge, because open-circuit sets consumed more oxygen and therefore had a limited range. Whether or not he had been made a full member of the climbing team, Tenzing was now at the centre of John Hunt's thinking.

The plan demanded a lot from Bourdillon and Evans: to succeed they would have to climb 3000 ft from the South Col to the summit and return on the same day. Some team members, notably Michael Ward and Alfred Gregory, thought it totally unrealistic, but the two chosen men were willing to try; Tom Bourdillon maintained that the closed circuit sets were powerful enough for such a task. Charles Evans had been impressed with their performance on the Lhotse Face reconnaissance. At the very least, he believed, even if they did not get all the way to the top, such a 'scouting' attempt might bring back valuable intelligence for the second pair.[14]

Before those summit attempts could take place, there was plenty of work to do. The important role of preparing a porter route on the Lhotse Face was allocated to George Lowe, George Band and Mike Westmacott. When they were finished, Wilfrid Noyce and Charles Wylie would lead two teams of specially selected Sherpas up to the South Col with over a ton of supplies. After that John Hunt and Alfred Gregory would follow in support of the two summit parties. Michael Ward, the expedition doctor, would act as reserve.

When John Hunt called for comments there was an awkward silence before Michael Ward spoke up, with what James Morris described in his book, *Coronation Everest*, as 'a vehemence that almost knocked me off my seat'. He told John Hunt that he was the weakest link in the plan and warned that he wasn't fit enough to climb up to the South Col. If he fell ill again, he might jeopardise the whole expedition.

Ed Hillary put Michael Ward's intervention down to frustration at being designated the reserve. Charles Evans did not comment on his motivations but he disagreed with his assessment. Charles recognised that for all John Hunt's frailties, he was 'tough as nails'. If he took it easy for a while, he would be up to the task. Michael Ward, for his part, genuinely thought that John Hunt was not. Only a month earlier he had been treating him with antibiotics for a suspected bout of pleurisy. Could this ashen-faced forty-two-year-old really get to the South Col, let alone further?

John Hunt clearly thought so and paid no attention whatsoever. Instead, after another mug of tea, he went back to his tent to write a long letter to his wife, Joy, in which he admitted that he had been tempted to go for the top himself.

Tom Bourdillon was very pleased to have been offered the first crack at the summit but when he filled in his diary that night he was, as ever, thinking about his wife, Jennifer:

If we get up it is just possible that we might fly back, which would be very good. Too happy and too unlikely to think about it. But anyway it is getting much nearer.[15]

On the following night, at 5p.m., John Hunt spoke by radio to George Lowe, who was at a camp in the Khumbu Icefall. Before he could announce the plan, Lowe delivered some bad news: George Band was ill and had not been able to get out of his tent that day. He would have to go down and, for the time being, would not be able to play any role in the attack on the Lhotse Face.

John Hunt would have to adjust his master plan – and they hadn't even started.

Chapter 8

THE LHOTSE FACE

At the age of ten, George Lowe tumbled off the verandah at his home in Hastings, New Zealand, and broke his left arm. The family doctor was away that weekend and the limb was not set properly. After enduring eighteen months of painful operations in which the bone was repeatedly broken and reset, George was left with one arm that would not bend fully. It was a turning point in his life: instead of following the usual destiny of Lowe males into farming, he stayed at school and eventually became a teacher.

If Alfred Adler, the German 'common sense' psychiatrist famous for his concept of the inferiority complex, had met him in his late teens, he might have wondered about the long-term effects of George Lowe's accident. In a macho society like the New Zealand of the 1940s, it would have been very difficult to be declared the family cripple. A weaker personality might have crumbled but George Lowe was determined not to be defined by his physical handicap. Mountaineering gave him the chance to prove himself. He started working as an assistant mountain guide just after the end of the Second World War and was soon spending most holidays in the mountains. His bad arm meant he had to adapt his ice axe technique but it did not stop him from climbing hard and fast. At twenty-eight, George was tall and strong, with a short beard and a brow that frequently wrinkled in laughter. He was ambitious too, both for himself and his best friend, Ed Hillary.

They met in the late 1940s and soon became friends, and eventually climbing partners. George was the loud one with the funny stories and a way with women; Ed was much quieter and shy. Together they had gone with Earle Riddiford to the Garhwal Mountains of India in 1951 and to Cho Oyu in the following year. Both had been thrilled to be invited to join the 1953 Everest expedition and equally shocked to hear of Eric Shipton's sacking.

George and Ed got on well with everyone on the British team but were amused by their reserve and their rather formal manners. They were also quite convinced that New Zealanders were better mountaineers, for these conditions at least. The Poms might be great rock climbers, but there wasn't that much rock on this side of Everest. It was all snow and ice, just like the Southern Alps of New Zealand, which they both knew so well. The long ice axes they carried always raised a smile from the British climbers, but they were perfect for the hard job of step-cutting, which George was expert at and which would be so important on the next stage of the climb: the ascent of the Lhotse Face.

George's plan was simple: find the route, prepare it, set up intermediate camps and then step aside to let twelve of the expedition's best Sherpas carry 400 lb of gear up to the South Col in one 'big carry'. Everything possible had to be done to make the route easy for the Sherpas because, unlike their British escorts, they would have to make the journey without oxygen. George Lowe was disappointed that leading the effort on the Lhotse Face meant that he would be too exhausted to play any significant role in the final summit attempts but it was an important job which he could complete easily. Or so he thought.

As soon as John Hunt announced his master plan, it seemed almost as if Everest had decided to make life harder for them. The most prominent landmark in the Khumbu Icefall, a large pillar in the middle, disappeared. Alfred Gregory nearly lost a Sherpa when a huge *serac* collapsed moments after he had passed it. There were massive new crevasses in the Atom Bomb Area and several of their log bridges began to sink into the crevasses they spanned. Then there was the weather.

A few months before leaving Britain, John Hunt had arranged for special Everest weather forecasts to be transmitted on All India Radio and the BBC Overseas Service in Singapore. The final three British Everest expeditions of the 1930s had been defeated by the early arrival of the monsoon snows, so accurate weather reports were vital. The BBC started broadcasting at the beginning of May. There were no reports of the monsoon yet but the afternoon storms, which had hampered their efforts in the icefall, suddenly intensified, dumping huge amounts of snow on to the Lhotse Face and making George Lowe's job more difficult. On most days there were at least three inches of fresh snow, on some days up to nine. If this weren't enough, there was the problem of finding a good assistant.

Not only did George Lowe lose young George Band to 'base camp-itis' but when he left Advance Base on 10 May to begin the attack on the Lhotse Face, Mike Westmacott started to feel very weak. Like many other first-timers in the Himalayas, he found it hard to adjust to the altitude. On the following day Mike stayed behind in Camp 5 at 22,000 ft, while George Lowe and four Sherpas ploughed up through endless waist-deep drifts. It took them five and a half hours to climb the final 600 ft to Camp 6, leaving George so exhausted that he slept for fifteen hours.

His temporary home was a small platform on top of a prominent bulge in the Lhotse Glacier. At 23,000 ft it was almost level with the summit of Pumori, at the other end of the Western Cwm. There was barely space for one small tent, so three of the Sherpas had to remain lower down at Camp 5, leaving George and Ang Nyima to do most of

Map 3 Camps on the Lhotse Face

the hard work above. Ang Nyima was a chain-smoking dandy who had
come up with a consignment of oxygen in late April, having brawled,
drunk and fornicated his way through the Solu Khumbu. At first he

was not well liked, being regarded as lazy and unenthusiastic, but he was one of those rare people whose temperament improved the higher he went. He soon proved himself to be an excellent companion and a stalwart mountaineer.

It was slow going. The heavy snowstorms continued on 12 May, turning movement into a real struggle. John Hunt acknowledged in his diary that the weather was 'atrocious' but he could not contain his impatience. It was five days since the planning meeting and three days before they were due to make the first summit attempt. On 13 May, he decided to pay a visit to George Lowe's tiny red tent in the middle of the Lhotse Face to see for himself why everything was going so slowly.

It was a beautiful morning when he left for Camp 6 but as Hunt and his Sherpa, Ang Namgyal, ploughed their way up, the going became progressively harder. The steps that George Lowe and Ang Nyima had so painstakingly cut were filled in with snow. John was dressed in what was to become his uniform for the next month: a check shirt over a rayon string vest, a white floppy hat and lashings of sun cream to protect his pale skin from the relentless sun. As usual, he had a Contax camera hanging around his neck, the case open. For the climbers, photo stops were a good excuse for a rest but as they struggled up the final slope towards George Lowe's tent, John Hunt and Ang Namgyal found themselves in the camera's eye.

George Lowe had not intended to do any cinematography when he began the expedition but by the end he was so competent that he considered taking it up as a career. Tom Stobart had brought several small 'gun' cameras, as well as his main camera, a 16mm Beaulieu. The gun cameras were easy to operate and virtually unbreakable – perfect for novice cameramen. Charles Wylie used one occasionally but George Lowe was Tom Stobart's most enthusiastic pupil. He developed a particular passion for filming other climbers in an advanced state of exhaustion. On this particular day he guessed that

John Hunt was coming up to chivvy him along, so when he saw his leader struggling through the snow, George was only too pleased to immortalise his obvious discomfort. To add to John Hunt's embarrassment, when the sequence was eventually incorporated into the official Everest film, extra-loud panting was dubbed on to the soundtrack.

Once he had got his breath back, John Hunt relaxed for a moment to take in the view. To the right was the snowy shoulder of Everest's western flank, to the left, the immense ridge connecting Lhotse to Nuptse that he had first glimpsed many weeks ago. Down below in the Western Cwm, their tents looked minute, while up above, the summit of Everest 'looked very close indeed'. Once he had received a progress report, John Hunt turned to descend. However impressive a perch, this was not the sort of place where anyone wanted to hang around.

Down at Advance Base, John Hunt went back to his plans. George Lowe was doing well under the circumstances but it was now time, Hunt decided, to bring in some fresh blood. That night he radioed Wilfrid Noyce and Michael Ward, inviting them to come up to assist George Lowe. John Hunt accepted that there was little chance of sticking to his 15 May target but he hoped that, with their aid, the schedule would not slip too much.

The next morning, as Wilfrid and Michael came up from Base Camp, George Lowe and Ang Nyima made a breakthrough. Alternating the lead, they plugged their way through heavy snow to reach the icy platform at 24,000 ft where, in autumn 1952, the Swiss had placed their main transit camp. It was big enough for several tents and roughly halfway up the Lhotse Face, making it the perfect break point for the 'big carry' to the South Col. That night, during the regular 6p.m. radio conference, George was pleased to report that at last they had made some significant progress. He told John Hunt that he planned to have a rest day before making the

The 1951 Everest Reconnaissance: (left to right) Eric Shipton, Bill Murray, Tom Bourdillon, Earle Riddiford, Mike Ward (seated), and Ed Hillary (seated).

October 1951: Eric Shipton and Ed Hillary climb Pumori to see the southern face of Everest for the first time.

Eric Shipton, 1935.

John Hunt, 1953.

Hillary leads a group into the Western cwm.

The 1953 Everest team.

Ed Hillary uses a builder's ladder to cross a crevasse.

26th May, c. 1.00 p.m.: Charles Evans on the South Summit of Everest.

26th May, c. 4.00 p.m.: Bourdillon and Evans return to the South Col defeated.

29th May 1953, c. 11.30 a.m.: Tenzing on the summit of Everest.

30th May 1953: John Hunt leaps on Hillary and Tenzing.

The Sherpas greet Tenzing like a returning God.

Laying about: George Band, Ed Hillary, Charles Evans (with pipe), and Mike Ward.

20th June 1953, Banepa: John Hunt, Ed Hillary and Tenzing are garlanded with flowers.

final push for the South Col. John Hunt was encouraged but he still thought reinforcements were needed. So on 15 May, the day that he had pencilled for the first attempt on the summit itself, he sent up Wilfrid Noyce to relieve Ang Nyima.

Like George Lowe, Wilfrid Noyce was a schoolmaster but that was where the similarity ended. While Lowe was loud and assertive, Wilfrid was quiet and serious, with pale blue eyes and a thatch of unruly blond hair. He taught modern languages at Charterhouse, the school where the British climber George Mallory had worked before his mysterious disappearance on Everest in 1924. On the walk in, George Lowe and Tom Stobart had entertained everyone with funny stories and anecdotes while Wilfrid wrote poetry and read the classics of world literature.

As a mountaineer, Wilfrid was much more daring than his persona might have suggested. He had climbed extensively in the Alps and survived some serious falls. It had been a slightly frustrating expedition so far but now he had an important job and he was keen to do it well. When he reached George Lowe that afternoon, his priority was to get a good night's rest. Like several other climbers, he had begun to use sleeping pills to overcome the effects of altitude, which made sleep very difficult. As they were turning in, Wilfrid took out a tin and offered his new tent-mate a small green lozenge. George Lowe had not recently had any trouble sleeping but in the spirit of comradely experimentation, he decided to try one.

The following morning, Wilfrid Noyce woke at 6a.m. but George Lowe was as still as the grave. At first Wilfrid was not too worried. Everything took longer at high altitude and no one ever wanted to swap their cosy sleeping bag for the bitter morning wind. Eventually, George stirred and began to pump their Primus stove to melt some water but when Wilfrid glanced at him a few minutes later, he had gone back to sleep – on his knees. Wilfrid got on with his own breakfast but as the sun came up he started thinking about the nightly radio conference. John Hunt would undoubtedly expect great things today but right now they were going nowhere.

A few minutes later George Lowe woke up again and slugged back some tea but he was still bleary-eyed when they finally left camp at 10.30a.m. George knew the route so he took the lead, but he went very slowly and periodically had to stop to rest on his rucksack. Wilfrid was beside himself: what could he do to get George Lowe going? Then he had an idea: more food might wake him up. So Wilfrid handed George a small tin of sardines, a coveted treat on the expedition. He started to tuck in but a few minutes later Wilfrid looked up and saw that he had fallen asleep again, with a limp sardine hanging out of the side of his mouth. At this point Wilfrid Noyce finally admitted defeat and they beat an untimely retreat.

As predicted, John Hunt was not at all pleased. It was 16 May, D-Day plus one and his troops hadn't even reached the beach. If everything had gone according to plan, they should now have a camp on the South Col and the first attempt should be under way. As he reviewed the situation, he realised that more and more, the success of the expedition seemed to be falling on the crumpling shoulders of one man. In the icefall, different parties had taken turns to pioneer particular sections but all their efforts on the Lhotse Face were channelled through George Lowe, who no longer looked like a safe bet. Griffith Pugh did nothing to reassure him, speculating that George Lowe's brain might have been affected by a prolonged stay at high altitude. If things did not improve rapidly, John Hunt resolved to bring George down and let Wilfrid Noyce take over.

Although George Lowe came in for some criticism at the time, this was the stage when John Hunt's planning went awry. Like the leaders of the two Swiss expeditions, he had underestimated the difficulties of getting up the Lhotse Face. This was particularly odd in view of the difficulties that Tom Bourdillon and Charles Evans had experienced on their reconnaissance. Climbing on oxygen, it had taken them three days to reach 24,000 ft but John Hunt seemed to expect George Lowe and his assistants to prepare a route from 22,000 ft and 26,000 ft in a week, entirely under their own steam.

Fortunately, on 17 May, George Lowe woke up much recovered. He and Wilfrid Noyce climbed up again and set up two tents on the site of the old Swiss camp, Camp 7 for the British team. This time, the nightly radio conference was much more optimistic; George Lowe claimed that they would reach the South Col within two days. The BBC forecast added further encouragement, with good weather predicted for the coming days.

At this point John Hunt made a serious mistake. Wilfrid Noyce and George Lowe were going well but instead of leaving them to finish the job, he called Wilfrid down to rest and get ready a group of Sherpas for the 'big carry' to the South Col. In Wilfird's place, he sent up the reserve climber, Michael Ward. Ward was a very good, technical mountaineer but he hadn't acclimatised well on the 1951 reconnaissance expedition and this time it was no different. By the time he reached George Lowe, Michael had slowed to one step for every five breaths.

On 18 May, the weather looked ideal. As John Hunt scanned the Lhotse Face through his powerful binoculars, he saw George Lowe and Michael Ward appear from behind the *seracs* that hid their tent, begin to ascend and then retreat a short time later for no apparent reason. At Advance Base it was calm and warm, the perfect conditions for climbing; what were they playing at? That morning Tom Bourdillon went up to deliver some food and fuel. On his return, he reported that Michael Ward and George Lowe were suffering from the extreme cold and showing early signs of frostbite; Michael Ward's left hand and George Lowe's toes were affected. Not everyone was convinced, as Ed Hillary confided to his diary:

Apparently windy and cold but it seemed to us at IV [Advance Base] that there was a certain lack of drive.[1]

To add to John Hunt's woes, there was a sudden outbreak of illness. Charles Evans developed a severe stomach bug and Gyalzen, Tom Stobart's personal Sherpa, started spitting blood and had to be sent down to Base Camp with a suspected ulcer.

The only positive news was the arrival of Thondup, the expedition chef, who quickly installed himself in the cookhouse. Gap-toothed and wizen-faced, Thondup was no climber. That morning, he had given the other Sherpas a good laugh when he donned his crampons with the spikes pointing inwards. Thondup's cooking was much appreciated but food was no distraction for an increasingly anxious John Hunt. He spent more and more of his time staring up at the Lhotse Face, counting the days and hoping that he might see some progress. George Lowe's radio set appeared to have died but John Hunt didn't have to speak to him to figure out that something was very wrong.

They were significantly behind schedule, leaving Hunt with two choices. He could send up a member of one of the summit parties to complete the route to the South Col, at the risk of weakening them. The alternative was to dispatch the main team of Sherpas with the supplies and equipment for the South Col camp before the route was fully prepared. Whichever choice he made, he had to do something before the weather changed and his plans unravelled completely.

After much deliberation, Hunt decided on the second option. He asked Wilfrid Noyce and Charles Wylie to get ready to lead the 'big carry' to the South Col. This was the moment when the Sherpas had to show their mettle. The best fourteen were split into two groups. Even the toughest would only be able to climb the Lhotse Face once without oxygen, so everything had to go perfectly. The number of tent spaces at Camp 7, in the middle of the Lhotse Face, was limited, so the two groups were scheduled to make their ascent to the South Col twenty-four hours apart.

On 19 May John Hunt woke to crystal-blue skies but there was no visible movement from George Lowe and Michael Ward. A revived George Band went up to deliver food and a spare radio set; he reported that it was so cold and windy that they had decided not to leave their tent. A rest day before renewing the attack? Too cold? What on earth was going on? In John Hunt's diary 'chagrin' turned into 'exasperation'.

Although everyone shared Hunt's worries and frustrations, 19 May was a busy but exciting day of packing and organising. It was hot and sultry at Advance Base; some of the Sherpas were bare-chested as they sorted out their loads. Tom Stobart filmed as Tenzing wrapped a series of flags around the shaft of his ice axe: the Union Jack, the red and black flag of Nepal, the blue and white of the United Nations and the red and green of an Indian flag, given to Tenzing by his friend Rabindranath Mitra in Darjeeling.

At 4p.m., Wilfrid Noyce left with the first party of eight Sherpas, aiming to get one camp higher that night before making a determined push for the top. John Hunt accompanied him for the first hour. Before they parted, he took Wilfrid aside and told him that he must, at all costs, make the breakthrough to the South Col, even if it meant leaving most of the Sherpas in camp and taking only Annullu, the strongest climber. The others could be escorted up by Charles Wylie the next day, if absolutely necessary. It was crucial to prove to the Sherpas that the Lhotse Face could be climbed, or they would undoubtedly become demoralised. Any Sherpa who reached the South Col would be paid a bonus but as John Hunt knew from his career in the army, fear was a powerful deterrent.

On the morning of 20 May, Hunt was at his familiar post, staring up at the Lhotse Face. At 9.45a.m. he saw Michael Ward and George Lowe come out, only to turn back after barely half an hour. Elation quickly turned to despair. John Hunt couldn't work out what was going on. Why couldn't they finish the job? His only comfort was the thought that Wilfrid Noyce must be close by.

If John Hunt could have witnessed the scene at Wilfrid's camp, a few hundred feet below George and Michael's, he would not have been so confident. Wilfrid Noyce had got up at 6.30a.m. full of purpose but his Sherpas took two hours to start. He pushed them hard but they were heavily laden, carrying not only the supplies for the South Col but also quantities of personal gear. Their average load weighed 50 lb, a huge amount for this altitude.

To add to the pressure, this was the first time that Wilfrid Noyce had used oxygen since the acclimatisation climbs a month before. He found his set very bulky and uncomfortable. More alarmingly, when he paused after a few hours to check his oxygen cylinder, there was only a third left. He found two more bottles in the snow near Camp 6, but they were the old-fashioned type that didn't have a built-in pressure gauge. The only way to check how full they were was to connect them to his set, a time-consuming and awkward task that brought more bad news: both bottles were half-empty. His only hope was that there would be more supplies at George Lowe's next camp.

A few hours later, Wilfrid Noyce met Michael Ward and George Lowe on their way down. The encounter did nothing to raise his spirits: George Lowe admitted that they had made no progress that morning and, to make things worse, informed him that there was very little fuel left higher up. The normally imperturbable Wilfrid was thrown into a panic. There was nothing he could do but send down two of his most reliable Sherpas with George and Michael, to bring back some fuel, while he and the others continued their ascent.

Camp 7, at 24,000 ft, was a miserable sight, clearly too small for all the Sherpas Wilfrid Noyce had brought up. They pitched two more tents and got the stove going to brew some tea. Wilfrid found a flask of lemonade but cursed his luck when the Sherpas noticed it as well and he had to pass it around. When he found a tin of sardines at the bottom of a tent pocket, he ate the lot, convincing himself that there was too little to share. High altitude was not good for moral probity. A few hours later Ang Norbu and Ang Dawa II, the two Sherpas he had sent back, returned with a few much-needed tins of kerosene.

At around the same time George Lowe and Michael Ward trudged back into Advance Base at the foot of the Lhotse Face. Tom Stobart filmed a heavily bearded George, tired but managing to raise a smile.

John Hunt did not reciprocate, as Michael Ward recorded in his diary on 20 May:

> John EXCESSIVELY RUDE to George who had been up about ten days and working damned well. Quite ashamed to have him in the party which has been very friendly so far.[2]

It was a rare moment of anger on an otherwise happy expedition. If John Hunt did let fly at George Lowe, the New Zealander took no permanent offence. Far worse was the silent criticism that hung over the camp; everyone seemed to feel that he had somehow failed especially after, as George Lowe admitted in a letter to his sister Betty, he had been so cocky early on.

That evening Wilfrid Noyce managed to get through on the radio. He was barely audible but reported that several oxygen bottles seemed to be leaking. Another oxygen crisis seemed to be looming but was Noyce a reliable judge? Tom Bourdillon was not convinced; he worried that Noyce might have inadvertently discharged the bottles or worse, left them open. With radio contact lost or intermittent at best, there was nothing that anybody could do but wait until the following morning and hope for the best. And worry.

The bad weather earlier in the month had given way to a much more settled spell but they were nowhere near ready to exploit it. In recent nights the forecasts on the BBC had been accompanied by messages of support from friends and admirers. Maurice Herzog, the leader of the French team that had climbed Annapurna in 1950, wished them luck. A few days later the Swiss climber Raymond Lambert echoed his encouragement. What would he say if he could see them now?

Colonel, you're going to have big problems.

The warning Raymond Lambert gave John Hunt when they met in Zurich four months earlier seemed even more like a prophecy than a challenge.

At Base Camp James Morris felt the tension growing. While almost everyone else had moved up to Advance Base, he had decided to stay put, to be as close as possible to the small army of runners that he employed to send messages back to Kathmandu. At night he made notes on the radio conferences. Sometimes reception was good enough for him to speak to John Hunt, at other times he could only listen. He was comfortable enough, with a double sleeping bag, a wireless receiver that picked up the BBC and his own cook, Sonam, but by late May his lonely vigil was not quite so lonely.

Mr Tiwari, the Indian policemen in charge of the telegraph station in Namche Bazaar arrived with several flunkies and a freelance journalist who was working for the *Daily Telegraph*. A few days later, Peter Jackson, a Reuters correspondent, turned up. He was an old friend and James Morris was happy to have tea with him. Morris was less happy when his guest informed him that he had rented a small house at the Thyangboche Monastery for the duration of the expedition. How many rivals would he have to fend off?

In Britain, the press coverage of the expedition had intensified. The dramatic story of Ralph Izzard's plimsoll-powered solo expedition had appeared in the *Daily Mail* at the beginning of May, followed by a series of reports on the expedition's progress, based on the plans that Hunt had announced a month earlier. On 16 May Ralph Izzard announced in the *Daily Mail* that the assault on Everest was about to begin with a bombardment of the Lhotse Face by the expedition's two-inch mortar.

Mercifully, the time delay in getting information to and from London kept Hunt ignorant of some of the more wildly speculative articles now appearing in the press but his letters home revealed his anxieties and his increasing desperation. On 20 May, after consulting with Charles Evans and Ed Hillary, he decided on another significant change of plan. The next day, if Wilfrid Noyce did not make good progress, Hillary and Tenzing would go up to give the South Col teams a final boost.

This went against Hunt's instincts and the grain of his plan. For the last two weeks he had been very protective of his two summit pairs, arguing that they had to be held back until the last moment. However, the expedition had reached crisis point: if the Sherpas could not get the supplies up to the South Col in the next few days, there would be no summit attempts.

On the following morning the camp was terribly tense: would Wilfrid lead the first band of Sherpas to the South Col or would there be yet another delay? After a sleepless night, George Lowe was up at first light. He joined John Hunt at his post, binoculars at hand, staring up at the Lhotse Face.

8.30a.m. – nothing

9.00a.m. – nothing

9.15a.m. – nothing

9.30a.m. – nothing

On the Lhotse Face all was clearly not well. Annullu had brought a bowl of porridge to Wilfrid's tent at 8a.m. but his news was not so welcome. The other Sherpas were ill, hungry and unenthusiastic. When Noyce called for volunteers to go to the South Col, only two men raised their hands, and one dropped out a few minutes later. Wilfrid had no alternative but to move to Plan B. He sent two Sherpas down with a message for John Hunt. Fifteen minutes later he and Annullu hauled on their oxygen sets and moved out.

From Advance Base John Hunt first saw the two Sherpas leave Camp 7 and begin to descend. Down. Descending? What was going on? Could things be getting worse? Then he saw a second pair, moving slowly upwards. It had to be Wilfrid and Annullu. This was a huge relief but what were the implications? Had the Sherpas refused to go on or was there some other problem? A few hours later the two Sherpas arrived at Advance Base. In a letter to his sister George Lowe described the ensuing panic:

> A note arrived from Wilf to say that several oxygen bottles were leaking & that the Sherpas at VII refused, in a body, to push up - saying they were all sick. John tore his hair [out] & retired to his tent, Charles Evans, his chief lieutenant went to console, Tom Bourdillon began pacing around & shouting over the wireless – 'Camp IV calling Camp VII – Report my signals – This is urgent – Over!' – Repeat, repeat, repeat! Tom is oxygen officer & wanted to try & save the oxygen. For three hours or so the place was like a battle control-room & the battle was going badly.[3]

Mercifully, Wilfrid Noyce had no sense of the panic that his note had created. He climbed upwards with Annullu, passing the fresh ropes that had recently been fixed by George Lowe and older ones left by the Swiss. He felt excited to be breaking new ground but aware of the huge responsibility he had shouldered. If they could get to the South Col, everything would be back on track but if they failed, the expedition would run into very serious problems.

At the top of the main slope they were halted in their tracks by a vast, eight-foot-wide crevasse. Wilfrid walked along the edge, searching for a snow bridge to get them across but he found nothing.

He tried the other direction. Nothing. High up on the Lhotse Face there were no tree trunks or aluminium ladders. The crevasse was too wide to jump and there seemed to be no way around it.

Then Wilfrid noticed a point where icy lips projected from either side of the crevasse, narrowing the gap to three feet. Would they hold a man's weight? Wilfrid gingerly prodded the near side with his ice axe. It seemed solid enough but what about the other one? There was only one way to find out. Annullu took a firm stance. Wilfrid took a few steps back, ran and jumped.

He flew through the air and jammed his ice axe in hard on the other side. He had made it. Nothing could stop them now. He brought Annullu over and together they traversed to the rocks of the Geneva Spur. It was amazing to feel something solid under their boots after several weeks of climbing on snow and ice. Slowly and carefully, they worked their way up to the crest.

A few hundred feet below them lay their goal: the South Col, a miserable, wind-swept plateau, about 400 yards square, swept clear of snow by the endless wind and covered in dirty grey boulders and sheets of blue ice studded with small stones. That day it was surprisingly calm, bizarrely reminding Wilfrid of a winter's day on Scafell Pike, in the Lake District. Towering above them on the left was the South-East Ridge that led to the summit of Everest, 3000 ft above, hidden behind a wall of mist. Mindful of their return journey and the many others to come over the next few days, Wilfrid hammered in an ice piton and attached a five-hundred-foot rope, which they unfurled on the way down. It was strange to be descending after such a climb up the Lhotse Face.

Up close the South Col looked unwelcoming. Six months of gale-force winds had reduced the Swiss camp to a few tattered and torn strips of yellow cloth hanging from skeletal tent poles, amid a frozen chaos of food, oxygen cylinders and equipment. It was an eerie, threatening sight. Then something very strange happened.

Annullu saw an abandoned Swiss rucksack, stuffed with a pair of felt boots, and pulled it free of the ice. Tenzing had told him that if he reached the South Col he could take whatever he wanted from the Swiss camp. Annullu was so bent on plunder that he was prepared to descend without oxygen if it meant being able to carry more. Wilfrid looked on disapprovingly but this was no place to have an argument. He took several photographs and picked up a few spoils of his own: another tin of sardines, some cheese, a few Vita-Weat crackers and a precious box of matches. Twenty minutes later they took hold of the rope and pulled their way back to the crest before descending to Camp 7 amid the cheers of the Sherpas they had left behind. It was a key moment in the expedition: the South Col had been reached and now they could get on with the final stage of the climb.

That night the tents were crammed full of Sherpas and climbers. Wilfrid Noyce was surprised to see Ed Hillary and Tenzing, who had come up after pestering John Hunt into letting them give an extra boost to the 'big carry'. This time there was no shortage of fuel at the camp but precious little food to cook. For his hero's dinner, Wilfrid Noyce ate the sardines and Swiss cheese that he had collected a few hours earlier. Charles Wylie spent the afternoon sorting loads and offering the Sherpas tea, sympathy and handfuls of the 'pep' pills given to him by Michael Ward. These, together with the successful return of Wilfrid Noyce and Annullu, boosted morale but there was still much grumbling. Tenzing's presence was vital: he worked hard with the Sherpas, alternating sweet talk with inspiring words.

It was a windy, cloud-free night that left their tents coated in thick frost. The Sherpas were up at 5.30a.m. but no one had the energy to cook anything more than tea, with handfuls of Grape-Nuts thrown in for sustenance. Charles Wylie ate his watery breakfast with a spanner.

At Advance Base John Hunt was at his usual post on the ice, craning his neck up to check what was happening. He had been thrilled to see Wilfrid Noyce and Annullu getting so high on the previous day but their success would mean nothing if they weren't followed by the Sherpas this morning. At 8.30a.m., he saw two tiny figures emerging from behind the *seracs*. Hillary and Tenzing, just identifiable through Hunt's powerful binoculars, were taking the lead. Next came the Sherpas, one after the other, until eventually there were no fewer than seventeen men high up on the Lhotse Face, heading for the South Col. If they all made it, it would be an incredible achievement, double the number of Sherpas that the Swiss had got up in the previous year.

High above Hunt, Charles Wylie, Ed Hillary and Tenzing were glad to be wearing oxygen sets but they found it very tiring to kick and cut extra steps for the men behind them. The Sherpas had reduced their loads to 30 lb but even that was a phenomenal weight at this altitude, especially because they had eaten so little over the previous twenty-four hours. By the time they reached the top of the Lhotse Face, almost everyone had slowed down markedly. Some were flat out on the snow; two looked so weak that Hillary and Tenzing offered to take part of their loads.

One Sherpa stopped just before the top of the Lhotse Face, saying that he could not continue; Charles Wylie took his pack. A few minutes later Charles's oxygen ran out. It was too awkward to change the cylinder, so he had to climb the final few hundred feet unaided.

Ed and Tenzing were first to the South Col, quickly followed by three Sherpas. They dumped their loads close to the remnants of the Swiss tents and then retreated as quickly as they could. Ed looked around in awe, as he recorded in his diary:

What a place! The South Summit looks absolutely terrifying from here.[4]

On the descent they picked up the Sherpa who had halted and escorted him to Camp 7. Most of the Sherpas stayed the night but Ed and Tenzing continued on to Advance Base after a short rest and a drink.

At the bottom they met John Hunt, on his way up with Charles Evans and Tom Bourdillon, the first summit party. Hunt was shocked to see how tired Ed Hillary looked. However, he didn't stop to talk for too long. After two weeks of tension, his main feeling was joy and huge relief that the summit attempts were under way. As he wrote in his diary:

We are off on the big adventure.[5]

The beginning of that adventure was more eventful than he might have wanted. The first crisis occurred on the second day, when Charles Evans changed the soda lime canister on his closed-circuit set. Within minutes, ice formed on the delicate valves that controlled the flow of oxygen, leaving him desperately breathless. Fortunately, Tom Bourdillon was close by and quickly resolved the problem but it was a nasty scare, a reminder of how dependent they were on their oxygen sets.

On the following day John Hunt was at the centre of the drama. In the middle of a difficult ice slope he suddenly felt spent and absolutely unable to continue. Tom Bourdillon and Charles Evans were close by but it took a long time and much effort to get him to a safe position. When Tom Bourdillon examined Hunt's oxygen set, he found that one of the supply tubes had developed a kink and cut off the supply of oxygen. No wonder John Hunt had felt terrible. He had been shouldering a 50-lb load and wearing an uncomfortable mask to no benefit whatsoever.

On the late afternoon of 24 May they reached the South Col, with only a few hours to pitch their tents before the sun went down and it became punishingly cold. The wind made it nearly impossible to attach guy ropes. John Hunt's oxygen ran out almost immediately and Charles Evans took off his set, thinking that it would make it easier to get things done. This was a serious mistake, as John Hunt wrote in his diary that night:

This was a fantastic struggle with each of us falling about with lack of oxygen and unable to work for more than a few moments at a time. And all the time that fiendish wind – deadly cold – was tearing the tent over our hands and blowing away anything we chanced to lay down on this desert stony waste.[6]

John Hunt fell over and lay face down in the snow, unable to move for several minutes. When Tom Bourdillon's oxygen ran out, he too collapsed from oxygen starvation. It was like the decompression chamber at RAF Farnborough where they had trained five months before but this time no gentle doctor chivvied him awake with fresh oxygen; there was only the relentless wind and a voice in the back of his head telling him that if he didn't get up soon, he might never do so.

Tom Bourdillon eventually managed to attach one end of a climbing rope to the top of the tent and the other end to a large boulder. Their two Sherpas stumbled down on to the South Col; the heaviest, Ang Tensing, nicknamed 'Balu' (after Kipling's *Jungle Book* bear) because of his unexpected bulk, collapsed inside the half-erect tent and acted as an impromptu ballast. It took them over an hour to erect the main pyramid tent and a further thirty minutes to put up a smaller tent next to it. Then they turned on their stoves, melted some ice and made hot drinks. Soup, lemon juice, tea, coffee: anything that warmed them and relieved their terrible thirst. They were so exhausted that they could not possibly stick to the schedule and make their attempt the next day, so they decided to wait for twenty-four hours, even if it meant using more food and supplies.

When they woke on the morning of 25 May the weather was tantalisingly good, with barely a breath of wind and clear blue skies. There was much to do but nothing could be done quickly. Tom Bourdillon later told Michael Ward that it took them about three times as long to perform a task on the South Col as it did at lower altitude. Tom painstakingly prepared their oxygen sets. Charles Evans kept the stove running and updated his diary. On the eve of his big day he took the time to write a postcard to his young nephew Martin. Charles drew a picture of their small tent on the South Col from where, he wrote, they would have 'a look at the route towards the top'. John Hunt was happy to potter around, tidying up the camp and unpacking some special photographic plates for measuring cosmic rays, given to him by a scientist in Zurich. He was amazed to be able to walk from one end of the South Col to the other in just his down socks, with a couple of woollen pairs underneath. At one point he stood on the edge, waving down towards the Western Cwm, in the vain hope that someone might be looking up. No one reciprocated. When he found a Swiss tin of tuna fish, he hid away in the small tent they had put up that morning and scoffed the lot. Like Wilfrid Noyce, he discovered that high altitude was not good for his moral fibre.

That evening, John Hunt gave a short but stirring speech to Charles and Tom about the great day ahead. From tomorrow, John Hunt would stop working with Bourdillon and Evans and become entirely focused on the second summit team. With Ang Nyima and Balu, he would attempt to carry the first few loads to Hillary and Tenzing's final camp, 1500 ft higher up on the summit ridge.

If everything went perfectly of course, there might not be a second attempt. Tom Bourdillon and Charles Evans would stand on the summit of Everest and crown the efforts of thirty years of British expeditions. Then they would go home, salute the Queen, kiss their loved ones and spend the rest of their lives as the toast of the climbing world. If everything went perfectly.

Chapter 9

FIRST UP

Dawn was bitterly cold on 26 May 1953 but nothing could dampen the British team's excitement. After six weeks laying siege to Everest, and eight months of preparation, they were finally ready. From Camp 8 on the South Col, 26,000 ft above sea level, Tom Bourdillon and Charles Evans were to make the first assault. To succeed, they would have to climb 3000 ft, over largely unknown ground and get back down, all in one day. It was a daunting task but they were quietly confident. Like everyone else, Tom and Charles were tired of waiting. Today was the day; no more plans and meetings, no more worrying about the monsoon, just the two of them and Everest.

They woke at 5a.m., when the first rays of the sun hit the edge of their tent. They had slept in their clothes, in order to get going quickly, and shared their sleeping bags with their soda lime canisters, to prevent them from freezing. During the night, the temperature had plunged to −20 °C, causing Charles Evans to lose all feeling in his toes. He was glad to put on his huge high-altitude boots, with their soft leather outer layer, which made his feet look elephantine. Although they both longed for a hot drink, neither attempted to light their Primus stove. Instead, they made do with a couple of flasks of lukewarm lemon juice brewed the previous night.

Boots, gloves, a handful of boiled sweets, crampons, a few more swallows of lemon juice, snow goggles, camera … by 6a.m., they were ready. Charles poked his head out of the tent into the biting wind. Tom passed him his oxygen set but as soon as he put it on, it froze. He crawled back in; Tom lit a candle to begin the careful work of thawing the valves that controlled the flow of oxygen. It was not an auspicious start but neither man was either surprised or worried. Throughout the expedition there had been minor problems like this and Tom had always managed to sort things out. Within a few minutes, Charles was back on the Col, lifting the heavy frame of the oxygen set on to his back and preparing to move off.

As soon as he inhaled, Charles Evans felt an indescribably awful choking sensation. He ripped off his mask and gasped hoarsely. In the thin air of the South Col, it took minutes to get his breath back. He croaked to Tom that it had felt as if he were about to die. 'I expect you were,' Tom replied, coolly. He wasn't going to let a technical problem dent his enthusiasm, even if this was their second false start of the day. Charles was shaken. He took his set off again and the two men huddled around it to find out what was wrong.

A few feet away John Hunt was in another tent. He had problems of his own. That morning he was due to follow Tom and Charles up the South-East Ridge, with 90 lb of tents, supplies and equipment but Ang Tensing was refusing to start. Lower down he had been happy to throw his weight around but since he had arrived on the South Col, he had been a nervous wreck. Instead of playing his part this morning, he would stay on the South Col and Hunt and Da Namgyal would carry even heavier loads.

The minutes ticked by.

Tom Bourdillon and Charles Evans had planned to leave at 6a.m. but an hour later, they had not discovered the fault. Charles spoke to John Hunt but his leader had other things on his mind. Today he was in battle mode: if the first assault was turning out to be a damp squib, his priority, as expedition leader, was to prepare for the second. Just after

7a.m., Hunt and Da Namgyal set off with 45 lb of oxygen and equipment each, destined for Hillary and Tenzing's top camp on the South-East Ridge.

Shortly afterwards Tom Bourdillon identified the problem with Charles's set. In his final report, months after the expedition, he wrote that someone had inadvertently damaged the oxygen supply valve, in a 'mistaken but well-meant attempt' to improve its efficiency. That 'someone' was probably Charles Evans but 7.15a.m. on the South Col, on the morning of their summit attempt, was neither the time nor the place to hold a full inquest. With blood covering his frozen fingers, Tom replaced the valve and a few minutes later they were on their way.

In front of them lay the South-East Ridge, a precarious staircase of uncertain snow and steep rock. Tom and Charles's earlier excitement was tempered with gloom but to their surprise, they began moving well. Ahead of them they saw Hunt and Da Namgyal making their way towards a gully at the foot of the ridge. Before long they had overtaken them. Up they went in a steady rhythm, kicking and chopping steps into the hard snow. When it became too steep, then they moved on to the rocks. Like all good climbers, Tom and Charles enjoyed both the intellectual challenge of finding the best route and the physical challenge of overcoming difficult terrain. Charles had marginally more Himalayan experience than his younger partner but Tom was very self-assured and, as everyone said, amazingly agile for a man of his size.

As they came up over a crest in the rocks, they were greeted with an eerie sight. On a small platform hacked into the ice were the skeletal remains of a small tent: a few wispy poles topped with torn strips of cloth, which thrummed in the wind like ancient prayer flags. A year earlier Tenzing and Raymond Lambert had spent an awful night at this spot, with neither sleeping bags nor anything to eat. Tom and Charles paused briefly to look down; like everyone who followed, they were amazed how steep the Lhotse Face looked and how precarious their camps seemed. They didn't stay long.

Tom and Charles's confidence was returning. At the very least, they would break Lambert and Tenzing's altitude record from the previous year and reach the unclimbed South Summit, the prominent peak in the ridge, just 300 ft below the summit. As they made their way upwards, weaving between the rocks, they constantly calculated how much oxygen they had left and how much further it would take them. They had started late but now were moving at a phenomenal pace, making 1000 ft an hour. If they could keep that up, the summit would be within their grasp.

Their optimism was premature. The slopes became much steeper and the rock increasingly uneven. They had to use their hands most of the time. Their short-pointed crampons did not grip well into the patches of hard, polished ice and the thick covering of powder snow elsewhere made the going even slower. At about 11a.m., they found a sheltered spot, a snowy hollow roughly halfway between the Swiss tent and the South Summit. Charles Evans stopped and made the sensible, but fateful, suggestion that they should change their oxygen cylinders and soda lime canisters.

He knew this was early in the day but after all the problems that morning and his experience on the Lhotse Face three days before, Charles Evans didn't want to risk running out of oxygen in the middle of a dangerous slope and having to make the change in a less controlled environment. Tom was not so sure; their canisters were not yet empty and to replace them now meant abandoning precious oxygen and soda lime and therefore reducing their endurance. Charles Evans was convinced that this was the right course of action; after the change, they would still have five hours of oxygen left. By his calculation, if they kept going at this rate, they would reach the summit in an hour and a half and have enough to get back safely. Tom Bourdillon was not so certain but there had been enough delays already and his priority was to maintain their momentum.

These were tense moments but the change went smoothly and

they carried on, 20 lb lighter. Tom was back on track, with every rock pitch leading him closer to his goal. Charles, however, soon regretted making the change.

After ten minutes he began to feel light-headed and breathless. This was not the sudden choking sensation that he had experienced earlier that morning but rather the strange feeling that no matter how deeply he inhaled, he was not getting enough oxygen. The sensation intensified until he could no longer go on. Tom turned repairman once again.

Valves: fine. Tubes: fine. Oxygen cylinder: full. Re-breathing bag: soft and malleable. He could not find anything wrong, so he started again. Valves, tubes, oxygen, mask ... There was only one thing left: the new soda lime canister. Tom and Charles had taken so much care but now they had a defective canister. It was a bitter blow: the oxygen cylinder was fine but the broken canister caused carbon dioxide to accumulate in the re-breathing bag every time Charles exhaled. Worst of all, there was nothing that Tom could do about it.

Incredibly, Charles Evans kept going, though he could not match Tom's pace. The two men grew further and further apart, until sometimes there was a rope length between them. Tom was in a desperate hurry; he knew that after changing so early, the rest of the day would be a race against time. It was a dangerous tactic: if Tom slipped, Charles might not be able to hold on to him.

To add to their problems, the route became increasingly uneven and the conditions much worse. Sometimes they had to wade through thick snow, sometimes they had to tackle slippery rock. Despite the difficulties, they pressed on, oblivious to their audience.

A thousand feet below, on the Lhotse Face, Ed Hillary and the members of the second assault team watched their progress as they made their way up to the South Col. George Lowe spotted them first and shouted joyfully to the others. Alfred Gregory was equally excited and felt immensely proud at the thought they might go all the way.

Hillary and Tenzing's emotions were more complicated; excitement tempered with uncertainty. If Bourdillon and Evans were to succeed, would their attempt take place? Lower down, Ed Hillary was heartened to spot two more tiny figures, moving slowly up the South-East Ridge. It was Hunt and Da Namgyal, carrying supplies up to what would become Ed and Tenzing's final camp. Evidently John Hunt still expected a second assault.

John Hunt and Da Namgyal were equally unaware of the excitement. They had only an intermittent view of Tom and Charles and no means to communicate with them. When John Hunt glimpsed them moving rapidly upwards he was surprised at how steady they looked. In his diary, he later wrote that his climb up the South-East Ridge was the hardest thing that he had ever done. It was such a physical strain that he wet himself:

> Gasping and moaning for breath was an experience I'll never, never forget: a real fight for life. Bodily self-control vanished as I struggled to get back into my lungs that vital element of oxygen. Never have I been put to such physical strain.[1]

At about 10.15a.m., John Hunt and Da Namgyal paused at the remains of the Swiss tent. They were in such a poor state that they rested for half an hour. Then they clambered up another hundred feet, until Da Namgyal could go no further. Hunt spotted a ledge a little higher up and cajoled his weary Sherpa into one final effort. The ledge was barely wide enough for the two men to stand on, never mind pitch a tent but they put down their loads and built a flimsy cairn to identify the location. Selflessly, they took off their oxygen bottles and added them to the equipment pile. Then they began to make their way down.

Their descent was as difficult as their ascent. They moved slowly and unsteadily. By the time they reached the Swiss tent, John Hunt was so concerned about the next stage that he connected a second oxygen bottle, which he had hoped to hand over untouched to the second assault team. This was a mistake. The main supply tube on his set had become clogged with ice; far from improving the situation, the faulty set made things worse. Eventually, he realised that there was something wrong and took off his mask. The weather worsened. In the gully leading down to the South Col Hunt and Da Namgyal descended painfully slowly, stopping frequently to belay each other.

By the time they reached the relatively easy ground of the South Col both men were almost played out. As they tottered back towards the tents of Camp 8, Hunt noticed Hillary and Tenzing coming towards them. They had just arrived on the South Col and had taken off their oxygen sets, but seeing Hunt and Da Namgyal's hesitant progress, they rushed out to help them. A few moments before their saviours reached them, John Hunt's legs gave way and he collapsed on the ice in tears. Once he was back on his feet, Ed put John Hunt's arm over his shoulder and held him around the waist. Even with the big New Zealander's assistance, Hunt was too weak to walk. Ed plied him with lemon juice from Tenzing's flask but it was no good.

Sensing that something was seriously wrong, Ed Hillary headed back to the tents and grabbed an oxygen set. Hurrying wasn't easy at 26,000 ft and it was some minutes before Hillary returned. He strapped the mask on to Hunt and adjusted the valve to peak flow. Fortunately, the medicine had some effect; ten minutes later Hunt and Da Namgyal made it to the tents. Hillary removed Hunt's mask but left the cylinder open, aiming to flood the tent with oxygen. Tenzing brought a hot drink and Hunt hoarsely murmured his gratitude. After a commotion outside George Lowe poked his head through the tent flaps. He and Alfred Gregory had just run down to the South Col.

'They're up! Tom and Charles have made it!' he exclaimed.

Barely a few minutes earlier, while George Lowe and Alfred Gregory were making a final traverse on to the South Col, the clouds had parted to reveal two tiny figures climbing steadily up and over the South Summit. Gregory and Lowe were so excited that despite the altitude, they ran all the way down to the tents.

Hunt was instantly revived by the news. Gregory and Lowe came in positively 'jubilant', as Hunt underlined in a letter to his wife, Joy. The Sherpas caught the mood. Ang Nyima, who had come up with Hillary and Tenzing, exclaimed in slang Hindi, 'Everest has had it!' Several of the Sherpas had found getting up to the South Col very hard. Even the 'Tigers', who had been kept back for the final stage, had struggled with the altitude. Now they celebrated what they thought was the end of the expedition. They didn't realise that Tom and Charles had only reached the South Summit and had another 300 ft to go.

Outside, on the Col, the wind picked up as the clouds rolled in, obscuring the South Summit and the two men who had just reached it.

Blue skies above; rolling banks of cloud below. A thin layer of snow covering everything, crunchy underfoot. Higher up, the wind whipping the enormous cornices on the ridge, sending plumes of snow soaring into the air. No sound except the relentless roar of the wind and the hiss of their oxygen sets. Tom and Charles gazed around in exhausted awe. For a moment they forgot the hard work of getting to the South Summit and simply revelled in the wild beauty before them. They were the highest men in the world: over 2000 ft higher than Herzog at the summit of Annapurna in 1950, several hundred feet higher than Tenzing and Lambert in 1952.

Charles removed his oxygen mask to suck some boiled sweets and Tom brought out his camera. He took a photograph of Charles sitting on the snow, looking into the distance, and then a more formal shot of him kneeling on one knee, with his arm resting on the other. In front of him his ice axe was plunged into the snow, with his rope coiled around it. Charles took off his mitten, revealing a watch poking from under his glove. It was 1.20p.m.

Before them lay the final three hundred feet of rock and ice that led to the true summit. For Tom, it was a beautiful, exhilarating sight, 'a wilder and more fantastic ridge than either of us had seen before in the Himalayas or the Alps'. Charles took a photograph of Tom, staring upwards, his back to the camera. Could they go on or should they head back? They had about six more hours of daylight, probably enough to get the summit and back. But did they have the oxygen?

Tom and Charles were not the only men considering what they should do next. Down on the South Col, the excitement of seeing them so high had given way to more sober reflection. Should Tom and Charles carry on? A few days earlier, the two assault teams had discussed this situation. When Hillary asked Tom and Charles what they would do if they reached the South Summit late in the day, Tom had assured him that they were 'both sensible chaps with a desire to go on living' but Hillary was not entirely convinced.

He trusted Charles Evans absolutely but although he rated Tom Bourdillon highly as a climber, he worried that his fierce determination might override his better judgement. Ed wanted the first assault to succeed but more important they had to return safely, both for their sake and the sake of the expedition. No one wanted a repeat of Mallory and Irvine's disappearance in 1924. No one wanted the second assault to turn into a rescue mission.

Although Tom Bourdillon and Charles Evans had been partnered for much of the expedition, they were quite different. Tom was a brilliant rock climber, who had made his name in the Alps, climbing the difficult routes the previous generation of British climbers had avoided. He and Michael Ward were founder members of the Alpine Climbing Group, whose rules included automatic retirement at the age of forty and bi-annual scrutiny of every member's climbing record, to make sure that their standards were high enough.

Charles Evans was five years the older; bitter experience had taught him to be cautious in the mountains. Just a few years before, he had survived an accident on Mont Blanc that had killed his friend, Richard Hull. Like Eric Shipton, his great joy lay in exploring blanks on the map and uncharted regions, not bagging peaks or scaling impossible cliffs. He was a natural leader and although Hunt never stated it publicly, it was clear that he had deliberately partnered him with Tom Bourdillon so that the two men might balance each other. Tom would push Charles to his limit but Charles, Hunt hoped, would always be strong enough to know when to say 'no'.

As Charles Evans looked at the ridge before them he estimated that it would take them three hours to reach the top – but they only had two and a half hours of oxygen left. If they succeeded, they would run out of oxygen on the summit and would have to make the return journey unassisted. Tom and Charles didn't have the luxury of Hillary and Tenzing's extra camp on the South-East Ridge, so they had to get all the way down to South Col by the end of the day. To Charles, this was utterly unrealistic. They had achieved their objectives: they had climbed to the South Summit and scouted the route for Hillary and Tenzing. It was time to turn back.

Tom disagreed. They had come this far, how could they not go on? He regretted following Charles's suggestion to change their oxygen and soda lime canisters so early in the day; it had lost them an hour of vital oxygen and considerably reduced their margin of error. However, they still had a slender chance to seize the greatest prize in mountaineering; what climber would turn back now?

From the very first thing that morning, the two men had behaved very differently. At 7a.m., when he thought his oxygen set could not be fixed and the first assault would have to be called off, Charles Evans had walked over to John Hunt and offered to help carry equipment up to Hillary and Tenzing's ridge camp. Hunt declined and Tom Bourdillon carried on working on the fault until, eventually, he managed to get Charles's set working again, albeit at a reduced flow rate.

Charles Evans had never been entirely convinced by the closed-circuit system and none of the events of that morning had given him more grounds for confidence. All oxygen sets were unpredictable but the closed-circuit variety seemed to be particularly capricious and too fragile for this kind of expedition. When Charles later wrote about closed-circuit sets, it was always with distrust; he described them as 'heavy and vulnerable' and 'covered in sharp edges' that invariably snagged on everything in their path. The bulky design and the tight mask were utterly alien to a climber like Charles Evans, who loved the companionship of mountaineering and the sense of communion with the environment.

Charles did not believe that getting to the summit was the be-all and end-all of climbing. In a revealing letter to his friend and fellow doctor Anne McCandless, sent in February 1953, just before he left for Everest, he wrote:

> As to success – putting someone on the top – I don't think it is so important – though it would not do to broadcast that opinion.

Then he added:

> It would be possible, wouldn't it, for a man to stand on top and yet to have failed.[2]

It was a cryptic comment but looking at his climbing record, it is obvious that for Charles Evans, mountaineering was not just about bagging peaks, it was also about doing everything in the right style and for the right reasons.[3]

Tom Bourdillon was not an obsessive peak-bagger but despite his shy demeanour he was very determined. For Tom, oxygen sets were a means to an end and on Everest, that end made the problems worthwhile. As for the peculiarities of the closed-circuit system, he felt utterly differently. He had, after all, developed and hand-built the sets together with his father.

For months the two Bourdillons had worked to perfect their system. After Tom had left for Everest, his father, Robert, a distinguished research scientist at Stoke Mandeville hospital, continued to work on the design, sending test reports to his son. Whereas Charles had experienced constant problems, Tom's set had worked more or less perfectly. If they got to the summit today, it would be a vindication of all his work. Tom would be crowned both as a brilliant climber and a ground-breaking engineer.

What should he do about Charles Evans? Tom realised that his partner was in no fit state to continue but could he go on alone? This was the question that Tenzing had fielded in Kathmandu many weeks earlier, but for Tom Bourdillon, there was nothing hypothetical about the current situation, and there were precedents on Everest.

In 1924 Edward Norton had left his sick partner, Howard Somervell, high up on the North Face and carried on alone for another hour, until exhaustion and double vision persuaded him to turn back. Nine years later, in 1933, Frank Smythe left the young Eric Shipton prostrate on the rocks below the famous First Step and continued on; meanwhile Eric Shipton made his own way down to camp. Frank Smythe wrote that at the time it did not strike him as 'strange' to be making a solitary attempt. 'There was nothing brave or bold about it,' he said. 'We had come to Everest to climb it and, if possible, it had to be climbed.'

There were two major differences between Tom's current dilemma and that of his predecessors. First, he and Charles Evans were already far higher than any of the pre-war teams. Second, crucially, they were using oxygen. Smythe and Norton had both eschewed artificial aids but the 1953 team had committed themselves to a very different path. If Tom were to leave Charles to return alone, not only would he have to descend almost 3000 ft of difficult ground with no one to belay him but, if the problems continued with his oxygen set, Charles would have to conduct the running repairs that Tom had carried out that morning.

Charles Evans wasn't only worried about himself; he was also concerned about Tom and the expedition as a whole. If Tom wanted to continue by himself, Charles believed that his partner wasn't thinking logically. John Hunt had briefed them that in circumstances like this they should only carry on if they were sure that they had enough oxygen and it was safe to do so. As he consistently maintained, this expedition was a team effort. Better for them to come back and tell Hillary and Tenzing what lay ahead than to take unnecessary risks.

Charles was proud of what they had achieved in reaching the South Summit; after all, they had established a new world altitude record. Now their priority had to be getting down safely; it was his job to persuade Tom to face facts. He spoke up, with dramatic effect:

If you carry on going, you will never see Jennifer again.

Jennifer, the young wife whom Tom loved so much. He thought about her all the time and felt very guilty about being away. She had accompanied him to Nepal on the previous year's Cho Oyu expedition and everywhere he went reminded him of their time together. On the top line of his diary, whose pages he sent home regularly, he counted down the days to their next meeting:

10th March 1953, Bhadgaon – Banepa, 146: Greeted by a very persistent English speaking man who met us last year. A good meal and then to sleep. Sad because no wife.

15th March 1953, Manga Deorali – Karantichhap, 141: It is 141 days
to go now, less when you get this, and then I will be able to hold you again.
It is difficult telling you about loving you on paper.

9th April 1953, 116: I WILL NEVER COME OUT AGAIN
WITHOUT YOU.[4]

What would his diary entry be tonight?

It wasn't just a question of how he treated his climbing partner or his own willingness to face danger. Charles Evans's stark warning was an attempt to remind Tom of the one thing in his life that was more important to him than mountaineering. But Tom was a rational scientist; he knew that this was essentially a question of litres and flow-rates, not sentiment. He had discussed the hazards of mountaineering with Jennifer. They both accepted that danger was part of sport but there was a difference between taking a calculated risk and being reckless. He returned to his calculations. Even if he had enough oxygen to get to the top, could he get back safely? Was he absolutely sure? However, 28,700 ft high on the South Summit of Everest was not an easy place to do mathematical computations.

Although later he regretted it bitterly, at 1.30p.m., Tom Bourdillon turned his back on Everest. The first assault was over; the nightmare was about to begin.

Charles Evans's oxygen set was still malfunctioning, so Tom attempted to bypass the soda lime canister and convert it to an open-circuit set. It did not work so Charles continued to breathe a noxious mixture of carbon dioxide and oxygen. On the steep rocks, he slipped several times. Tom did his best to hold on to him but he too started to tire. When they reached the site where two hours earlier they had changed oxygen cylinders, they stopped to suck snow and glucose tablets. It did not occur to them to remount the soda lime canister that Charles had discarded earlier in the day.

After a few minutes they set off again, with Charles Evans in the lead and Tom Bourdillon as anchorman. Then, without warning, Tom lost his footing and slid straight into Charles's back. The two men hurtled down the mountain uncontrollably. Charles tried to arrest their fall by plunging his ice axe into the snow but it was no use. In their exhausted state, there was nothing they could do but wait until the slope eased and they came to a stop. They lay on the snow, panting, for several minutes. Then Tom hauled himself up wearily and climbed thirty feet back up the slope to the ledge where his ice axe had fallen. Charles later wrote ruefully that whenever one of them caused an accident, he apologised punctiliously to the other; even on Everest, manners were manners.

At the Swiss camp site, they made a 'most solemn pact' to take the dangerous final snow gully very carefully. Rope length by rope length they eased themselves down, taking turns to lead and driving their ice-axes deep into the snow to belay each other. Suddenly, they had their second major slip. Charles fell and within a few seconds was sliding past his partner on the hard-packed snow. He waited for the rope to go tight but all he felt was a slight tug around his waist: Tom had come off too! Below them lay the South Col, to their right was the Lhotse Face and a sheer drop of 6000 ft.

At Camp 8 George Lowe and Ed Hillary watched the events unfold with utter amazement. The clouds played their usual tricks. They saw Tom and Charles at the top of the gully and breathed a huge sigh of relief. Then the mist rolled in, totally obscuring them. When it cleared, ten minutes later, the two men were at the bottom. At first they couldn't believe it: how on earth could they have got there so quickly? As Tom and Charles well knew, they were lucky to have survived the descent. They later joked that they had 'yo-yoed' their way down the slope, a technique most definitely not included in reputable climbing manuals.

As Tom and Charles stumbled across the South Col, George Lowe filmed them; first a wide shot of two tiny figures and then closer shots of two utterly weary men. It was just after 3.30p.m. Bourdillon and Evans were safely back. But could they have made it to the top? It was unlikely but no one knew for certain. Should they be celebrating or commiserating?

George Lowe and Ed Hillary went to meet them. The returning men, according to Ed, looked like 'figures from another world',[5] covered from head to toe in tiny icicles. Charles was in the lead with Tom close behind, both men walking very slowly. Ed Hillary, overcome with emotion, threw his arms around them and 'muttered some familiar abuse'. Eventually, they reached a large rock and sat down. Tom and Charles were just a few yards from the tents but so tired that they could not go on. Alfred Gregory photographed them and George Lowe took a few more shots before abandoning his camera to greet the men in unprintable slang. 'We should have gone on, we should have gone on', Tom muttered. Tenzing came out with hot lemon juice. Charles and Tom kept looking at Everest.

More hot drinks, more questions, more photographs, more weary steps. In the main tent they peeled off their outer clothing and told the story of their ascent to the South Summit. Everyone was relieved: there would neither be a rescue mission nor a wake. Ed Hillary later admitted to somewhat mixed emotions; he was thrilled by what they had achieved but felt guilty over what he called a 'regrettable feeling of satisfaction'[6] that they had not gone all the way. Tomorrow he and Tenzing would have their day.

For Tom and Charles, the ordeal continued. To give the second assault team as much space as possible, they left the main tent to them and crammed into the small tent with John Hunt. It was barely big enough for two men, never mind three. The wind that night was remorseless, pummelling the canvas and making it impossible to rest. Nearby Hillary and Tenzing breathed supplementary oxygen to help them sleep but Tom and Charles had no such luxury.

They'd had their day; it was time to take second place. Charles was relieved to have made it back alive and cheered by the warm welcome of the others but Tom spent the night churning over the events of the day. If only he had prepared the oxygen sets better; if only he had ignored Charles's suggestion to change cylinders; if only he'd gone on alone. A sleepless night on the South Col was the last thing he needed.

The following morning the wind was so ferocious that Hunt was forced to postpone Hillary and Tenzing's move up to their high camp. This left him with a problem: Tom and Charles. They had to go down; on the South Col they were a drain on precious food and fuel. Tom Bourdillon, however, was not sure if he was fit to leave; he was exhausted by yesterday's exertions and emotionally drained.

When Ed Hillary struggled over to their tent, he found Tom in what he later described as a 'a vague state of mental depression from which he would emerge every now and then with a new set of figures and times to prove that he could have done it'.[7] Hillary asked them again about the final stretch of the South-East Ridge but neither had good news. When Hillary was out of earshot, Charles told George Lowe that it looked impossible.

By mid-morning the wind had abated, so Tom, Charles and Ang Temba prepared to descend. Ang Temba had been on the South Col for less than twenty-four hours but felt so ill that he had go down. Their first problem was to get off the South Col. To get back on to the Lhotse Face, a climber first had to climb *up* an icy 300-ft slope that led to the rocks of the Geneva Spur before beginning their descent proper. Normally, this was not a problem; the Sherpas in particular were usually so glad to leave the South Col that they scurried up as if it were flat. For Tom Bourdillon, that morning, it was a slope too far. He roped up to Charles and Ang Temba and they slowly moved off. In order not to use more oxygen, they had decided to climb down unassisted. They had only been going for a few minutes when Tom lurched forward and collapsed flat on his face in the snow. For a few moments he didn't move. Then he picked himself up and staggered forward before collapsing again.

Ed Hillary was more and more worried. As he hurried over to them, he had visions of a full-scale mountain rescue. Could they carry Tom Bourdillon down the Lhotse Face? Ed and Charles Evans left Tom with Ang Temba and headed back to camp. John Hunt was in the pyramid tent, with George Lowe, when they burst in. They told him that Tom was in a critical state, 'possibly dying'. Charles Evans assembled an oxygen set and hurried off, leaving the others to work out what to do next.

Even if the oxygen revived him, it was clear that Tom would not be able to get down without someone to help him but who could be spared? Alfred Gregory or George Lowe? Both men were needed to help Hillary and Tenzing set up their final camp the next day. John Hunt chose George Lowe but instead of meekly following orders, George Lowe had the temerity to say no.[8] He pointed out that Hunt was exhausted and would not be able to play a role in establishing Hillary and Tenzing's top camp. Better to have a fit climber like him, who had been on the South Col for one day, than a weakened leader with no reserves left.

John Hunt stood firm and George Lowe reluctantly began packing his gear. In spite of his doubts about his fitness and age, Hunt was as passionate as anyone about climbing Everest. As far as he was concerned, he had sacrificed his ambition to be on one of the summit attempts for the good of the team. The second assault was about to begin, there was work to be done and decisions to be made. He wanted to be on the South Col, at the heart of the action. What happened next was a small but crucial moment in the expedition, which showed how good a leader John Hunt was.

In the official expedition book, *The Ascent of Everest*, he played it down:

My post was here on the Col, to see the big assault safely launched and decide, if need be, on a further postponement or, possibly, a withdrawal. Yet I was supporting the first Assault, and by sending either Greg or George would only weaken the second Assault's chances. I decided I must go.[9]

In a letter to his wife, Joy, written a week later, he was more candid about the emotions involved:

I turned to Greg and George, it must be one of them. Then in their chagrin, I saw my mistake. I was finished, they were fresh ... I must go down but it was a bitter decision to take.[10]

A full twenty-five years later, in his autobiography, *Life is Meeting*, John Hunt wrote that this was the 'worst moment of all' for him. He wanted to stay but he realised that he had to go down. Ed Hillary was enormously impressed: this was John Hunt at his finest, showing real leadership and a real commitment to the good of the expedition, whatever his personal ambitions:

I have never admired him more than for this difficult decision.[11]

As he assembled his gear, John Hunt had a final word with Ed. He told him to put safety above everything but to try his damnedest to get to the top. Thousands of people around the world, he said, were backing this expedition and had put their hopes in a British success. Suddenly, he remembered something: deep in his rucksack was a small crucifix, given to him by a Benedictine monk a week before he left Britain, with the request that he should plant it on the summit. John Hunt was a spiritual man and, at this time in his life, a committed Christian. He later wrote that on Everest he felt 'as though guided along a pre-destined track, a curious sensation of confidence answering to Faith'.[12] He pressed the crucifix into Ed Hillary's hand before wearily plodding out of the tent to join Charles and Tom.

Ed Hillary followed, offering to carry Hunt's pack. It was not an encouraging sight: John Hunt wove drunkenly from side to side, unaware of his enfeebled state. As soon as he joined the others, he tried to take charge, announcing that he would go to the back, to shepherd them down. Despite being given oxygen, Tom Bourdillon had collapsed for a third time and was far from recovered. Charles Evans, by contrast, seemed much more solid. It was further proof of the psychological dimension of expedition climbing. Arguably, the previous day had been physically harder for Charles, because of the problems with his oxygen set but he had not made the same emotional investment in reaching the summit, so had not been as devastated when they failed. Gently but firmly, Charles steered Hunt into the middle position on the rope, with Tom in front and Ang Temba behind. With a final wave, the four men set off.

As they watched them stagger up the slope, Hillary and Lowe felt anxious: was John Hunt strong enough to get down, never mind help Tom Bourdillon? If anything went wrong, Hillary warned Lowe, it would be his fault.

Fortunately for George's conscience, the first assault team managed to climb down the Lhotse Face with only one small incident. Just above Camp 7 on the Lhotse Face, Ang Temba slipped and fell head first into a crevasse. Charles Evans held on tight but he wasn't strong enough to pull Ang Temba out. John Hunt was so weak that he could only stand and watch. To everyone's great relief, they saw Wilfred Noyce coming up towards them. Fortuitously, he and Michael Ward were at Camp 7, conducting breathing experiments. Wilfred was able to remove Ang Temba's pack and haul the poor Sherpa out.

Smiles, kind words, cups of tea, questions, more questions and overwhelming weariness. After an hour Charles Evans pressed on to Advance Base with Michael Ward but Tom Bourdillon and John Hunt were too tired. They followed a day later.

The first attempt had failed but although Tom and Charles had not reached the summit, they had made an amazing effort and lived to tell the tale. They had ascended 2700 ft in one day and managed to get back safely. The descriptions they were able to give of their route up the South-East Ridge were not especially helpful but the two bottles of oxygen that they had discarded on the way up most definitely were.

In the days and weeks to come Tom continued to regret everything that had gone wrong but most of his thoughts were on going home to Jennifer. Charles recovered quickly and looked forward to five more glorious months in the Himalayas, unencumbered by the expectations of a 'national' expedition.

Edmund Hillary was frightened neither by Charles Evans's descriptions of the South-East Ridge nor by his comments to George Lowe about the feasibility of climbing it. However, seeing Tom Bourdillon prostrate on the snow had been a powerful warning about the dangers of high altitude. He took out his tool kit and checked and rechecked the two oxygen sets that he and Tenzing would use, making sure that they worked perfectly.

If the weather held, they would climb up to their high camp tomorrow and make their attempt the following day. Two years earlier, in 1951, he had climbed 20,000 ft up Pumori with Eric Shipton and had his first proper glimpse of the summit of Everest. In two days' time he could become the first man to stand on its snows. As Ed Hillary knew well, it would not be easy.

Chapter 10

TO THE SUMMIT

The night of 27 May was another brutal reminder that on the South Col, the wind was king. It battered the team's tents and chilled them to the core. Even though Hillary and Tenzing were both using sleeping oxygen, neither could settle.

For Tenzing, there was a real sense that this, at last, was *his* moment. The first month of the expedition had been endlessly frustrating. He knew what an important job it was keeping the Sherpas in line but it didn't feel like it. He would have infinitely preferred to be out in the lead, with the *sahibs* of the climbing team. Then, on 7 May, John Hunt told him that he would be a member of one of the summit teams but the second, rather than the first. Were the gods toying with him? Over the next forty-eight hours he would get his chance. If all went well, he would climb to the summit of Everest. None of the other Sherpas understood his obsession with mountaineering but Tenzing had caught the bug and there was only one way to get relief.

The Swiss expeditions of 1952 had boosted his self-confidence and given him his first taste of fame. However, nothing had changed materially in his life. At the beginning of May he had received a disappointing letter from his friend Rabindranath Mitra, in India, telling him that a fund set up by well-wishers to buy him a house had collected very little money. There was a lot of talk but no action. At thirty-nine, Tenzing had two children and a wife, and nothing more to show for himself than a shack in a Darjeeling shanty town. If he could reach the summit, things would get better, wouldn't they?

Ed Hillary was also at an unsettled period of his life, although he didn't feel the same urgent pressure of poverty. He had grown up in the shadow of a difficult, demanding father. The newspapers loved to describe him as a 'humble bee-keeper' but he was neither a country bumpkin nor the 'typical Dominion type' that John Hunt had thought on their first meeting.

His mother had been a teacher; his father, a journalist who ran a local newspaper before moving into the honey business. Ed went to one of the best grammar schools in New Zealand and to the University of Auckland for two years. However, apart from a brief stint in the Air Force during the Second World War, he hadn't managed to break away from the family home and the family business. His younger brother Rex had married but, at thirty-three, Ed had had only one serious relationship. The minimal wages his father paid would not have enabled him to set up by himself.

Ed was not driven by a great hunger for fame but mountaineering was the part of his life of which he was most in control. Now he had the opportunity to realise his ambition to climb Everest and fulfil the dream of so many of his heroes. His diary entries show he had a strong sense of destiny. He recorded not only his activities but also everyone else's, as if he knew that one day he might write a book. The entry for 27 May, with the story of Tom Bourdillon's collapse on the South Col, was a stark reminder of the dangers of Everest and how easily a man could be brought to his knees, destiny or no destiny.

Tom and Charles Evans had been far from encouraging in their descriptions of the final 500 ft but Hillary realised that this was the expedition's last chance. If they didn't get up now, they would have to leave it to the French, who were due in the spring of 1954. In theory,

John Hunt had the capability to launch a third attempt but other than Wilfrid Noyce, and perhaps Annullu, no one was strong enough to take part. And the monsoon was approaching.

At around 4a.m., for a brief moment, the wind stopped. Ed Hillary woke up, thinking that this was a good sign but it wasn't long before the gusts started again. Tenzing slept on, enjoying hallucinatory dreams of yaks and white horses and a far-off mountain. Then he too stirred and the two men began the long, painfully slow process of making breakfast and preparing to leave. Ed went to tell George Lowe and Alfred Gregory that he and Tenzing were ready. Then he heard some crushing news. Pemba was ill. After a night of vomiting, he was clearly in no state to go on, never mind carry a load.

Hillary and Tenzing should have had George Lowe, Alfred Gregory and three Sherpas to carry their gear to the high camp. Now they were down to just one Sherpa, Ang Nyima, a true stalwart. They had two choices: reapportion the loads or give up.

Frustration gave way to grim determination. Ed told everyone to go through their rucksacks and remove anything that wasn't absolutely necessary. Even a few extra pounds made a huge difference at this altitude. George Lowe reluctantly abandoned his camera and film stock but Ed couldn't quite bear to leave the 'luxury' foods that he had taken from the South Col and hidden from the others. There might not be any footage of their final camp but they would eat well tonight.

At 8.45a.m. George Lowe set off with Alfred Gregory and Ang Nyima, promising to cut a trail for Hillary and Tenzing to follow in roughly an hour's time. Over the last few days George had made a magical recovery and was very happy to be in the lead, after the frustrations of the Lhotse Face. It was hard work: each member of the support party left with at least 40 lb on their back.

Ed gave their oxygen sets a final once-over. Tenzing was unusually talkative that morning; exactly a year earlier he had made his dash for the summit with Raymond Lambert. He told Ed about how hard that day had been and how much affection he retained for his Swiss friend. If only he were here today, was his unspoken thought.

Although they had been partners for several weeks, there was no warmth between Hillary and Tenzing. They respected each other's abilities but there was always a distance. Although Ed was more pushy than most of the British team, he could also be reserved and slightly awkward.

For Tenzing, this expedition had been very different from that of the previous year. It would be wrong to suggest that in 1952 the Swiss had seen the Sherpas as complete equals – they were still *sahibs* even if they spoke French – but they had come to the Alps without the British team's imperial baggage and huge burden of expectations. The Swiss undoubtedly wanted to succeed but they did not see it in terms of national destiny. They were easy-going and friendly; as John Hunt later wrote, their warm camaraderie contrasted with the proverbial reserve of the British.[1] On the other hand, it must have been obvious to Tenzing that this was a large and well-prepared team that stood a high chance of succeeding and enabling him to realise his ambition.

Hillary opened the valves and let the oxygen flow. It gave them a huge boost; soon they were climbing steadily up the South-East Ridge, rhythmically moving from step to step. The wind had stripped the slopes of snow cover, exposing the bare ice and making the going much harder. To be able to follow in George Lowe's tracks made a huge difference but it didn't make their packs any lighter.

After half an hour Tenzing saw something sticking from the ice. He tugged the rope and they moved across to investigate. It was an oxygen set, perfectly preserved and almost full. It must have been abandoned in November 1952, during the second Swiss attempt. Who could tell: it might have been Tenzing's. Was this a gift of oxygen from the gods or a warning that technology and engineering were no match for Everest's elemental power? Either way, they moved on. They simply could not carry any more cylinders.

Before long Hillary and Tenzing started to catch up with George Lowe's party but the closer they got, the more hazardous it became. Chips of ice dislodged by the men above spun down the slope and bombarded them with freezing shards. It became so bad that they stopped for a moment and hacked out a small seat in the slope. For a few precious minutes Hillary and Tenzing enjoyed the view of Pumori and the Western Cwm.

At around 11.45a.m., at 27,300 ft, they caught up with George Lowe and the advance party at the wreck of the Swiss tent that Tenzing and Lambert had shared a year earlier. It was a spectacular spot and for a few minutes Ed Hillary and George Lowe indulged in what they later called 'an orgy of photography'.

Everyone was tired but they couldn't stop. They weren't high enough and John Hunt's pile of stores was some way further on. In the first few months of the expedition the climbers marked their ascent in thousands of feet but at this altitude, every few yards mattered. When they reached Hunt's hard-won cache at 27,395 ft they made another painful readjustment of their loads. Ed Hillary took a tent, increasing his load to more than 60 lb, a stupendous feat at this altitude. Alfred Gregory drew the short straw; he added a large black RAF oxygen cylinder, which weighed 20 lb on its own, to his load.

George Lowe went back into the lead and began chopping yet more steps. Another hundred feet. They still couldn't find a suitable place for their camp. Another hundred. And another. Ed Hillary's oxygen ran out; he had to change the cylinder and use some of the precious oxygen he had wanted to save for the next day. Ed had started to worry that they might never find anywhere remotely flat, when Tenzing pointed to a place that he had noticed in the previous year. They followed him, ploughing their way through deep snow. It was not quite large enough for their two-man tent but George Lowe spotted a possible site fifty feet higher, where the angle of the slope eased a little. The new site was by no means perfect but it was now 2.30p.m.; if they carried on, their exhausted support party might find it very difficult to get down to the South Col. Ed Hillary was touched when Ang Nyima offered to stay, to help them down the next day but there was no room and also, Ang Nyima was clearly exhausted. After a few snatched handshakes, the support team descended, leaving Hillary and Tenzing alone at 27,640 ft.

They were the highest men in the world, far above the clouds, so high that they could look down on the summits of Nuptse and Lhotse, which had towered over them for the previous two months. There was no time to take in the view. As the snow fell and wind blew, they hacked out a small platform in the snow.

Four thousand miles away and thousands of feet lower down, in London the morning newspapers were being laid out in kiosks and corner shops. In late May 1953 there were plenty of other news stories: John Christie, the serial killer, was on trial in London; Senator Joe McCarthy was hunting Communists in America; and peace negotiations for the Korean War had stalled. Everest, however, was never far from the front pages. Over the last two weeks there had been numerous articles based on 'sources close to the expedition'. Nothing had been heard from the team since John Hunt's target date of 15 May, so many people assumed that the expedition was over. The *Daily Telegraph* reported on 25 May that a first assault, by George Band and Mike Westmacott, had failed. On 28 May, several British newspapers reported that Hunt's team had been defeated not once but twice.

In a letter to Michael Ward, Raymond Greene, brother of the writer Graham Greene and another climbing doctor, gave a flavour of the Everest hysteria:

> *There is immense excitement here, second only to the Coronation. The BBC is trotting out all the time-worn broadcasts and a lot of my*

secretary's time is taken up with deflecting newspapers from their hellish object of interviewing me about your chances. All the newspapers are full of inspired guess-work about exactly what you are doing at each moment of time. There is a feeling of urgency which I never saw before perhaps because the ascent at the beginning of the new Elizabethan Age has some metaphysical meaning in many minds and perhaps because of a feeling that if you don't do it somebody else will. Perhaps the Russians maybe with a battalion of expendable troops.[2]

Although they suspected that most of the reports were nothing more than speculation, inevitably the rumours and so-called 'reliable' reports made the members of the Himalayan Committee nervous. They had drawn up secret plans for a second expedition in the autumn, if the first failed. Now they began work in earnest.

The leader-in-waiting was Emlyn Jones, an experienced climber who was one of the official reserves for the main expedition. If the first team failed, he and three others would travel to Nepal in July, where they would join members of the current team and make a second attempt.

By late May Emlyn Jones's preparations were well advanced, with equipment at the ready, tickets reserved on a ship for India and three keen climbers waiting for the word. The Himalayan Committee drafted a press release, which, if needed, would announce the failure of John Hunt's expedition:

The news that Colonel Hunt and his party have for the time being been compelled to forego any further assaults on Everest does not mean that the Expedition will now return to this country. After the monsoon, the assaults on Everest will be renewed. A small reinforcement group which has been organising and training to meet this contingency will leave this country in July and will join the main party, selected members of which, meanwhile will have withdrawn from the mountain for rest and reorganisation. The whole Expedition will return to Everest early in September this year.[3]

On Everest, after two and half hours of hard labour, Ed Hillary and Tenzing were not thinking of press releases. It was unpleasant work: the icy slope that they had chosen was full of rocks that had to be removed one by one. Eventually, they cleared two strips a little over six feet long and three feet wide. Their platform was on two levels but just about good enough to pitch their tent.

While Tenzing melted ice for a hot drink, Hillary took his camera outside. In the evening light the nearby peaks looked serenely beautiful. Ed's eye was drawn to Makalu, the huge mountain to the east of Everest that he had coveted with Eric Shipton in 1952. Tonight its summit seemed almost close enough to touch. The South Col did not look quite so peaceful; the wind was up. Ed could make out the tents, battered and buffeted by the gusts. For the moment it was quieter on their icy perch but Hillary was anxious about what might happen later that night. It had been impossible to find somewhere to drive in their tent pegs, so they had resorted to weighing down their guy ropes with oxygen cylinders and attaching them to nearby rocks.

Ed tried to get a decent photograph of their final camp but the slope was impossibly steep. He gave up and retreated into the tent. With their small kerosene stove purring away, it was warm and fuggy. They drank cup after cup of chicken soup and sweet lemon juice. Ed delved into his rucksack and brought out the delicacies that he had been saving for the last three days. They were ravenous and made quick work of the dates and sardines. The climax of their feast, a tin of apricots in syrup, was not quite the treat that Ed had envisaged. When he removed the lid, the contents slid out as a solid block of ice and needed several minutes on the stove before they were edible.

Throughout the expedition everyone had taken special care to drink as much as possible. When Griffith Pugh looked into the records of previous expeditions, he discovered that climbers frequently complained of raging thirst at high altitude. Some had become so dehydrated in the final stages of their expeditions that they had gone for twenty-four hours without urinating. Pugh had drilled into everyone the importance of consuming lots of liquid and they had benefitted from an improved design of Primus stove that was much more efficient at melting snow. Ed Hillary's favourite tipple was lemon juice laced with sugar. In an article written for the sugar manufacturers Tate and Lyle, one of the expedition's supporters, Michael Ward revealed that on Everest their standard high-altitude rations included 14 oz of sugar per day per man. This reflected both a craving for sweet things and the value of sugar as an easily digestible carbohydrate. Although it might seem hard to consume so much, anyone who followed Griffith Pugh's recommendation to drink eight pints of liquids every twenty-four hours soon used up their allowance.

When they could eat and drink no more, they prepared the tent for what would undoubtedly be an uncomfortable night. When, earlier that evening, Ed Hillary had made an inventory of their oxygen supplies, he came to an awkward realisation. Someone had inadvertently taken down the special adaptor needed for the oxygen cylinder Alfred Gregory had carried up with such a struggle. Without it, the heavy black bottle was useless. They had no alternative but to use the dregs of two spare cylinders for their sleeping oxygen. Together, these provided a total of four hours but irritatingly, the bottles had to be swapped halfway through the night.

The wind continued to torment them, coming in ferocious gusts every ten or fifteen minutes. Their flimsy tent, so precariously attached to the slope, felt as if it would be blown off the mountain altogether if it weren't for their weight anchoring it. Ed Hillary straddled the length of the tent, with his long legs hanging over Tenzing's sleeping bag. Between gusts, he somehow managed to doze.

If it was uncomfortable on the South-East Ridge, down on the

South Col it was agony. After their heroic struggle with Hillary and Tenzing's gear, Alfred Gregory and Ang Nyima came down absolutely worn out. George Lowe was in a better state. As if to prove the point, he went ahead to retrieve his film camera and get some shots 'of really flogged men'. Fortunately for film-goers everywhere, he did not record the scene in the tent later that evening as Alfred Gregory strained to defecate into a tin while he lay nearby in his sleeping bag. This was the true romance of Everest! George Lowe was too exhausted to care; Alfred Gregory too dehydrated and too constipated to relieve himself. In his autobiography, *Because it is There*, George Lowe cheerfully recorded that Alfred Gregory rated this as his worst experience ever. After one and a half hours, he gave up.

Hillary and Tenzing's first batch of oxygen ran out at about 11p.m. For the next two hours they brewed more lemon juice, to keep warm. They hooked up their second cylinder at around 1a.m. and slipped into a fitful sleep. The gas ran out two hours later but they stayed in their sleeping bags for another hour until Ed Hillary stirred. He opened the flap at the end of the tent and Tenzing pointed out the silhouette of the Thyangboche Monastery, just visible in the early-morning light. Tenzing said a prayer and they brewed yet more lemon juice for breakfast. The air was still and calm; everything looked good for their attempt. However, before they could get going, Ed Hillary had to cook his boots.

For someone so meticulous, it was a strange mistake to make. Tenzing had kept his boots on overnight but after a long, sweaty day Hillary had opted for a comfortable night and removed his. Unfortunately, that night was the coldest of the expedition, down to −27 °C; when Ed Hillary woke up, his boots were frozen solid. He had no alternative but to thaw them over a naked flame, filling the tent with the stench of burning rubber and singed leather. Eventually they were supple enough to put on but it was not the start that they wanted.

Before they left Ed Hillary gave their oxygen sets a final check. Despite John Hunt's detailed preparations and the huge effort everyone had made in getting their stores high on the mountain, there was very little margin for error. They would each carry two oxygen cylinders: one full, the other partially used. Griffith Pugh had advised that the minimum useful rate for ascent at high altitude was four litres of oxygen per minute but when Ed Hillary did the calculations he realised that they could only afford three. Everything would have to go perfectly, otherwise, like Tom Bourdillon, they would return to the South Col cursing their luck, if they returned at all.

After yet more lemon juice and sardines, at 6.30a.m. they crawled into the crisp, cold morning, wrapped in all the clothes they possessed. Ed Hillary stuck to regulation issue: a woollen shirt, a string vest, woollen underwear, woollen socks and pullover, down trousers and jacket and blue windproofs to top them off. Tenzing's clothes were more eclectic and more personal. He wore socks knitted by his wife, Ang Lahmu, a pullover given to him by Mrs Henderson of the Himalayan Club in Darjeeling and a woollen hat from his expedition with Earl Denman, the maverick Canadian who had made an unauthorised attempt on Everest in 1947. He had the same windproof jacket as Ed Hillary but his boots and down jacket were from the Swiss expedition, as was his most precious garment: a red scarf given to him by Raymond Lambert.

There were only 1300 vertical feet between their final camp and the summit but it was not going to be an easy climb. Before them lay deep snow, topped with a hard wind-blown crust. Sometimes it held their weight but frequently the crust collapsed and they had to wade through. Neither could get into the steady rhythm that they liked and that made them such effective climbers.

When they reached 28,000 ft, they made a welcome discovery. Bourdillon and Evans's cylinders were visible in the small hollow where they had been left two days before. When Ed Hillary scraped the ice from their pressure gauges he discovered that they were still almost a third full. They would give Hillary and Tenzing a vital extra hour of oxygen, to be used on the way down, but would have been worth even more to Tom Bourdillon and Charles Evans, with their closed-circuit equipment. Further on, Tom and Charles' tracks were occasionally visible on the way up to the South Summit but two days of wind and snow had obliterated many of them.

The slopes below the South Summit, as both men later wrote, were the most dangerous area. To the left was a long section of precarious ribs of shattered rock, to the right a band of pure snow. Bourdillon and Evans, good English mountaineers trained on the slopes of Wales and the Lake District, had gone for the left, even though there were few obvious handholds and some of the rock looked very loose. Ed Hillary, a typical New Zealander, was more comfortable on snow and ice, so he chose the other option. Tenzing led off; soon, they faced severe problems.

Ed Hillary was not at all sure that they should go on, although his diary entry was a model of understatement:

> We commenced plugging up in foot-deep steps with a thin wind crust on top and precious little belay for the ice axe. It was altogether most unsatisfactory and whenever I felt feelings of fear regarding it, I'd say to myself 'Forget it! This is Everest and you've got to take a few risks'. Tenzing expressed his extreme dislike but made no suggestion regards turning back.[4]

Tenzing occasionally sank up to his waist and his tracks refused to compact because the snow was so powdery. To make things even worse, it looked as if it might avalanche; large chunks of crust slid down, sometimes carrying them along too. It was excruciating work, even though they regularly changed the lead. Tenzing later told James Ramsey Ullman, his American ghostwriter, that this was the most dangerous place he had ever encountered on a mountain.

These were moments that put the traditional arguments about mountaineering and safety into perspective. On the 1951 reconnaissance Ed Hillary had sometimes felt that Eric Shipton was over-cautious and that different standards were needed to get up Everest. Now he had to practise what he preached. His training told him they should not be on this slope but he knew that if they didn't keep going, they would never reach the summit. Tenzing was equally aware of the danger but he too realised that if they didn't carry on, they would have to go back defeated.

Their persistence paid off. The angle of the slope eased and the snow became firmer. By 9a.m. they were on the South Summit, pausing to take in the view and prepare for the final push.

Alfred Gregory was thrilled to watch their hesitant progress from the South Col, as he prepared to descend with Ang Nyima and Pemba. Exhaustion overcame any qualms about leaving George Lowe on his own. When, in mid-afternoon, Alfred reached Advance Base at the foot of the Lhotse Face, he felt a lot better and was pleased to be able to tell his anxious leader that the second assault was under way. John Hunt definitely looked like he needed some good news.

Michael Ward was very worried about Hunt's condition. He noted in his diary that when John Hunt came down on the 28th he had had 'a partial mental and physical collapse'. John Hunt had enormous reserves but they were stretched very thin. He confessed to his diary that he felt 'increasingly played out' and 'thoroughly whipped'.

If John Hunt had been at his customary position, binoculars in hand, outside the tents of Advance Base at around 9.30a.m., he might have made out two tiny black dots above the South Summit. However, even with the ears of a piano tuner, he could never have heard the distant shouts. Ed Hillary, suddenly overcome by the manic urge to communicate when he caught sight of the tents of Advance Base far below, had hollered and waved for a few moments before acknowledging the futility of the gesture.

Ed was allowed to go a bit crazy. They had broken the altitude record set by Bourdillon and Evans. The snow conditions were better than below the South Summit and, having jettisoned one oxygen bottle, their loads were considerably lighter. Lest they should become too confident, Tenzing had a scare when the outlet on his mask became clogged with ice. Ed Hillary cleared it quickly but it was a timely reminder to stay alert. Before them the crest of Everest stretched upwards for the final few hundred vertical feet. To the right, huge icy cornices overhung the Kangshung Face. To the left, the rock slabs dropped steeply away towards the Western Cwm, 8,000 ft below. Ed Hillary tried to plot a middle way, avoiding the cornices and climbing on the hard-packed snow whenever they could.

It wasn't just a physical effort. Ed Hillary continually calculated and recalculated their oxygen supplies, to determine the optimum flow rate. They were reduced to one bottle each, filled with 800 litres of oxygen. If they used three litres per minute, it should last roughly four to four and a half hours, just enough to get up to the summit and back to their top camp. Every time they stopped, Ed had to do the sums again.

After an hour and twenty minutes they arrived at the obstacle they had thought about for the last two months: the forty-foot rock face close to the top of the ridge. On a good day it was just visible from the Thyangboche Monastery, many miles away. Ed checked their oxygen cylinders: they had just over three hours' worth to get to the summit and back. If they couldn't get up this rock face quickly they would have to retreat and let someone else take the final step.

Ed reached for his camera and took several photographs. If this turned out to be the end of their climb, he wanted proof that they had set a new altitude record and climbed hundreds of feet above the South Summit. The rock face was about forty feet high, almost vertical, with no obvious hand-holds. A tricky pitch but the issue wasn't really the topography. As Ed later joked, if this were the Lake District, it might have been viewed as a fascinating problem for weekend climbers.

At approximately 28,900 ft it was a very different matter. They had discarded their first oxygen bottles but were still shouldering 20 lb of oxygen and wearing an unwieldy set. The flow rate was set at three litres per minute; good enough for grinding their way up the ridge but not so generous for difficult climbing.

Ed Hillary had avoided the other rock pitches on the South-East Ridge and found alternative routes. Here he had no choice. They could descend and try to work their way around but there was no guarantee of finding an alternative route and at this altitude every foot gained was a small victory that he was loath to give away.

Then he saw it. A possible way up but a very dangerous one.

On the far right-hand edge was a huge icy cornice, overhanging Everest's Kangshung Face. It had begun to detach and would eventually tumble down the mountain and be smashed on the glacier, 9000 ft below. For the moment it was still precariously attached, leaving a narrow gap between rock and ice, just wide enough to take a climber. Ed Hillary inspected it more closely and saw a few possible hand- and boot-holds on the edge of the rock. He might be able to lean back on the cornice and wriggle his way up. Would it take his weight or would he too tumble down the Kangshung Face?

'Don't give in unless it is unavoidable.'

Two days earlier, when they said goodbye, John Hunt had left Ed with a huge responsibility. It was make-or-break time for the British Everest Expedition of 1953. The rock face before them was unavoidable. The risks of the cornice breaking off were unavoidable. The choice they had to make was unavoidable. Take a big risk or turn back.

There was no need to speak. Both men knew what they had to do. Tenzing jammed his ice axe in hard and took a firm grip on the rope that connected him to his partner. Ed Hillary put his camera away and squeezed into the narrow channel. He stretched upwards to find the first hand-hold and started to lever his way up, jamming his crampons into the cornice behind him. It was punishing work, made worse by the thought that if at any moment he pushed too hard, the cornice might give way. Below, Tenzing had a firm anchor point for the rope but if Ed came off there was no guarantee that he would be able hold him.

A wiggle, a test of the snow behind him, a stretch, a probe with his ice axe, a sharp intake of breath as he hauled himself up another few feet … again and again. Stretching, digging in his crampons, hauling himself upwards until he reached the top, breathing hard but to his amazement, not feeling too bad.

This was the point at which Ed Hillary proved himself one of the world's greatest mountaineers and inscribed his name on the feature that would come to be known as the 'Hillary Step'. It wasn't an amazing feat of technical climbing. Arguably, the rock slabs on the north side of Everest, tackled by the British climbers of the 1920s and 1930s, were a much tougher proposition. Ed Hillary showed that morning that he could be cool under pressure, take a calculated risk and get it right. Other climbers might have turned back or attempted to climb directly up the rock, which undoubtedly would have taken much longer. Ed Hillary read the situation correctly, had the courage to take a risk, and found the best route.

Tenzing came up but there was no elation yet. The remainder of the ridge was not quite as steep but there was still no obvious summit. They plodded on, yard after yard, Hillary chopping steps, Tenzing holding him on a tight rope. Hillary hoped that each hummock would be the last but it never was. At the back of each undulation was always another one. They carried on for several hundred yards, gradually getting higher and higher. Ed Hillary's confidence began to ebb: would it ever end? Weary of constant step-cutting, he tried to crampon up the hummocks but a few slips convinced him that this was too risky. Out came the ice axe and on they went.

Finally, at 11.30a.m., they reached their goal.

The last few moments took them by surprise. Ed was cutting around another of the seemingly endless undulations when he noticed that instead of rising, the slope was falling away. Before them lay the vast emptiness of the Tibetan plain. To the right was a final bump, about forty feet high. It had to be the highest point but was it solid or was there another overhanging cornice? Tenzing took a firm belay and Hillary cut a last weary line of steps.

The top of the world was a small, rounded bump, big enough for both of them to stand on but not, as Hillary later joked, large enough to pitch a tent. To one side puffball clouds hung over Tibet, to the other lay the valleys of Nepal. The sky was a deep, intense blue, stained by high wispy clouds. Around them, enormous Himalayan peaks were reduced to acolytes.

Ed Hillary offered his hand 'in good old Anglo-Saxon fashion' but this was not enough for Tenzing. Echoing Bill Tilman's famous words to Noel Odell on the summit of Nanda Devi – 'we so far forgot ourselves as to shake hands' – Ed Hillary wrote in his diary:

Tenzing so far forgot himself as to embrace me. It was quite a moment.[5]

They stayed on the summit for roughly eighteen minutes, even daring to remove their oxygen masks. Contrary to the dire warnings, they did not keel over immediately and were not even particularly uncomfortable. Ed Hillary methodically set about recording their achievement. Tenzing unfurled the small flags wrapped around his ice axe and posed for three photographs. They were almost identical but Ed made sure that he had one 'front page' picture.

When asked why he hadn't asked Tenzing to take a photo of him, Hillary replied laconically that, as far as he knew, his partner had never used a camera in his life and this was not a good moment to start. Some thought this a rather odd explanation but it was typical of Ed Hillary. He wasn't climbing Everest for fame and glory, or to get his face on the front cover of the world's newspapers. The camera was there for objective reasons, as a method of proving that *they* not *he* had reached the summit. So he made sure to get a good shot of Tenzing with his flags and systematically photographed the slopes around, in case anyone doubted that they had really got there. Then he took a couple of photographs of Makalu, to the east of Everest, because he had noticed a possible route to its summit. Even on top of the highest mountain in the world, Hillary was thinking about the other climbs that he might make.

For Tenzing the view was more personal and his behaviour on the summit very different. The surrounding topography was a map of his life. To the north lay Tibet, where he had been born and made his first expedition with Eric Shipton in 1935. To the south, Nepal and the Solu Khumbu, the land where he had spent his early years herding yaks. On either side were the monasteries of Thyangboche and Rongbuk, revered sites for Sherpas. Under his feet was not Everest but Chomolungma, the Goddess Mother of the Earth.

In the months afterwards Tenzing was asked many times whether he met the Lord Buddha or any other mountain-top deities. He always said 'no' but it was a profoundly religious moment, in which he said he 'felt closer to God'. The language used in Tenzing's ghost-written autobiography today seems awkwardly home-spun but it was undoubtedly heartfelt:

> At that great moment for which I had waited all my life, my mountain did not seem to me a lifeless thing of snow and ice but warm and friendly and living. She was a mother hen and the other mountains were chicks under her wings.[6]

Ed Hillary also personified Everest but his choice of metaphor was much more raw and masculine. In his famous greeting to George Lowe a few hours later, he chose New Zealand slang to sum up their achievement: 'We knocked the bastard off!' For Hillary, Everest was fundamentally a challenge, an arena in which he could both compete with others and do what he enjoyed most: climb. Ed Hillary had been a scrawny kid, mocked by games masters at school but in mountaineering, he discovered a sport at which he excelled. Now, he was literally at the top of his game, fulfilling the dream of thousands of climbers but he didn't punch the air or whoop for joy. He was too controlled for that. As for the spiritual aspect, despite having once been the highest man in the world, Ed Hillary was, as many people remarked, a 'down to earth' character. He recognised the beauty of mountains and some of his friends maintained that he had a romantic side. Only rarely in any of his books is there any sense of the sublime in his response to landscape.

On the summit Ed Hillary's approach was more pragmatic than reverential: eat, look for any signs of Mallory and Irvine (the British climbers who had disappeared on their way to the summit in 1924), take photographs to prove he and Tenzing had reached the top, have a look at the nearby mountains and get down safely to tell the tale. Like all mountaineers, he knew that getting to the top was only half of the story. There was plenty of climbing to do before they could really celebrate. Tenzing thought back to the previous year and imagined Raymond Lambert standing next to him on the summit, remembering the phrase that he always used: *ça va bien*. He pulled tight the red scarf that his Swiss friend had given him; soon it would become one of Raymond Lambert's most treasured possessions.

As a final gesture, Tenzing scraped a hollow in the snow and left a personal religious offering: some sweets, some chocolate and a stubby red and blue pencil given to him by his daughter Nima. This reminded Hillary of the small crucifix that John Hunt had entrusted to him. He followed Tenzing's example and buried it in the snow. As he pointed out in later interviews, he did not do this for personal religious motives: 'It did not matter to me at all; I have no religious beliefs' he bluntly told the *Catholic Herald* in September 1953. He did it out of loyalty to his leader.

In his autobiography, *Man of Everest*, Tenzing did not remember the crucifix being planted in the snow. He thought that Ed Hillary had left the small black fluffy cat sent to John Hunt by his mother-in-law a month earlier. This went unnoticed by most readers but John Hunt wrote to Tenzing to tell him that although the cat had indeed made it all the way to the South Col, it had returned to Britain unscathed.

Hillary's final action on the summit had neither religious nor personal significance but would have made Griffith Pugh proud. It was so shocking that he didn't mention it until his third and final autobiography, *View from the Summit*, written almost fifty years after the event. He unzipped his fly and urinated. For the last forty-eight hours Ed Hillary had conscientiously heeded Griffith Pugh's warnings and drunk pint after pint of fluids. He just couldn't hold it in.

At 11.48a.m., just as Ed started to feel a little woozy, they turned the oxygen back on and prepared to descend. Tenzing took the flags off his ice axe and buried them in the snow, although with little hope that they would be there for long. Then they began a very careful retreat.

Almost an hour and a half later, at 1p.m., George Lowe saw them coming over the South Summit. For the last couple of hours he had waited alone for their return. George arranged his tent almost as if to receive casualties, neatly organising oxygen sets and sleeping bags side by side. Now he grabbed his movie camera, an oxygen set and two thermos flasks of hot drinks and ran out into the snow … or he would have done, if he hadn't been on the South Col.

After 400 yards George realised two things: first, he could not move quickly and second, Ed and Tenzing were still far away. They seemed to be moving steadily, so George shuffled back to his tent. He lay in the door, watching them and getting his breath back.

Ed and Tenzing had too much to think about to notice George on the South Col. Their descent was rapid but tense. Ed Hillary was tired and very glad that Tenzing was such a reliable and dependable companion, especially in the difficult snow slopes below the South Summit. At 2p.m., they stopped at their high camp for an hour, brewing up yet more lemon juice. Their oxygen supplies were exhausted, so they were glad to change to the cylinders left by Tom and Charles. Then wearily, after packing their things, they carried on.

At 4p.m., they reached the cold comfort of the South Col and a smiling George Lowe, laden with flasks of soup. As they crossed the icy ground towards their camp for the last time, they were met with more liquid offerings, this time tea, from Wilfrid Noyce. John Hunt had sent him up with Pasang Phutar to aid Hillary and Tenzing's descent.[7] For once George Lowe did not whip out his camera and record the tottering steps of exhausted men; he was too pleased and excited to see his best friend, Ed Hillary.

In the tent, Ed drank cup after cup of soup and lemon juice and slowly told the story of their climb. At first his voice was hoarse – his oxygen had run out as they reached the Col – but as he warmed up, the excitement and realisation of what they had achieved came through.

George was absolutely thrilled at Ed Hillary's success but for Wilfrid Noyce it was a bitter sweet moment. If Hillary and Tenzing had not succeeded, he would have been top of the list for a third attempt. Like everyone else, Wilfrid longed to get back to his family and felt proud of his contribution to the team effort but like any ambitious climber he wished that he too could have stood on the summit.

At about 5.30p.m., Wilfrid left the tent to perform one last duty. He took two sleeping bags and collected a reluctant Pasang Phutar from Tenzing's tent. The Sherpa had no idea what the *sahib* wanted or why he was leading him to the top of the South Col and the edge of the Lhotse Face. Wilfrid found a patch of snow, arranged the sleeping bags in a 'T' shape and asked Pasang Phutar to lie down on one of them. The Sherpas were famous for their sense of humour and their love of practical jokes but what on earth was this? A high-altitude bivouac? The final sign that the British were madmen?

In fact, it was a signal, agreed by Wilfrid and John Hunt: 'T' if Hillary and Tenzing had reached the 'top', two bags side by side if they had only reached the South Summit and one solitary bag if they had achieved nothing. For ten minutes Wilfrid Noyce and Pasang Phutar lay, shivering, as soft clouds swirled below. Wilfrid suspected it was a waste of time but felt compelled to carry out his promise.

His hunch was correct. At Advance Base, John Hunt stared up at the Lhotse Face but clouds ensured he could see nothing. Tom Stobart later wrote: 'You suffered just to look at Hunt.' The other climbers took it in turns to stare up with binoculars but Wilfrid's signal was never seen and they were forced to retreat to their tents.

John Hunt's mind was focused on the summit: if Hillary and Tenzing had failed, it was his job to regroup the team and organise a third attempt. But his resources were stretched very thin. If his two best climbers could not get up that final slope, who could? It did not bear thinking about but he just couldn't stop.

Chapter 11

SNOW CONDITIONS
BAD

Five tiny dots.

High on the Lhotse Face, moving slowly but steadily.

For John Hunt, the relief was immense. Five tiny dots meant that everyone was alive but what else? Had they succeeded or had they failed? Would there have to be another attempt?

When James Morris came up to Advance Base with Griffith Pugh, he was shocked to see how much everything had changed. In the Khumbu Icefall once-mighty towers had been reduced to dirty puddles as the temperature rose by just a few degrees. Just as the icefall had crumbled and cracked, so the men in the camp looked infinitely weary. Tom Bourdillon and Charles Evans were noticeably thinner and weaker, despite their outward cheerfulness. Almost all the climbers had lost over a stone and the heavier ones, like Tom Bourdillon, a lot more. John Hunt looked worst of all. According to James Morris, he was like a 'grizzled Hannibal', his hair turned from ginger to grey, his face caked in thick white sunscreen. John Hunt tried to carry on as if it were business as usual. He discussed the odds of getting news back to Britain before the coronation but his attention was elsewhere, high up on the Lhotse Face.

For Wilfrid Noyce, one of those tiny dots, the descent from the South Col had a 'holiday' atmosphere. They had abandoned much of the equipment and were travelling light. At Camp 7, in the middle of the Lhotse Face, they met Charles Wylie, waiting with mugs of freshly brewed tea. He was tremendously disappointed when Ed Hillary turned it down. Almost fifty years later Charles remembered this small, insignificant moment and couldn't work out why Hillary had said 'no'. Ed Hillary had nothing against Charles Wylie, with whom he stayed in contact for the rest of his life. He just didn't feel like tea. The others were thirstier; Wilfrid Noyce suggested that he and Pasang Phutar should stay behind to help to carry down the tents but Lowe, Hillary and Tenzing were in a hurry to get away and left after a few minutes.

For everyone below, the sight of only three men coming out of camp added to their anxiety. Why only three? Were the others hurt? Or exhausted? In the aptly named mess tent James Morris tried to distract himself by flicking through the tatty pile of newspapers. He scanned a part-finished crossword but it was hard to think about anything other than those tiny dots, slowly growing closer and closer.

At 2p.m., George Band tuned into *All India Radio* for the afternoon news broadcast. A solemn voice announced that the British Everest expedition of 1953 had failed.

Did someone know something that they didn't? This was no time to discuss the absurdities of the press. Seconds later, someone ran into the tent to say that the three dots had emerged from behind a ridge and were nearing the bottom of the Lhotse Face. Outside, James Morris heard the rattle of crampons and the hullabaloo of Sherpas about to leave camp. Tom Stobart was organising his camera porters and getting ready to meet the returning men. He was tired of waiting; after recovering from his bout of pneumonia, Stobart was probably the only person at Advance Base who felt fit and energetic.

'If they've made it, I'll wave my coat in the air,' he promised John Hunt. None of the other climbers offered to accompany him; they were either too tired or too tense.

Tom, and two Sherpas, crossed the first 500 yards quickly, hoping to get some shots of the three climbers coming down the Lhotse Face. Halfway, Tom carried on alone, leaving the Sherpas at Camp 5, a seldom-used way station just below the Lhotse Face, to brew yet more drinks. The returning men had been hidden by a series of snowy bumps but suddenly they emerged over the brow of a small slope. They smiled and waved their ice axes in the air. Tom Stobart was so excited that he almost forgot to film them.

Ed and George were interested neither in more liquid refreshment nor in Tom's plan to announce their success by waving his coat in the air. It didn't seem a fitting end to their heroic struggle. 'Wait,' said George Lowe, 'let us tell them ourselves.'

Tom tied on to their rope and trudged behind them. The terrain dipped and bulged, so they could be seen only occasionally. The returning men had made rapid progress down the Lhotse Face but now began to tire. Just before they reached the final snowy hummock above the tents of Advance Base, they stopped for a breather. Tom un-roped and got his camera ready.

The expedition hadn't gone well for him. Both he, and the team physiologist, Griffith Pugh, had frequently felt like hangers-on. John Hunt and the others tried to be helpful and co-operative but there was always something else to do. No one wanted to linger while Tom organised a shot in the icefall or Griffith Pugh set up an experiment when hot soup waited half an hour away and a snowstorm brewed above. Although he had been on mountaineering expeditions before, on Everest Tom had never gone above Advance Base. The really high-altitude filming had been done by the climbers themselves, principally George Lowe.

Now Tom Stobart was in the right place at the right time and, for once, in a position to direct the action for what he sensed would be a key scene in the Everest film. He told Hillary and Tenzing not to give a signal until he had the perfect shot lined up.

On the other side of the hump two figures walked towards them: Mike Westmacott in front and John Hunt a few feet behind, moving very slowly. When Lowe, Hillary and Tenzing came within sight, Hunt assumed that their silence meant they had failed. The closer they got with no gesture, the more convinced he became and the more he held back. In Tom Stobart's book, *The Adventurer's Eye*, he wrote that his 'eyes filled up with tears' at the thought of how happy his leader would be when they gave him the news. However, those few minutes were torture for John Hunt, who was once again thinking about the work involved in staging a third attempt.

Suddenly, Tom Stobart dropped the rope, moved out of the line and started filming. George Lowe raised his axe, Tenzing wobbled to one side and Ed Hillary smiled. For a few minutes, as John Hunt wrote in his diary, they 'temporarily went mad'.[1]

Mike Westmacott was first to meet them, grabbing their hands and shaking them vigorously. John Hunt had shuffled out of camp a broken man but he leapt on Hillary and hugged him tight for a moment and embraced Tenzing. He put his head on his shoulder and beat him on the back, all the time crying and laughing. It was the most extraordinary moment of release. After all those months of preparation and weeks on the mountain, it was over. No more days anxiously staring up at the Lhotse Face, no more tables to compile or plans to make. Everest was theirs:

> Such a scene as I've imagined but never dared believed it could come true – Everest was climbed yesterday by Ed and Tenzing at 11.30. We'd made it, exactly according to plan. We had crowned the efforts of our illustrious predecessors. We had stood at the apex of this pyramid of hard won experience and endeavour. What a tale to tell the waiting world![2]

Everyone crowded round, taking pictures, asking questions, laughing and smiling. The Sherpas held back, standing in front of the mess tent 'like Englishmen', according to George Lowe. Then Ed was among them, shaking their hands and smiling, endlessly smiling. When Tenzing went over, their mood changed again. They became quiet and were almost reverential towards him, bowing their heads and holding their palms together, one older man bending his head to touch Tenzing's hands.

These were wonderful, wonderful moments. When they calmed down, everyone crowded into the mess tent to hear Ed and Tenzing's tale. How did you feel at the top? How much oxygen did you use? What could you see? What about that rock step near the top? Of course you felt relieved but surely you must have felt something else?

Amidst the endless questions, James Morris realised something. It was mid-afternoon on Saturday 30 May. If he could get a message to Namche Bazaar by 1 June, there was the slimmest of chances that it would reach *The Times* by coronation day, 2 June. He had two and a half days and almost five hours of time difference to break the story of his career.

Mike Westmacott generously offered to escort James Morris to Base Camp and after a few last handshakes they set off. At the head of the icefall James Morris shed a tear to say goodbye to Everest, before pressing on, in the dark.

When they arrived several hours later, exhausted, James's first thought was to ask the Sherpas who had stayed there whether any journalists had come to visit. He was immensely relieved when they shook their heads. After a quick meal he typed a short message, to be carried down by a runner at first light.

During the last few months James Morris and Arthur Hutchinson, the second *Times* reporter, stationed in Kathmandu, had agonised many times over the best way to get news back to London. The Swiss had wrong-footed the press corps by sending their reports out via

Patna, over the border in India. With the British embassy and Arthur Hutchinson on hand, James Morris had chosen the more direct route via Kathmandu. Coded dispatches, carried by runners, took around eight or nine days to get from Everest Base Camp to Arthur Hutchinson. There was no evidence that any dispatches had been intercepted but no one had any illusions about their safety. As Arthur Hutchinson had written to his bosses at *The Times* a few months earlier:

> In the East every messenger, every cable office clerk and almost every government official has his price – and for the first news (however bare the details) of a successful [Everest] assault, the news agencies will be prepared to pay that price.[3]

Some old stagers at *The Times* suggested using carrier pigeons or Elizabethan-style beacons for the final message of success or failure but James Morris decided on a less poetic method. There would be no chance of getting a message back the usual way; even his quickest runners needed at least five days to get to Kathmandu but if he sent a message viá the Indian radio station at Namche Bazaar, there was a slim possibility that it might be forwarded to London in time. He knew that any message transmitted from Namche Bazaar was bound to leak, particularly as it had to go through both the British and Indian embassies in Kathmandu. All he could do to protect his scoop was to send it in code.

The standard code used by James Morris for his written dispatches was rather flippant. For John Hunt, James Morris typed 'Kettle' or 'Stringbag'; for the South Col, 'Fishmonger' or 'Manchester' and for Tenzing; 'Asparagus' or 'Carpenter'. In another version, Hunt was 'matchbox', 'refrigerator', or 'fugitive'; and Tenzing, 'drawer', 'patrician', or 'chairman'. It was clever and witty but it produced messages which were obviously encoded. When James Morris discussed the final message with John Hunt several weeks earlier, they came to the conclusion that the Indians at the Namche Bazaar radio station would be uncomfortable sending something that was very obviously encrypted. Heavens above, it would imply that they weren't trustworthy! James Morris devised a more subtle approach, again choosing specific words and phrases for each member of the team but in such a way that the code words could be combined to produce a perfectly plausible dispatch that contained a hidden message.

The most important part of the final message was the first phrase, which would indicate success or failure. According to Morris's code, if it began 'Snow conditions bad,' Everest had been climbed. If it was 'Wind still troublesome,' the attempt had failed and the team was withdrawing from the mountain. The code words and phrases that followed would reveal the names of the successful summit team or, in the case of failure, the climbers who had got highest.

On the morning of 31 May James Morris handed the message to one of his most trusted runners. A day later the runner arrived at Namche Bazaar. Just as Morris had anticipated, the message was soon in the hands of one of his rivals, Reuters's Peter Jackson, who had made it his business to befriend Mr Tiwari, the boss of the radio station. Jackson was not sure what to make of Morris's latest message:

Snow conditions bad stop advanced base abandoned yesterday stop awaiting improvement All well![4]

It seemed to confirm that the British team was about to leave Everest but there was something odd. If snow conditions were 'bad', why was 'All well'? After being so careful for so long, why was James Morris sending this message publicly? Peter Jackson was so uncertain that he decided to ignore it, rather than forward the message to Reuters. One of Mr Tiwari's assistants got on the bicycle that powered the radio station and the message was transmitted in Morse code to the

Indian embassy in Kathmandu. Before long it was in the hands of Indian journalists. They took it literally, as final confirmation that the expedition had failed, and typed their reports accordingly.

When the message reached the British embassy, at 5.45p.m., it received a very different reaction. Christopher Summerhayes, the British ambassador, immediately recognised the opening phrase 'Snow conditions bad' and quickly took out the hand-written sheet from James Morris with the code phrases for each member of the team. In his jubilation he made a mistake: he correctly deciphered 'awaiting improvement' as 'Tenzing' but misread 'advanced base abandoned' and wrote 'Tom Bourdillon'.

Mt Everest climbed 29 May by Bourdillon and Tensing. All well.[5]

The only record of his error is in a hand-written note in the archives of the RGS. One of the great scoops of the twentieth century could have ended as a famous blunder. Fortunately, Christopher Summerhayes was a diligent and meticulous man, so before sending the message on to London he double-checked and realised that 'advanced base' meant 'Ed Hillary'.[6]

The correct message was sent 4500 miles, and four and three-quarter hours back in time, to the Foreign Office in London. It was forwarded to *The Times* at 4.14p.m., just in time for the afternoon news conference. No one expected it. Only two days earlier they had received the final version of the Himalayan Committee's press release announcing the failure of the expedition, to be used once confirmation had been received. Amidst huge excitement, pages were quickly reset and new advertising put in place.

In the early evening, the news was delivered to Buckingham Palace in a red dispatch box and presented to the Queen. Her Majesty's secretary quickly drafted an official message to John Hunt, sent via the Foreign Office:

I have been commanded to transmit to you the following message from the Queen. 'Please convey to Colonel Hunt and all the members of the British expedition my warmest congratulations on their great achievement in reaching the summit of Mount Everest. Elizabeth R'.[7]

The Duke of Edinburgh's telegram was much less formal:

Everybody is delighted with the wonderful news. Well done. Congratulations to you all. Philip.[8]

The next stop for the news was the Himalayan Committee and a few family members. Basil Goodfellow, the Honorary Secretary of the Himalayan Committee, who had spent so much time setting up the expedition, was wide awake when he heard over the telephone at about 10.30p.m. The next morning, his wife draped a banner from their window:

Everest Conquered: Long Live the Queen[9]

When the news reached John Hunt's wife, Joy, at her cottage in Radnorshire, she was tied up with domestic duties:

I was giving the children a bath when the telephone rang. And they weren't in the slightest interested by the news.[10]

Whatever their initial reaction, the children perked up when Joy Hunt began telephoning to announce the news and organise a party. Within a few hours bonfires were lit and their small garden was full of carousing neighbours. The victory on Everest was celebrated in a small village on the Welsh borders long before the rest of Britain had any idea.

At 11.56p.m., the story finally reached the general public, when it was reported on the final bulletin of the BBC Home Service. All over Fleet Street front pages were scrapped and rapidly reset. When reports reached the United States, television and radio programmes were interrupted to announce the dramatic story of the British team's triumph. Soon it was sent around the world to all the newspapers who had bought syndication rights from *The Times*.

It would have made the front page whenever it was climbed but the coincidence of the news reaching London at the same time as the coronation added immeasurably to its impact. Everest was climbed on 29 May but for many it would forever be associated with June 2 1953, one of the most important days in Britain's post-war history. Many thousands of people first heard the news on the streets of London when, at around 6a.m., it was announced by loudspeaker to the crowds who had stayed up all night to line the route of the coronation parade.

The headlines in Britain on the morning of 2 June reinforced the link between Everest and the coronation. 'The Crowning Glory, Everest Climbed' proclaimed the *Daily Mail* and the *News Chronicle*. 'All this – and Everest too' exalted the front page of the *Daily Express*. 'Bulldog tenacity Beats Everest The Unconquerable. It will never be climbed again!' thundered the *Evening News*. In headlines and articles in newspapers all over the world, the first ascent was repeatedly referred to as 'a coronation gift', as if the British climbers had deliberately timed their attempt to coincide with events in London.

Famously discreet and serious in the 1950s, *The Times* did not have headlines on its front page. However, in the top right-hand corner of its coronation day edition was a small announcement: 'Everest Climbed'. Inside, the editorial was everything the Himalayan Committee dreamed of when, all those months ago, they had sacked Eric Shipton and appointed John Hunt to lead the great national expedition. Entitled 'Man's Challenge to the Heights', it began by comparing the news of the first ascent to Sir Francis Drake bringing back the Golden Hind to Plymouth Sound for the pleasure of Queen Elizabeth I. It went on to list the other great British mountaineers who had tried and failed to conquer the mountain.

The justice of the British victory was a central theme of the telegrams which began pouring into the RGS. The American Geographical Society sent a message of nationalistic fervour:

> The conquest of Everest is yours by right and is acclaimed by all American explorers and mountaineers. It also adds lustre to the crown of the second Elizabethan era. Long live the RGS![11]

The Chairman of the French National Mountain Rescue Committee, Felix Germain, declared that Everest was a British victory 'by right' and dramatically added:

> Sentimentally speaking, mountain climbing is veritably decapitated.[12]

On Everest, the climbers had no idea that their news had reached London in time. On the night of 30 May, they uncorked a bottle of rum and toasted the Duke of Edinburgh and Eric Shipton. John Hunt made an emotional speech to the assembled team before retiring to his tent in a very weak state. The next morning, they began the evacuation of Advance Base and the long haul down the Western Cwm and the icefall. No one was sad to say goodbye to the Lhotse Face but they were all dreading the icefall.

Mike Westmacott had worked diligently over the previous weeks to maintain a safe route but so much snow had melted that it was almost more dangerous than on the way up. A lot of supplies were simply abandoned in the Western Cwm, because no one wanted to force the Sherpas to make any more journeys up and down the Khumbu Icefall than was absolutely necessary.

By 1 June everyone was at Base Camp on the Khumbu Glacier, unpacking the gear that had lain in their bags for several weeks. John Hunt noted in his diary that he changed his clothes for the first time in six weeks and brushed his teeth for the first time since 26 March.

For Tom Bourdillon, the days after the return of Hillary and Tenzing were filled with pride and regret. As he listened carefully to Hillary and Tenzing's accounts he remembered his attempt a few days before:

They took 2½ hours from the S. Summit, 1 hour back to it. I was going faster on closed-circuit and if I had left Charles early and conserved the second canister I could have done it. Very miserable.[13]

His only consolation was that he would soon be back with Jennifer. Tom spent 1 June persuading John Hunt to send a telegram to the Himalayan Committee to suggest that the team should travel back to Britain by plane, rather than endure a long sea voyage. John Hunt was in such a good mood that he acquiesced.

While everyone back home celebrated their victory, Base Camp was in a little time bubble, almost a week behind the rest of the world. Wilfrid Noyce had a letter from his wife, Rosemary, telling him that it would be fine to stay on for the second attempt in the autumn. At lunchtime, a runner arrived with a telegram from the acting Prime Minister of New Zealand, congratulating Ed Hillary on progress so far and wishing him luck on the final assault. John Hunt joked that he wished that Winston Churchill, the British prime minister, could do the same.

At 4p.m. they turned on their radio to listen to the BBC's coronation broadcast. When the service finished, George Band retuned to All Indian Radio. To their utter astonishment they heard that James Morris's report had reached London. What was more, the newly crowned Elizabeth II and Winston Churchill had sent messages of congratulation.

The outside world exploded into their strange, cloistered existence. 'If the BBC says that we have done it, then it must be true!' quipped Ed Hillary. For the second time in two days, emotions, and their bottle of rum, overflowed. John Hunt drafted telegrams to thank the Queen and the Prime Minister for their support. Ever the poet, Wilfrid Noyce sensed that something fundamental had changed. As he wrote in his book, *South Col*, this was the moment when Everest transformed from the mountain of rock and ice that they had been trying to climb for so many months into something very different:

> *Everest symbol of Coronation Year, Everest climbed by a British party,*
> *Everest laid at the feet of our Queen for her Coronation Day. Everest*
> *whose top had first been trodden by Hillary and Tenzing – which?*[14]

No one gathered in the mess tent that night had any inkling of what would happen next. The story of the 1953 British Everest expedition was about to move into a new and in some ways, even more unpredictable phase, which would be as challenging to John Hunt as the events on Everest. For the last three months he had been in charge of the expedition and, both literally and metaphorically, in control of the official narrative. There had been many unpredictable factors, such as the weather and the performance of his team, but he had felt in command of the situation. Over the next two months, and indeed for several years to come, he would find that others would challenge the official narrative. On 3 June he wrote in his diary about the 'strange and thrilling thing that we have let loose'.[15] He had no idea how strange the next few weeks were to be.

Chapter 12

WHOSE MOUNTAIN?

As the members of the British team listened to the coronation service on 2 June, Tenzing was thirty-five miles away in the village of Thame, visiting his elderly mother, Kinzom. She was especially pleased to hear about his success; it meant that he would never have to risk his life on Everest again. Elsewhere in the Solu Khumbu, the reaction was similarly muted. As the Reuters correspondent Peter Jackson discovered, there was 'a little interest [among the Sherpas] at Thyangboche but at Namche none at all'.[1] If anything, the Sherpas were more downcast than elated, worried about their future job prospects. Now that Everest had been climbed, would any foreigner come back and employ them? Far away in Kathmandu and Darjeeling, in India, the news was treated very differently.

When he heard the news on the radio, Tenzing's friend in Darjeeling, Rabindranath Mitra, sent a runner to Tenzing's house to inform his wife, Ang Lahmu and his daughters, Pem Pem and Nima. Shortly afterwards a messenger arrived with official congratulations from the Governor of West Bengal. His statement, published in the press on the following day, was full of patriotic fervour, though it made no mention of British victories, coronations or 'The New Elizabethan Age':

Permit me madam to congratulate you on the glorious achievement of your husband Mr Tenzing Norkey who has set up a mountaineering record. As Head of the State of which he is an inhabitant I cannot but exult in his glory which will redound to the credit of all our countrymen in the eyes of the whole world.[2]

Over the next few days Indian newspapers were full of stories about Tenzing. Countless visitors came to pay their respects to the family of India's new folk hero.

The Statesman, the Calcutta newspaper, revived the fund to buy Tenzing a house. This time, they raised more than twelve thousand rupees in less than two weeks, more than enough to build a substantial property. There were reports that he had been offered a large cash sum by the state of West Bengal, as well as a life pension from the Nepalese government. Indian film producers were said to be considering various roles for him. Within a week of the ascent, a documentary film was in production entitled *Tenzing: Tiger of the Snows.*

Tributes both large and small came in: a group of Indian students at the London School of Economics was reported to have made an impromptu collection for a man they called 'an inspiration to us the youth'. At the other end of the scale, several Indian newspapers suggested that Everest should be renamed 'Mount Tenzing' or 'Tenzing Peak', in recognition of his achievement.

While he was lionised in the Indian press, in Britain, Tenzing's position was not so prominent. Newspapers were full of references to 'plucky' and 'indispensable' Sherpas but they were the support act, not the main players. When the first full account of the ascent was published in *The Times* on 8 June and syndicated around the world, one missing detail caused huge consternation and offence in India. It came in the description of Hillary and Tenzing's fifteen minutes on the summit:

Tensing produced a string of miscellaneous flags and held them high, while Hillary photographed them. They included the Union Jack, the Nepal flag and that of the United Nations.[3]

Where was the Indian flag? Tenzing had lived in Darjeeling for almost twenty years and was a proud citizen: surely he would have carried one? His friend Rabindranath Mitra remembered giving him a flag. Had it been taken from him?

The article confirmed something else that was to create much controversy in the coming weeks. On 6 June it was announced that the Queen intended to confer knighthoods on Ed Hillary and John Hunt. There was no mention of a future Sir Tenzing Norgay. Elizabeth II was said to be 'considering giving him an award', perhaps a George Medal,[4] but nothing was certain. Many in India and in Britain wanted to know why Tenzing was being treated differently. Especially if, as several Indian and Nepalese newspapers claimed, this valiant, humble, indispensable, plucky little Sherpa had reached the top first.

Who precisely had set foot on the summit first – Hillary or Tenzing – was never an issue for British journalists. In his initial account of the ascent for *The Times*, James Morris simply noted that at 11.30a.m. on 29 May 1953 'they stepped at last on to the snow-covered final eminence of Everest'.[5] When Peter Jackson interviewed Hillary and Tenzing at the Thyangboche Monastery on 5 June, he didn't bother to ask. For the British team, and for Hillary and Tenzing, it didn't matter who was in the lead. They ascended, two men climbing as one, a living embodiment of the idea cherished by mountaineers of 'the brotherhood of the rope'. However, for the Indian and Nepalese press, it was a crucial question, which became more and more important as the days went on.

In June 1953 Nepal was in the middle of a political crisis. There were widespread rent strikes in the eastern part of the country and the main political parties in Kathmandu were so riven by infighting that it was impossible to form a coherent government. In the midst of the chaos, Tenzing was universally acclaimed as a unifying figure, a local hero, championed by both Communist radicals and Nepalese Nationalists. The fact that India seemed to want to appropriate him as their national hero made the Nepalese drums bang even louder.

One of the first references to the summit controversy came in the *Gorkhapatra*, Nepal's oldest regular newspaper. Their edition of 9 June 1953 included a report that stated Tenzing was several hundred feet in front of Hillary on the final stage and had hauled his partner up to the summit. Though the *Gorkhapatra*'s circulation was limited, the story spread quickly. In Kathmandu schoolchildren were told by their teachers that Tenzing had beaten the Westerner to the great prize. The poet, Dharma Raj Thapa wrote a ballad that was quickly turned into a hit song, *Hamro Tenzing Sherpa Le*. It told how Tenzing 'guided Hillary through the confusing trails' and 'goaded Hillary to climb on'.

The 'who got to the summit first controversy' is often thought to have been cooked up by Nepalese politicians but the Indian press played a major part. The report in the *Gorkhapatra* originated not in Nepal but in India and arrived in the Kathmandu newsroom via the Hind Samachar,[6] an Indian news agency. Similar reports attributed to 'sources close to the expedition' appeared in India in *The Mail* (Madras)[7] and *The Leader* (Allahabad).[8] It is important to realise that the story did not come from Tenzing. There is no record of any Indian or Nepalese journalist interviewing him before he reached the outskirts of Kathmandu, more than a week after the controversy began. Like much of the earlier reporting of Everest, it was essentially wishful thinking.

For the local press, which had felt excluded since the beginning of the expedition, this was their Everest story. In March *The Times*'s monopoly had caused huge resentment and drove Indian journalists towards Tenzing for the simple reason that he was the only member of the expedition able to give interviews. Now, at the end, here seemed to be proof that they had backed the right horse. As Inder Malhotra, a young journalist who became one of the most respected figures in the Indian press, remembered fifty years later:

> The idea that white man is the leading one, oh no rubbish, this time, we have done it, our people have done it, Tenzing has done it and why should this credit be misappropriated by others. This was the feeling.[9]

As the story gathered momentum, the protagonists were making their way back to Kathmandu. After a brief stop at the Thyangboche Monastery, John Hunt set off on 5 June, with Tom Bourdillon and Alfred Gregory, leaving Ed Hillary and Tenzing to return with the others at a more leisurely pace.

En route, John Hunt was greeted by numerous runners, carrying messages of congratulation from all around the world. The British ambassador, Christopher Summerhayes, forwarded the news of his knighthood, together with a bottle of champagne. There were telegrams from Field Marshal Montgomery, the President of France, the prime ministers of New Zealand and Canada, and greetings from friends and well-wishers. On 9 June, one runner intercepted Hunt's party with a postbag containing no fewer than sixty-five telegrams.

With the congratulations, Christopher Summerhayes also forwarded the press reports about renaming Everest and the articles about who had reached the summit first. For John Hunt, who despite his exhausted state was pressing on to Kathmandu at twice the rate of the outward journey, the prospect of dealing with a press controversy must have been awful. However, he thought that he would be able to deal with the matter quickly, as he confided to his diary on 11 June:

> I intend to hold a press conference as early as possible and straighten out incipient inconsistencies, exaggerating facts. In particular I am worried

about Tenzing. There are already stories of his having guided us, which will grow enormously and fantastically if I do not scotch them now.[10]

If only it were so easy.

Hunt's party arrived at Banepa, on the edge of Kathmandu, late in the evening of Saturday 13 June, a day earlier than expected. There was no welcoming party and no way of getting in touch with the British embassy. As luck would have it, the climbers encountered a local reporter working for Ralph Izzard's paper, the *Daily Mail*, who gave them a lift to the embassy. Their story appeared two days later under the headline 'Daily Mail reporter meets heroes and gives them lift into town'. It contained little information other than the fact that the conquerors of Everest were amazed to see electric lights after three months on the mountain. It was a sweet victory for a newspaper that had been the team's pet hate since March.

At the British embassy, they were warmly greeted by Christopher Summerhayes but John Hunt was in no mood to relax. He was eager to hold the press conference at the first possible opportunity but he knew that he could not speak to the press without breaking his contract with *The Times*. He sent a telegram notifying the editor of his plans:

> *View worldwide interest consider impracticable and potentially harmful interests both expedition and Times to refuse information other press organs particularly Nepalese Indian.*

> *Desire specially emphasize danger of false impressions involving minor political implications due ignorance of facts (this tendency already apparent here) and resentment here of Foreign expedition withholding news of local mountain and Sherpa achievements.*[11]

The Times immediately telegraphed back insisting that John should stick to the terms of the contract. They could not possibly approve because they had syndicated their exclusive rights to dozens of newspapers around the world. John Hunt was so concerned that he decided to ignore them and go ahead.

He was appalled to see the expedition so casually misreported. Like everyone else in the team, Hunt thought that the issue of who had stepped on the summit first was absurd but he was also irked by repeated references to Tenzing 'having guided' the British team. The Everest victory was the result of teamwork and everyone had played a role. There had been no guides; one of John Hunt's first decisions, in October 1952, had been to revoke Eric Shipton's invitation to the New Zealander Harry Ayres precisely because he was a professional mountain guide.

Although John Hunt embraced the idea that there was an international competition to get to the top of Everest, he was modest and magnanimous in victory, at pains publicly to express his debt to the Swiss team, as well to the British and European mountaineers who had climbed in the Himalayas. When Vincent Auriol, president of France, sent him a message of congratulation on 15 June, he immediately replied that the French ascent of Annapurna in 1950 *'a fourni inspiration notre reussite'*[12] (had been the inspiration for our success). John Hunt's choice of Hillary and Tenzing for the main attempt on the summit was an archetypal Commonwealth project: a New Zealander, to represent the remaining dominions of the British Empire, partnered with a representative of a former colony, the Republic of India, on an expedition organised and led by Britain, 'the Mother Country'. This might be fanciful; a simpler explanation is that he chose Hillary and Tenzing because they were the fittest and best climbers available at the time. One thing is certain: John Hunt would never have dreamed that one day Tenzing and the Sherpas would be portrayed as competitors in the 'Race for Everest'. And as Hunt knew, the Nepalese and Indian press had one small but significant detail wrong: Tenzing had not reached the summit first, Ed Hillary had.

John Hunt had been through the story of the final ascent in person; unlike the journalists, he wasn't reliant on 'sources close to the expedition'; he was the expedition leader. Hunt was adamant that the issue was utterly irrelevant but if it had become a moot point, he intended to tell the truth.

The press conference at the British embassy late on 14 June was a tense affair. When asked whether Tenzing had reached the summit first, Hunt said no, although he qualified his answer by insisting that the precise order of the climbers did not matter. With regard to the flags displayed on Tenzing's ice axe, he confirmed that there had been an Indian flag and regretted that it had not been mentioned in the first reports. When it came to the issue of Tenzing's role as a guide, Hunt committed a *faux pas* that would make the controversy last much longer.

He categorically rejected the idea that Tenzing had ever guided the British on Everest. This was consistent with his previous comments but as if to rub salt into wounded pride, when asked to compare Tenzing to an experienced Swiss mountain guide he replied, candidly rather than diplomatically:

> *Tenzing, brilliant climber [that] he was, was not the equal of more experienced European alpine mountaineers.*[13]

A report in *The Statesman* included a phrase that, although seemingly innocuous, had a lasting impact:

> *Tenzing, Sir John said, was astonishingly excellent in courage and determination and physically wonderful. 'Within the limitations of his experience, Tenzing is a brilliant climber and an excellent companion'.*[14]

What exactly did he mean by 'the limitations of his experience'? It was one thing to deny that Tenzing had reached the summit before Hillary but with this phrase John Hunt seemed to imply that he wasn't even a very good climber. Hunt did not want to belittle Tenzing but this was not a good answer. Obviously, a self-taught Sherpa was not going to have the same technical skills as trained and certified Swiss guide but Tenzing had reached the highest point on earth, a mountain that was almost twice the height of any in the Alps. Bearing in mind the obvious adulation of Tenzing, this was the worst thing John Hunt could have said.[15]

When Joy Hunt arrived in Kathmandu, flown out courtesy of Alfred Bird and Co., custard kings and manufacturer of the expedition's favourite cereal, *Grape-Nuts*, her first words, according to the *Daily Express*, were: 'Darling, your nose is peeling.' John Hunt had bigger problems to deal with. Far from killing off the story, the press conference made things worse. Scenting that there was a new Everest 'angle' that *The Times* could not control, the British press widely reported the summit controversy and added a few twists of its own. The left-wing *Daily Worker*, not known for its mountaineering coverage, ran articles about the iniquitous rates of pay for Sherpas and reported that Tenzing's wife, Ang Lahmu, who had also arrived in Kathmandu, had told John Hunt that 'world fame is a poor consolation for poverty'. On 16 June, the *London Evening Standard* reported that Tenzing was so insulted not to be awarded a knighthood that he planned to turn down the George Medal.

As usual, 'sources close to the expedition' were only too pleased to speak for Tenzing.

The *Manchester Guardian* took up the story with an editorial on 17 June that complained about the seeming inequality of offering Hillary a knighthood and Tenzing the George Medal, which they described as an obscure award that had most recently been given to policemen who had arrested armed criminals. The controversy spread to the House of Commons, when the Tory MP Robert Lindsay asked the Prime Minister, Winston Churchill:

Is the Prime Minister aware of the general disappointment that it has not been thought appropriate to offer the Indian subject, Tenzing, an award comparable with that given to the New Zealander?[16]

Winston Churchill's reply – 'That does not entirely rest with Her Majesty's government' – did nothing to appease the critics or dampen the controversy.

The issue of Tenzing's 'missing' knighthood generated much argument over the next month and, since 1953, has continued to be held up as proof of British snobbery. Ed Hillary wrote in his autobiography, *View from the Summit*, that he was unhappy about the inequality and wished that Tenzing had also been given a knighthood. 'Some people claimed at the time', he wrote, 'that Indian and Nepalese citizens were not permitted to accept foreign titles but I don't believe that this was completely true.'[17] Did the British establishment cheat Tenzing of his due or, as Winston Churchill intimated, was it more complicated? Only now, with the release of previously closed government files, is it possible to address this question more fully.

The official papers are surprising in several ways. They reveal that the idea of offering Ed Hillary a knighthood did not come from the British government but from the Prime Minister of New Zealand, Sidney Holland, who was in London for the coronation. He recommended Ed Hillary for a knighthood on 4 June. Initially, government and palace officials resisted and suggested that it would be more appropriate to award him a George Medal. Sidney Holland was adamant and eventually won the day. At this point officials at the War Office were asked if John Hunt could also be given a knighthood. They were unsure, because serving military officers were not eligible for certain honours but eventually this point of protocol was overcome and John Hunt was also knighted, although with a slightly lesser honour than Ed Hillary. (Because of his military rank John Hunt was made a Knight Bachelor. Ed Hillary was made Knight Commander of the Order of the British Empire, KBE.[18])

There are no documents to suggest that Tenzing was ever considered for a knighthood but government papers reveal that, as Winston Churchill's statement indicated, the British felt that this matter was out of their control. Under the complex rules that governed the honours system, both an individual and their national government had to agree to accept an award but Tenzing's nationality was far from clear. At first he was thought to be either Pakistani or Nepali, until it was realised that Darjeeling was within India. This complicated matters considerably, because if Tenzing were an Indian, he could not possibly accept a British knighthood.

During the 1920s and 1930s, in the twilight of the British Raj, a very elaborate honours scheme had been created by colonial officials. Titles had been handed like baubles to India's numerous royal families to keep them loyal to the Empire. Nationalist campaigners demanded that Indians should refuse to accept British honours. After independence in 1947 this was enshrined in the Indian constitution, Part III Section 18(2), which stated:

No citizen of India shall accept any title from any foreign state.

With the Indian press and politicians claiming that Tenzing was one of their citizens, there was no point in considering a knighthood for him. It took many weeks and much consultation before the Indian government allowed Tenzing to be awarded the George Medal. At the time, the diplomatic activity was *sub rosa* but even if the truth had come out, the feeling that Tenzing was victimised would have persisted. By the middle of June a new narrative had been created in India and Nepal, in which the ascent of Everest was framed as a battle between the plucky East and the patrician West. The issue of the knighthood was yet another example of British *hauteur*.

As the arguments raged in Kathmandu and London, the two protagonists were wending their way towards Kathmandu. For Ed

Hillary and the members of British team, the most important issue was not who got to the summit first but getting hold of fresh food and eating as much as possible. Their group fantasy was to find a village that would sell them enough poultry for each man to have a whole chicken for his evening meal. The sudden change of diet, unsurprisingly, wreaked havoc on their stomachs but did not blunt their hunger.

The closer they got to Kathmandu, the more extravagant the welcome that Tenzing was given. He had been joined by his elder sister, Lhamu Kipa, and her daughters, who appeared happy to minister to his every need. The world's most famous Sherpa occupied a large tent replete with a rug and tea-making equipment, like 'an oriental potentate', according to Wilfrid Noyce.

Tenzing first became directly embroiled in the summit controversy on 19 June, at Dolalghat, two days' march from the capital. When he arrived the village was decorated with flowers and ornamental arches to welcome the returning heroes. Among the adoring crowds were several journalists who were keen to interview Tenzing but also there was another group, of young Nepalese men, who rudely pushed the pressmen away.

Their aim was to get two signed statements from Tenzing. The first affirmed that he had indeed beaten Hillary to the summit of Everest, the second, and perhaps more important, asserted that he was Nepali, not Indian. Tenzing later said that he was so confused and unprepared for their questions that he signed the paperwork to stop them pestering him.[19]

Brandishing their so-called signed documents, the crowd of young men rushed back to Kathmandu, pausing only to rough up any Indian journalists they met on the way. That night Nepalese radio reported that Tenzing had confirmed that he had reached the summit first, adding that Hillary had taken a full five minutes to climb the final slope.

After a brief rest in the small town, the rather frazzled team carried on to Hukse, where they stayed the night. John and Joy Hunt came to join them on the final day's march, as did several journalists from British and American newspapers. The Himalayan Committee had telegraphed John Hunt suggesting that that he should offer Tenzing a contract to work for the expedition for the next few months in return for agreeing to abide by their exclusive press deal with *The Times* (that is, in return for his silence). It was too little, too late. At Hukse, Tenzing met journalists from *Life* magazine and the large American press agency UPI, who made it very clear that they were willing to pay for his story. When John Hunt put the Himalayan Committee's offer to him, Tenzing turned it down. As he later commented in his autobiography, *Man of Everest*, he was for once in a position to make a lot of money, so why shouldn't he?

Tenzing told James Burke of *Life* magazine about his humble origins and the fact that he was still very poor. He was worried and confused by the nationality issue, which had not mattered in the past but he thought that he had a solution to the summit controversy:

If I say Hillary first, Indian, Nepal people unhappy. If I say I first European people unhappy. If you agree, I like say both got top together almost same time. If everybody write that, no trouble.[20]

The language was simple and much less florid than his later biography but there was no doubt of Tenzing's sincerity.

Ed Hillary was also approached by a representative of a British newspaper and asked if he would sell his story for several thousand pounds. Ed explained that he was contracted to *The Times* but the journalist persisted, until Ed threatened to punch him. As the British journalist Rawle Knox wrote years later in the British magazine, *Punch*, Ed was equally forthright about the summit question:

'We were a ＿＿ team, so what the ＿＿ does it matter who got to the ＿＿ top first. I couldn't have ＿＿ done it without him and vice ＿＿ versa.

'Steady on, Ed' said his fellow New Zealander George Lowe, who was standing by, 'you're a ＿＿ knight now'.[21]

This quotation sounds a little too polished, and a little too profane to be verbatim, but there is no doubting Ed Hillary's exasperation at the time. Next day at Banepa, on the edge of Kathmandu, the crowd was even bigger. Charles Wylie intervened when Tenzing was pulled away by a particularly insistent group:

I was next to Tenzing and the other side was a reporter who was really aggravating him and in those days the Nepalese had shaven heads, except for the tupi, a sort of bit of hair left on top, so I leant over and pulled his tupi. At once there was a deathly hush throughout the crowd and I realised I'd done something terrible. I'd quite forgotten that the tupi, after you die that is what you're hauled up to heaven with. And so you shouldn't touch anybody's tupi but I'd done it! Anyhow, I waited to be lynched or whatever was decided by the crowd but they just muttered and murmured and Tenzing and I backed out of the crowd and we got away with that one.[22]

This was the last Wylie saw of Tenzing for several hours; he was almost immediately whisked away by one of the official reception committees, asked to don Nepalese clothes and hustled into a jeep. John Hunt and Ed Hillary were crammed into the back, with Tenzing standing up, leaning on the roll bar with his hands clasped together in a gesture of greeting. As they drove into Kathmandu, huge crowds lined the road to witness Tenzing's return, shouting: 'Shri Tenzing Zindabad' (Long Live Tenzing). During the previous week large ornamental arches had been built along the route; many were festooned with images of Tenzing on the top of Everest. Hillary was either nowhere to be seen or sprawled out a few feet below, being hauled up by his Nepali partner. At first, Ed thought that the posters were funny but gradually, he became more and more irritated.

A day earlier the first summit photographs had been published in *The Times* and flashed around the world. Ironically, they seemed to confirm the idea that Tenzing was the main climber. The most widely disseminated image showed Tenzing on the summit, holding his ice axe, with the flags fluttering in the wind. It was a powerful, iconic photograph, which seemed to allocate the glory to Tenzing, even though it had been very carefully stage-managed by Ed Hillary. There were no photographs of Hillary on the summit and the low-angle shot of Tenzing showed that his partner was below him (which of course he was).

When the Everest heroes reached the temples of Bhadgaon, they stopped for a display of devil dancing in the main square, before Tenzing was invited to speak. Overwhelmed, he didn't manage to say very much. Nevertheless, he was given a rapturous reception. John Hunt received some muted applause for his short speech but Ed Hillary was greeted with a hostile silence.

Three miles from Kathmandu the heroes of Everest were compelled to swap their jeep for an ornately carved state carriage led by a brass band flanked by four brightly-dressed female outriders. Thousands of people lined the streets and hung off the balconies of nearby buildings, desperate to see their hero. Months later, in the expedition film, the scenes in Kathmandu were intercut with coronation crowds. It is easy to see why: that was Tenzing's day, crowned as Nepal's new national hero.

In an account for *The Times*, James Morris captured the frenzied atmosphere:

Riding in dubious triumph through a crazy Persepolis, with his colleagues of the expedition trailing along behind rather like Tamburlaine's captured Kings ... [23]

It was raining and according to Nepalese superstition Saturday was an unlucky day but nothing could dim the enthusiasm of the crowds. Once again Tenzing stood at the front, while Hillary and Hunt were crammed below. The other members of the British team, ignored, had to beg lifts from the press or local officials. A few had gone back to the British embassy for the cold beers that they had thought about for so long. Others were corralled into a jeep that followed the main carriage, amidst the deafening clamour of the crowds. At the front the main carriage was continually showered with red *holi* powder, giving everyone an increasingly unworldly look.

After stopping for more speeches in Kathmandu, at about 7p.m. they reached the royal palace, where they were escorted through gloomy, chandelier-lit rooms to the King's chamber. It was a surreal moment: on one wall stood Tenzing, Hillary and Hunt, stained red with *holi* powder, against another was a line of climbers, dusty from the trail and dressed in a motley collection of shorts and plimsolls. Griffith Pugh, most eccentrically of all, wore his very faded blue pyjamas. At the front King Tribhuvan was surrounded by the resplendently dressed royal family. The King made a speech, in which he congratulated Tenzing for reaching the summit first. He then handed out decorations. Tenzing was given the Nepal Tara, the highest award in the country and Hunt and Hillary were given a lesser decoration, the Order of the Bracelet of the Right Hand of Nepal. The other members of the team were given nothing.

As it grew dark, John Hunt and the others retired to the British embassy. Tenzing went with his family to a government guesthouse.

The next day the team was invited to a public meeting at Kathmandu's main military parade ground but there was only one star of this show. As *The Times* commented, 'scarcely one out of 40 speeches and addresses given during the afternoon gave any indication that any persons other than Tenzing were present on Everest at the time of the ascent'. There was one breakthrough that day: Hillary, Hunt and Tenzing agreed a common formula for the story of their climb to the summit. Later Tenzing read it on Nepalese radio. The issue of who had arrived at the summit first was fudged:

> As we climbed upwards to the south summit first one then the other would take a turn at leading.
>
> We crossed over the south summit and moved along the summit ridge. We reached the summit almost together.

This phrase 'almost together' was distinctly ambiguous but it seemed to take a little heat out of the debate.

Another phrase was much more damaging: 'a good climber *within the limits of his experience*'. When Tenzing was told about John Hunt's comments of a week earlier he was hurt and angry. On the evening of 21 June, he turned down the opportunity to attend a party at the British embassy and instead held a press conference at which he refuted Hunt's statement, asking bluntly: 'Is there any living man that has been on Everest seven times?' *The Times* claimed that the various controversies were stoked by 'sponsors' whose 'main interest on the subject of Everest seems to be the possible political capital to be made out of the success'. However, there is no doubt that Tenzing was deeply wounded by what he perceived to be John Hunt's insult to his climbing skills.

Over the next few days the atmosphere in Kathmandu continued to be volatile. There were several reports of armed gangs beating and threatening Indian journalists and even claims that Tenzing had gone into hiding after death threats. Much of this was exaggeration and fantasy but there is no doubt this was a very turbulent moment in

Nepal's history. Tenzing's return to Kathmandu came only a few days after a change of government and the appointment of a new prime minister. The arguments over Tenzing's nationality fed into a wider political debate over Nepal's relationship with India, a deeply divisive issue in 1953.

The strain of the public adulation and the political pressure was obvious on Tenzing. The man whose smile was his trademark never looked less comfortable than he did in late June 1953. For Ed Hillary, the pressure was not quite so great. He had picked up a dose of dysentery and did not mind keeping a low profile but as the summit controversy grew he became increasingly irritated. When a journalist working for *The Observer* asked him what he felt about it, he said that 'it didn't matter a damn'[24] but when pressed, said that Tenzing was roughly forty feet below him, on the other end of a rope.

The crunch came when Hillary wrote his account of their summit climb for *The Times*. Everyone knew that the line 'we reached the summit almost together' had fudged the issue. He had to tell his story to a 'newspaper of record'. Would he tell the truth?

Buried deep in the archives of the RGS is a three-page memo based on Ed Hillary's account for *The Times*. It gives a fascinating insight to the final moments of the climb and the process of editing that went on afterwards. It begins with the following paragraph:

To save time I tried cramponing without cutting steps but quickly realised our margin of safety on these steep slopes at this altitude was too small, so went on step cutting. I was starting to tire a little now. Tenzing was moving very slowly. As I chipped steps around still another corner, I wondered rather dully just how long we could keep it up and then I realised that that ridge ahead instead of still rising, now dropped sharply away and far below I could see the East Rongbuk Glacier. I looked upwards to see a narrow snow ridge running up to a sharp summit.

This is the text that appeared in the final article but the next paragraph was significantly changed, on the advice of John Hunt and the Ambassador, Christopher Summerhayes. The first version read:

> *Still fearful of cornices but with an air of hopefulness, I got Tensing to belay me carefully while I chipped a path up this ridge. As I climbed higher, I realised that there was no cornice and with added confidence cramponed up the ridge and stepped on top of Everest. My initial feelings were of relief: relief that there were no more steps to cut, no more ridge to traverse and no more humps to tantalize us with hopes of success. I quickly brought up Tensing beside me ...*

The final version was considerably shorter and less detailed, making everything seem to happen much more quickly:

> *[I looked upwards to see a narrow snow ridge running up to a sharp summit.] A few more whacks of the ice axe in the firm snow and we stood on the summit. My initial feelings were of relief ...*

As the front page of the memo states, this revised version was 'accepted by *Times* in view of leader's (John Hunt's) insistence which was due to a desire not to cause offence to Nepalese nationalists and smooth over the dispute as to who got there first'. The phrasing is awkward but it is notable that Hunt and Hillary decided to keep the original version and create a formal document for the historical record.

For John Hunt, this was a very difficult time. The expedition had left him physically and emotionally exhausted and the aftermath was totally unexpected. One day he was receiving messages of congratulation from all over the world, the next he was opening hate mail. His fragile state was revealed in a candid letter to Lawrence

Kirwan at the RGS on 23 June. After recounting the latest developments in Kathmandu, he continued:

> I would ask you, without diffidence to be as careful with me as you can. I have had a pretty strained time for well over a year now with no respite at all and the final outcome of our expedition, triumphal though it has been has produced something like a relapse or reaction in myself; I am not as full of energy, mentally or physically, as I was before leaving London. So far I have not been able to put pen to paper on the Times articles and do not feel sure they will be ready by the time I return. I have had a pretty bad time over the last few days with this political trouble and the deliberate attempts to discredit the expedition.

He had led a brilliant attempt on Everest but now John Hunt was in uncharted territory. As leader, he felt that he had to be in control but events had moved much more quickly in Kathmandu than they had on the mountain. He had won the 'Race for Everest' but the trophy was much harder to collect than he had anticipated.

On 24 June, Hunt left for Calcutta, with Ed Hillary and Alfred Gregory, hoping that with a change of scenery, the controversy might die down. Even as they left Nepal, the divisions in the team were clear. While Tenzing and his family flew in the Nepalese royal family's private plane, the British climbers went on a commercial service. In Calcutta, the capital of West Bengal, the atmosphere was slightly less feverish but, as in Kathmandu, the focus of the celebrations was Tenzing. He was presented with the cheque for 12,000 rupees by *The Statesman* and, more significantly, the state government announced its intention to build a mountaineering school in Darjeeling, with Tenzing as its first director. *The Times* reported that there was a 'notably happier feeling in the air' but one very important question remained to be resolved: would Tenzing accompany the team to Britain to celebrate their victory?

John Hunt had invited Tenzing in early June, soon after the ascent, but as the controversy developed, this invitation became another bone of contention. Some newspapers reported that Hunt had threatened to withdraw the offer unless Tenzing endorsed Hillary's story, others that Tenzing didn't want to go because he was unhappy. This was closer to the truth.

The question was unresolved when they moved on to Delhi for more celebrations. The crowds were bigger than ever; an estimated twenty thousand people turned out to greet Tenzing at Delhi Airport. As he emerged from his plane, hundreds of people burst through the police cordon and mobbed him on the runway. When the mayhem subsided, Tenzing was driven to the Nepalese embassy.

That evening a new figure entered the drama, who was to play a crucial role in Tenzing's life over the next decade: Pandit Nehru. A protégé of Mahatma Gandhi, during the 1930s and 1940s he was a key figure in the Indian independence movement. In 1947 he was appointed India's first prime minister and impressed everyone with his statesmanlike qualities.

Nehru had been out of the country for much of June, attending the coronation in London and the Commonwealth Prime Ministers' conference that followed, so he had not intervened publicly in the debate over Tenzing's nationality. At their first meeting, however, he immediately warmed to Tenzing and decided to take an active interest in his affairs.

For Tenzing, Nehru seemed like a politician who genuinely cared for him and was willing to listen. In *Man of Everest* Tenzing gave Nehru a fulsome tribute:

> *He was warm and kind and unlike so many others, was not thinking of what use he could make of me but only of how he could help me and make me happy.*

Looking back, it would be naïve to think there was no political opportunism on Nehru's part. He, as much as anyone, realised the importance of national heroes and figureheads and saw Tenzing as an inspirational figure for India's youth. Nehru seems to have had a genuine affection for Tenzing and clearly felt that the recent 'Everest controversies' were deeply distasteful. In a letter to his chief ministers he wrote:

> The final ascent of Everest has been a great achievement in which all of us should take pride. Here again there has been pettiness and the narrowest type of nationalism shown over them … It does not make the slightest difference to anybody whether Tenzing first reached the top or Hillary. Neither could have done so without the other … For us to show a narrow and deplorable nationalism in such matters is not to add to the credit of our country but to lead people to think that we are petty in outlook and suffering from some kind of inferiority complex.[25]

Nehru's most important intervention came over Tenzing's proposed visit to London. When he left Kathmandu, 'will he? won't he?' still hung in the air. On 24 June John Hunt had telegraphed the Himalayan Committee in London to say that Tenzing would definitely not be coming but a few days later he informed them that the visit would happen. Changing Tenzing's mind had taken the combined persuasive powers of Pandit Nehru and another leading politician, Maulana Azad, India's education minister. Tenzing had not been enthusiastic and kept raising his demands. First, he had not wanted to go at all, then he had agreed to do so on condition that his wife and children came too. No sooner had this been agreed than Tenzing came up with another demand, insisting that he be allowed to take a Sherpa friend from Darjeeling, Lakpa Tsering, who was acting as his secretary.

This might have been a sign of Tenzing's growing assertiveness but newsreel images and photographs from India tell a different story.

Tenzing was clearly unhappy in the public eye and looked confused and upset by the huge crowds and the sudden adulation. He wanted to go back to Darjeeling, where he felt comfortable; if he couldn't, he wanted to surround himself with his friends and his family.

Eventually, *The Times* agreed to meet the cost of everyone's flights to London. When Nehru discovered that Tenzing had few clothes to travel in, he took him to his wardrobe and offered him his own. Nehru was clever enough not to offer one of his Congress Party white caps, which would have been too obvious, but he was happy to give Tenzing one of his trademark collarless suits, a subtle reminder of his association with the great climber.

On July 1, Tenzing and the British team left Delhi on a BOAC aeroplane which had been specially rerouted for them. On the way to London they stopped several times and were everywhere greeted by cheering crowds but the halts were short. Everyone was glad to relax, away from the intense press focus of the last few weeks. When they stopped in Rome, as a reporter in *The Times* quipped, John Hunt and Tenzing came down the steps from the plane together, 'almost as if to avoid any argument about who had been the first to touch Italian soil'. When their plane stopped in Zurich, the British party was greeted by several members of the 1952 Swiss team bearing bottles of champagne. Tenzing was thrilled to meet Raymond Lambert again and everyone on the British team was moved by the Swiss men's generosity. Fifty years later Alfred Gregory remembered it with real emotion, 'I don't think we would have done that for them had they climbed it … it was just marvellous.'

Amongst the camaraderie was one final sour note for the last leg of their journey home. As usual, the press was involved. This time it was the *Daily Express* that chose to reignite the controversy just as the British team was on its way to London. On 1 July, it announced on its front page that over the coming days it would print a series of articles telling 'Tenzing's side of the Everest story', based on syndicated interviews carried out by United Press International in Calcutta a few days earlier. Tenzing's secretary, Lakpa Tsering, had been instrumental in organising the deal and had set up further interviews in London.

The first article, on 2 July, concentrated on the tensions between the British team and the Sherpas at the beginning of the expedition. It revealed how the Sherpas had been billeted in a garage at the British embassy in Kathmandu and how they had 'dirtied the road in front' before detailing the early arguments over clothing and equipment. When John Hunt read the story on the flight to London, he was not amused.

As far as he was concerned, these were minor issues from a long, long time ago. Why was anyone bringing them up again? Hadn't there been enough bickering? John Hunt and Tenzing had a candid discussion, which Tenzing later said cleared the air but for John Hunt it was another problem that he had not anticipated. In a few hours they were scheduled to arrive in London. Surely it was time for the controversies to end?

When the plane landed, they assembled on the tarmac at London Airport and posed for the cameras. The smiles were not quite so innocent any more.

Chapter 13

BRINGING EVEREST
HOME

The plane carrying the Everest team touched down at London Airport almost half a day late, just before 1p.m. on Friday 3 July. As *The Times* reported, there were 'chaotic scenes' and 'spontaneous cheering'. After the regular passengers had disembarked, running the gauntlet of more than a hundred journalists, John Hunt was first down the stairs. He held an ice axe adorned with a small Union Jack taken from one of the Humber limousines at the British embassy in Kathmandu.

The waiting crowd was cordoned behind a rope but once this barrier had been breached, by Griffith Pugh's daughter, who dashed across the tarmac and leapt into her father's arms, the remainder followed suit. Eric Shipton presented a bouquet of bananas to Ed Hillary[1] and there were hugs and kisses all around. It wasn't quite the pandemonium of Delhi Airport but as Lawrence Kirwan, Secretary of the RGS, later wrote, it looked 'like a bit of a revolution at the time'.

Inside the terminal there was a strong military presence. Having played down John Hunt's military credentials at the beginning of the expedition, there was now a distinct change of policy. The list of dignitaries invited to the airport included two generals from John

Hunt's regiment and Sir Anthony Head, Secretary of State for War, the government's official representative. In his welcoming speech he emphasised the importance of the expedition to both the country and the Commonwealth and reminded everyone of John Hunt's status as a serving army officer.

After the print journalists had put forward their questions, the BBC and Pathé Newsreel took over. When Tenzing was asked how he felt at the summit Charles Wylie stepped in to translate: 'I felt very happy.' John Hunt was characteristically modest, crediting both Eric Shipton and the 1952 Swiss Everest Expedition as major contributors to the British victory.

Amongst the good humour and the back-slapping, the controversies of the previous fortnight were not quite forgotten. John Hunt was invited to comment on 'the empty arguments' over who reached the summit first. He did not take the bait and replied that the success of the expedition was down to teamwork. Ed Hillary was quizzed about the day he fell into a crevasse on the Khumbu Icefall and had to be helped out by Tenzing. This had been reported in the *Daily Express* that very morning, under the headline 'Hillary Slipped'. What had seemed like a minor incident two months earlier had been turned into a near-death incident that climaxed in a dramatic rescue. Ed Hillary graciously replied that it proved how strong a partnership they were.

There were more questions and more photographs. As *The Times* noted, 'Tenzing himself was in Col Hunt's keeping and the two were often locked together in comradeship as they faced the cameras.' Whether Hunt was more concerned to protect Tenzing or keep him away from reporters went unanswered.

The next day the *Daily Telegraph* rather spitefully reported that John Hunt had mounted the Union Jack on his ice axe upside down. However, finally, the partisan reporting of the previous month gave way to a more benign appreciation of the British team's achievement.

The Himalayan Committee sought to retake control of the Everest narrative. Instead of the crude jingoism of a 'Race for Everest' or talk of a coronation gift for the Queen, the first ascent was presented much more subtly. It was a victory for mankind, in which Britain played a leading role, an inclusive victory from a team that carried the flag of the United Nations as well as the Union Jack.

If members of the British team were promoted as twentieth-century heroes, they were described as the epitomes of modesty and reserve, not boastful conquerors. This was easy to achieve because the team was genuinely full of modest men who did not court publicity. As they would quickly discover, even playing the role of modest heroes involved a lot of work and a large appetite.

The celebrations began with a round of banquets and parties, hosted by the organisations most directly involved in the expedition. In rapid succession they were fêted by the RGS, the Alpine Club, the Lord Mayor of London, Lloyds, and several other firms and guilds from the City of London that had contributed to expedition funds. These early celebrations climaxed with a royal garden party at Buckingham Palace on 16 July. On a wet Thursday afternoon the Everest team joined 2000 people and a cohort of overseas debutantes who had come to meet the new Queen and the Duke of Edinburgh.

The ceremony at which Hillary and Hunt received their knighthoods, and Tenzing was awarded his George Medal, was private and low-key. Tenzing's daughters Pem Pem and Nima were a little worried when they saw the Queen brandishing an ornamental sword but Ang Lahmu giggled when the Queen asked her how she had reacted to the news that her husband had just climbed Everest. With Charles Wylie translating, Ang Lahmu told the Queen that she had gone out and bought him a present.

'What was it?' enquired the Queen.

'A tin of condensed milk,' replied Ang Lahmu.

That evening, the team was invited to a state reception at Lancaster House preceded by a private meal with the Duke of Edinburgh and various dignitaries. It was a grand occasion, replete with displays of Everest photographs, a large Everest model and organised photo calls. Press photographers were excluded from most of the event for fear that they might take photographs of politicians drinking, which might cause future embarrassment.

The rest of Tenzing's fortnight in London was relatively quiet, marred by the illness of his daughter Pem Pem, who developed such a bad lung infection that she had to stay in hospital for several days. He and his family stayed at the India Services Club and when they weren't attending official functions, went sight-seeing and shopping, much to the fascination of the British press. They were offered numerous free gifts and Tenzing was frequently asked for his autograph. The hero of Everest cut a stylish figure in London, alternating between Western clothing and traditional Nepalese dress. Once, he managed to slip out and walk anonymously along the Strand, dapper in his newly acquired flannel trousers and check coat. He later wrote how cheered he was by the response of ordinary Londoners, who were much more welcoming of him than the citizens of Kathmandu had been of the British team.

For the diplomats of the Commonwealth Relations Office, however, Tenzing was still a 'cause for concern'. Their main worry was that he would leave early, before all the official functions had been held. When they heard rumours that he was unhappy and 'isolated and at the mercy of film and press men (particularly the *Daily Express*)',[2] Charles Wylie was drafted in to cheer him up and organise some social events.

Ed Hillary created no such worries. He and George Lowe stayed with another New Zealand climber, Norman Hardie, just outside London. Ed had plenty of friends to visit and two other members of the Hillary clan were in Britain: his brother Rex, who had made the trip from New Zealand especially for the occasion and his sister,

June, who had lived in Britain for several years. Ed was the star turn at many of the official events but, like the others, he found the lavish hospitality a little overpowering after almost five months of army rations in Nepal. Tom Stobart later estimated that they attended twenty banquets in two weeks; writing in his autobiography, *The Adventurer's Eye*, he commented that muscles which had been wasted by altitude were replaced with 'smoked salmon and caviar. And fat.' In *Nothing Venture, Nothing Win* Ed Hillary was more scathing, writing that his meetings with the rich and powerful offered 'little to envy or, indeed, much to admire'.[3]

In late July the team headed north to spend a weekend at the Outward Bound school at Eskdale in the Lake District, at the invitation of its new director, Eric Shipton. The Himalayan Committee had gone out of their way to include him in the London celebrations, billing him at official functions as 'Britain's greatest living explorer' whilst quietly ignoring the fact that they had sacked him a few months earlier. Eric took it all in very good grace and if he felt any resentment, did not show it.

With a BBC news crew in attendance, the visit to the Outward Bound school went well until George Lowe lost his front teeth when a canoe that he was paddling capsized. Anticipating the public lectures to come, George Lowe asked the Himalayan Committee's Treasurer for a loan to pay for his dental work but with characteristic penny-pinching wit, R.W. Lloyd reminded him that he couldn't possibly put any money towards his 'dining room furniture' because 'your teeth are your private affair'.[4]

At the beginning of August Ed Hillary and George Lowe returned to New Zealand to a rapturous reception. Thousands of people came to welcome them back to Auckland and hear them speak. The newly knighted Sir Edmund Hillary was presented with a large white armchair with a sharply-pointed back, to commemorate his ascent of Everest.

There was much pride in the two local boys who had been at the heart of a global event. When the Prime Minister, Sidney Holland, first heard the news he proclaimed:

I hope this terrific example of tenacity, the spirit of endurance and fortitude in this our Coronation year may be regarded as a symbol that there are no heights or difficulties which the British people cannot overcome.[5]

In 1953, as Ed Hillary acknowledged, New Zealanders still regarded themselves as essentially British.

After a few days in Auckland Ed Hillary and George Lowe went on a hastily arranged lecture tour, which raised the unprecedented sum of £4000. Originally, this had been destined for the coffers of the Himalayan Committee but, displaying a new-found munificence that undoubtedly would have sent R.W. Lloyd apoplectic, the money was donated to the New Zealand Alpine Club to fund a trip to the Barun Valley of Nepal in 1954, which Ed Hillary was due to lead.

At that moment Ed Hillary had something very different and much more important on his mind: Louise Rose. Twelve years younger than him, she was a beautiful brunette, studying the viola at a music school in Sydney, Australia. Her father was Ed's old friend Jim Rose, the former president of the New Zealand Alpine Club. Her mother, Phyllis, was a big fan of Ed Hillary and was thrilled when he told her that he wanted to marry her daughter. When it came to it, Ed was too shy to pop the question during a long-distance telephone call, so his future mother-in-law did it for him. Louise said yes and a few weeks later, on 3 September, they were married in Auckland.

George Lowe was the best man. Outside the chapel his friends from the New Zealand Alpine Club created an archway of ice axes for the newly-weds to pass under. Ten days later Ed and Louise arrived in London to begin a 'honeymoon' organised around Ed's Everest lecturing commitments.

John Hunt, meanwhile, was burning the candle at both ends. As his friends remarked again and again, he was the kind of person who never did things in half measures. This time, his challenge was to hammer out the expedition book in record time. It was scheduled for release in 1954 but the publishing company were keen to put it out as soon as possible and brought the date forward to November 1953, which meant delivering the manuscript in just over a month. The worry that Tenzing might be persuaded to write his own expedition book undoubtedly added to the urgency.

In characteristic fashion, John Hunt tried to turn it into a team effort. He wrote to everyone to ask for diary extracts and rather plaintively enquired if they could remember any humorous incidents on the expedition when they had said, 'this should go into the book'. Ed Hillary was invited to write the chapter on the summit attempt and everyone else was asked to contribute to one of the book's numerous appendices. Even Charles Evans was tracked down in Nepal to be asked for comments on certain chapters. He warned John Hunt that he was being asked to work too quickly and that the writing would suffer but the great work went on. At one stage John Hunt was hammering out a chapter per day.

The final manuscript was a triumph of perseverance and dedication but as the American writer and critic, James Ramsey Ullman, wrote in his review, it was rather a dry book, especially compared to Maurice Herzog's *Annapurna*. Most of the facts were there but there was very little emotion or drama. Having endured months of stress, John Hunt played everything down. His public persona and his literary voice were those of a controlled, tightly buttoned soldier even though, on the mountain and in his diary, he had shown himself to be a passionate, emotional man. The book contained little mention of the controversies at the end, or the early friction with the Sherpas but there was one, revealing, battle that John Hunt was willing to fight, over the book's title. At the producers' insistence the official film was called *The Conquest of Everest* but John Hunt fought to have it changed. As Joy Hunt remembered:

John could never abide the idea of conquering a mountain. Mountains are just too big and just too beautiful ever to be conquered.[6]

Ultimately, John Hunt lost the battle over the film but succeeded with the book, which was more modestly titled *The Ascent of Everest*.

No sooner had he delivered the manuscript than John Hunt began preparing for the first batch of lectures in London. They were an enormous success. In the first four months there were no fewer than eleven lectures at the Royal Festival Hall and more than sixty all over Britain.

William Hickey's review of the first gala event, in the *Sunday Express*, captured the low-key tone:

No glamour. No excitement. Not really a gala premier. Just a handful of very brave men pretending that they had not been brave at all.[7]

At John Hunt's insistence, wherever possible the climbers appeared in pairs or in threes, to emphasise that it had been a team effort. Increasingly, however, as the lectures went on, it became clear to the promoters, and the RGS, that Ed Hillary and John Hunt were far more in demand than any of the others. No matter how hard Hunt tried to present the expedition as a supreme team effort, the media and the public wanted their heroes in the singular, rather than the plural.

The official film, *The Conquest of Everest*, was a much more ponderous and puffed-up record of the expedition than was John Hunt's book. The music was provided by the elderly British composer Ralph Vaughan Williams and the commentary by the poet Louis MacNeice. Its highlight was Tom Stobart and George Lowe's photography. *The Conquest of Everest* had its royal premiere in Leicester Square in November and by the end of the month was competing for audiences with the live Everest lectures.

The focus moved abroad, with various members of the team

lecturing all over Europe. Ed Hillary went to Iceland and Scandinavia; Charles Wylie, to Yugoslavia; and Wilfrid Noyce lectured in Italy, Germany and Greece. Alfred Gregory, a French speaker, lectured in francophone North Africa and even did a twelve-date tour of the Belgian Congo.

The foreign appearances and showings of the Everest film were not as lucrative as the British lectures but there was no doubting their value as British propaganda as far as the Foreign Office was concerned. Officials wrote to Lawrence Kirwan at the RGS, praising the Everest team's efforts, and helped set up lectures and film showings. There were Everest exhibits at European trade fairs and much was made of the companies that had developed and contributed equipment to the Everest expedition.

As for the climbers, most were happy to be involved, although they did become bored with the endless repetition. In compensation, they were paid twenty-five guineas plus expenses for each official event; a decent fee, especially when several lectures were strung together. George Band's friends at Cambridge University joked that he gave more lectures than he attended. With quantities of money unexpectedly pouring in, the Himalayan Committee paid Ed Hillary a small stipend and agreed to cover any losses to his honey business arising from his lecture commitments. George Lowe was appointed expedition secretary, to look after the post-expedition paperwork and the lecture scheduling.

The public appearances eventually took their toll on John Hunt. He had been appointed deputy commandant of the army staff college at Camberley in autumn 1953 but still maintained a very hectic lecture schedule. When, after an appearance in Scotland, he was asked by the *Glasgow Evening News* when the lecture tour would end, he joked:

I presume we go on lecturing until we go mad.[8]

In late November Hunt went to Paris for three major public lectures at the huge auditorium the *Salle Pleyel*. It was a fun-filled couple of days, with Ed Hillary lecturing in schoolboy French and John Hunt's friends from the French climbing world taking everyone to Pigalle, Paris's red-light district. There they laid on a special entertainment, starring a group of beautiful young women who, clad only in a few slender ropes, danced and sang in front of a snowy backdrop draped with Union Jacks.

However, it was exhausting: in four days John Hunt delivered five lectures, attended three official lunches, two cocktail parties and one official dinner, gave interviews to the press and French television, and was presented to the King of Belgium and the Prime Minister of France. When he finished, he flew back to 'work' at 6.45a.m. This kind of schedule couldn't be sustained but the invitations kept coming.

On 30 November an article appeared in the *London Evening Standard* announcing that Hunt would not give a charity lecture at London University and that his place would be taken by Tom Bourdillon and Mike Westmacott. After months of tension in the build-up to Everest, a physically demanding expedition and the problems at the end, John Hunt was, quite simply, exhausted. Even though the term at the army staff college at Camberley was almost over, his doctors ordered him to cancel all engagements until March in the following year. For someone who prided himself on always writing that extra letter, always making that extra appearance, it was a major blow but no one who knew John Hunt was surprised. As Wilfrid Noyce commented, it was amazing that he had carried on for so long.

With John Hunt temporarily unavailable, the Everest show moved into its final phase: the biggest and most important foreign tour, to the United States, in early 1954. It had been assumed that Ed Hillary and George Lowe would go to the United States but initially the Himalayan Committee had hoped that John Hunt would also be available. As

Edwin Herbert wrote to Field Marshall Alexander on 2 October 1953, there was an important, if delicate, issue to be considered:

> *Much as we all love the Dominions, I cannot think it right that the story should be presented to the American public only by New Zealanders and that the American audiences should only hear a New Zealand accent.*[9]

When John Hunt became ill, they turned to Charles Evans. In late January 1954, he set off with Ed and Louise Hillary and George Lowe on a tour that would take them from New York in the east to San Francisco in the west. In between they performed in twenty-four cities, with Charles Evans opening the lectures, George Lowe delivering the middle section and Edmund Hillary bringing it to a climax.

The real tension in the US came from a fundamental question of what the tour was about: was its primary purpose to further British prestige or was the real motive to make as much money as possible? Having existed for so long on a relative shoestring, no one on the Himalayan Committee expected to reap huge financial rewards from the 1953 expedition. The cash, however, kept rolling in: by February 1955 they had amassed over £121,000 from the lectures and royalties for the book and the film. This created an unanticipated problem: if the purpose of the Himalayan Committee had been to organise Everest expeditions, what was their job now and what should they do with the money? Should it go to the RGS, the Alpine Club or into the pockets of John Hunt and his team? In what would become one of the great legacies of Everest 1953, the Himalayan Committee created a body whose aim was to support 'exploration of the mountain regions of the earth': the Mount Everest Foundation (MEF).

Though they would never admit it, from the outset the American tour was established on a sound commercial basis, with the profits going to the future MEF. Rather than letting their transatlantic equivalents – the American Alpine Club or the American Geographical Society – organise the events, the Himalayan Committee put the tour out to tender and awarded it to the promoter who guaranteed the highest return. Instead of the relaxed leisurely trip they had been promised, with opportunities for sightseeing and climbing in California's Yosemite Valley, Ed Hillary and the others were rushed from venue to venue in planes, trains and automobiles. Between shows they spent much of their time shaking hands with dignitaries and meeting climbing clubs. If it hadn't been for James Morris, who had been invited to accompany them as their general spokesman and 'fixer', tempers would have undoubtedly become very strained. The Himalayan Committee's fear that the starring roles of Ed Hillary and George Lowe might lead American audiences to think that Everest was essentially an Antipodean triumph were not realised. As James Morris dryly noted, most Americans 'had never heard of New Zealand and took it to be one of the more obscure border counties [of England]'.[10]

The US tour was notable for John Hunt's first public appearance for three months, albeit a brief one. On 10 February he flew to Washington to join Ed Hillary for a ceremony at the White House, in which the team was collectively awarded the Hubbard Medal, the National Geographic Society's highest accolade. Whereas the ceremony at Buckingham Palace had been conducted discreetly, behind closed doors, this was done in the full glare of national television.

Hunt and Hillary were given VIP treatment and taken to the White House by limousine but when they met President Eisenhower, it was obvious that he had forgotten who they were and what they were doing there. An aide reminded him and 'Ike' was all smiles but when it came to presenting the medal he introduced his first guest as 'Sir Edmund Hunt', before Ed Hillary corrected him. Then, to the bemusement of Hunt and Hillary, President Eisenhower proceeded to repeat the presentation of the Hubbard Medal several times for the cameras, each time with the same sincere smile. Although they had both encountered the media many times by now, Ed Hillary was still shocked by how 'undignified' these public events seemed to be.

As well as the collective award for the whole team, John Hunt and Ed Hillary were given personal replicas of the Hubbard Medal. A third one was struck and sent thousands of miles to Darjeeling, where it was presented to Tenzing by the American ambassador.

While the British team lectured around the world, Tenzing kept a relatively low profile. After leaving England in July he spent two weeks in Switzerland, climbing with Raymond Lambert and his old friends from the 1952 expedition. Then, when he returned to Darjeeling, he moved out of his old one-room house into a flat while he waited for a large house to be built, using the money that had been raised in public appeals.

Though he never made an explicit public announcement, it was clear that Tenzing had decided that his future lay in India, not Nepal. After visiting the Solu Khumbu in 1954, he brought his mother to Darjeeling and invited her to live with him, together with Tenzing's sister and other members of his extended family.

Tenzing continued his close association with Pandit Nehru but it was a mixed blessing. In return for becoming a hero of modern India, Tenzing found himself having to sacrifice a measure of personal freedom. The publication of his autobiography was held up by the Indian government lawyers who had been appointed to help negotiate the contract. At one stage Nehru himself was to write the introduction, and his niece was mooted as Tenzing's ghost-writer, but in the end neither happened and a lot of time was wasted.

In the mean time, an unauthorised biography, *Tenzing of Everest*, appeared. This caused a brief stir and once again threatened to damage his relationship with the British team. It was written by Yves Malartic, a minor French novelist and translator, and published by the Scorpion Press of Paris.

Malartic embroidered and exaggerated the stories that had first appeared in the United Press interviews,[11] criticising Hunt's team whenever he could. His central theme was the arrogance of the British, who he claimed continually patronised the valiant Sherpas and did everything they could to rob them of their glory. Malartic turned the incident of Hillary falling into a crevasse into a three-page drama. He also came up with the entirely new idea that Tenzing had planned to abandon the British team on 27 May and realise his 'secret project' to make a solo dash for the summit from the South Col. Clearly Scorpion Press felt that there was still money to be made from Everest scandal stories.

The Conquest of Everest by the Sherpa Tenzing was released in France in late September 1953 and offered to publishers in Britain and Germany. When Lawrence Kirwan and John Hunt saw it they were appalled but they weren't sure what to do. Kirwan checked with lawyers, who said that although scurrilous, it was not quite libellous. John Hunt worried that if they tried to take any action against Yves Malartic it would give the book extra publicity and confirm the impression of British high-handedness.

When John Hunt wrote to Tenzing to ask if he was aware of the book, he replied that he had had nothing to do with it and had only met Yves Malartic very briefly at a press conference in Switzerland. He was equally disturbed to hear of its contents. The French publishers of John Hunt's book, *The Ascent of Everest*, which was not due to be published until November 1953, took action against the Scorpion Press, claiming that they had erroneously implied that Tenzing was involved in their book and had breached the RGS's copyright by using photographs without permission. The French courts upheld their case and ordered that Malartic's book should be withdrawn, only, a month later, to allow the book back in the shops with the offending material removed. *Tenzing of Everest* was subsequently published in Germany but no British edition went ahead. It was released in the

United States but there too was the subject of legal action, when its American publishers used a copyright image on the cover without obtaining permission.

While Yves Malartic's unauthorised biography went in and out of courtrooms, Tenzing's autobiography continued to have problems. Ghost-writers came and went and it wasn't until the early summer of 1954 that the book really got under way. The man asked to put Tenzing's life on to the page was an American, James Ramsey Ullman, a well-known author who had written a history of the pre-war Everest attempts as well as several other books with mountaineering themes.

Tenzing was enthusiastic but hard to pin down. James Ramsey Ullman spent three weeks with him in Darjeeling, accompanied by a stenographer and Tenzing's friend, Rabindranath Mitra. Then he followed him to Switzerland in the summer of 1954, where Tenzing was attending a Swiss climbing school. On his way back to America, James Ramsey Ullman dropped in at the RGS to have a look at the Everest photographs. After the battles over Yves Malartic's book, Lawrence Kirwan, the Secretary of the RGS, was worried that Ullman's book would be another anti-British account and their meeting did nothing to assuage his fears. Ullman told him that he intended to expose the colonial attitudes of the British team and give a 'Tenzing version' of the final climb to the summit. Lawrence Kirwan was so worried that he considered refusing Ullman access to the Everest photographs and lecture slides but John Hunt disagreed.

Hunt was wary of the arguments and believed that it would be totally counterproductive to take such an aggressive approach. He made a suggestion: rather than sending the images to Tenzing by courier, why not hand them over in person? He was planning to be in the Alps in the summer of 1954 with George Lowe and Wilfrid Noyce, and offered to meet Tenzing before he returned to India. It was a typical John Hunt idea: if he could surround Tenzing with his old friends from the British expedition, then his heart was bound to melt.

Ullman's book, *Tiger of the Snows*, didn't come out until 1955, by which time the public's appetite for Everest had waned. John Hunt's *The Ascent of Everest* was a big hit around the world and Ed Hillary had just gone into print with his first autobiography, *High Adventure*. James Ramsey Ullman's book had none of the spitefulness of Yves Malartic's effort but it was clear that Tenzing was hurt by certain aspects of the coverage of the expedition. He particularly resented Ed's description of hauling him up the Hillary step 'like a giant fish' that had appeared in *The Times* and *The Ascent of Everest* and was offended by the comments that John Hunt had made on his climbing ability. As in Yves Malartic's book, there was a long passage about how Tenzing rescued Ed Hillary from the crevasse on the Khumbu Icefall and a full account of the garage incident in Kathmandu but these critical passages were balanced by respectful comments towards John Hunt and the British team.

For the most part there were few new revelations about the 1953 expedition except for one major point: for the first time Tenzing acknowledged in print that Ed Hillary had reached the summit first. In his book, *High Adventure*, Hillary stuck to the formula: 'a few more weary steps and a few whacks of the ice axe, we were on top' but Tenzing and Ullman decided that now was the time to write the truth:

> *I did not say to myself, 'There is a golden apple up there. I will push Hillary aside and run for it'. We went on slowly, steadily. And then we were there. Hillary stepped on top first. And I stepped up after him.*[12]

Tenzing's voice had been translated into James Ramsey Ullman's folksy prose but the book's insistence that 'only the truth is good enough for Everest' was an admirable sentiment after the years of controversy. Surprisingly, Tenzing's admission that Ed Hillary had reached the summit first did not seem to cause much fuss.

When Lawrence Kirwan reviewed the book for *The Times Literary Supplement* he did not even mention it. *Tiger of the Snows* sold reasonably well but it had nothing like the success of John Hunt's book.

By the end of 1955 the world had moved on. The Himalayan Mountaineering Institute had opened in Darjeeling and was taking most of Tenzing's attention. Ed Hillary had been back to the Himalayas, to revisit the Barun Valley, and was preparing to head south to Antarctica to take on a very different sort of challenge. John Hunt was about to leave the Army for a change of career. The other members of the team were pursuing their different interests inside and outside the climbing world. The Himalayan Committee held its final meeting in spring 1955. It was the end of an era. Britain was enjoying the warm glow of the New Elizabethan Age but that June morning when the coronation day crowds had heard the news of the first ascent of Everest was fading inexorably into distant memory.

EPILOGUE

In 1952 and 1953 there was much talk about the symbolic importance of the British Everest expedition. There were claims that it would do everything from initiating a New Elizabethan Age to radically transforming the sport of mountaineering. Looking back, it is perhaps not that surprising to discover that the hyperbole of the period was not matched by a real, long-term impact.

In Britain, there is no doubt that for the millions of people who read the books, saw the film, attended the lectures, or simply read about it in the papers, the 1953 ascent was special. In the history of exploration, the word 'first' has always been crucial and the first ascent of Everest helped create a 'feel-good factor' in Britain, as demonstrated by the letters sent by the public to John Hunt, telling him how much it meant to them. The optimism of the coronation, with which Everest was so closely linked, ran through the 1950s, a decade that saw significant improvements in the average Briton's standard of living.

Abroad, the first ascent of Everest helped boost Britain's prestige but real power has always been based on economic and military strength, not symbolic sporting or geographical victories. The first ascent of Everest possibly raised Britain's international profile for a few months, maybe even a few years, but getting a team to the highest point in the world did not stop the gradual decline of Britain as a global force.

The attention created by the first ascent had a significant effect on Nepal, which over the next few decades was transformed from a mysterious backwater into a Shangri-La for the new generation of global tourists. In 2007 over half a million foreigners visited the country, while approximately the same number of Nepalis were involved in the tourist industry. Today mountaineering and trekking are a very important part of the modern Nepalese economy, particularly in the Solu Khumbu region. Although there is still a small community of Sherpas in Darjeeling, the centre of gravity of the mountaineering business has moved to Kathmandu, where an increasing number of Sherpas live.

India, Nepal's dominant neighbour, has changed enormously over the last fifty years. It is now one of the biggest of the Asian 'tiger economies' and is becoming an ever-more-important player in the world of international politics. As Pandit Nehru wrote after Everest, for India to really prosper it needed to rise above petty nationalism. Today, with the rise of Indian multinational companies and the export of Indian culture, India is playing a much more important global role and is regularly described as an emerging superpower.

In terms of mountaineering, the impact of the expedition was not quite as predicted. In the immediate aftermath of the expedition, there were some who thought that after the first ascent, Everest would lose its allure. In a letter home in June 1953 John Hunt wrote that the 'Epic of Everest is ended' and in an article written just after the expedition, Eric Shipton, 'Mr Everest', told the *Sunday Express* that he hoped that once Everest had been climbed 'a new era of mountaineering in the Himalayas' would begin. The next two national expeditions to Everest, by the French in 1954 and the Swiss in 1955, were cancelled. Since then, apart from a brief period at the end of the 1960s when the Nepalese government refused to allow any expeditions, Everest has become busier and busier.

Its image, however, has changed significantly. In many ways Everest has followed the pattern set in the Alps in a previous age. Before the Matterhorn was climbed in 1865, many thought it invincible but twenty years after Whymper's first ascent, dozens of climbers were reaching the summit every year and his pioneering path up the Hornli ridge was described as an 'easy route'. Similarly, by the 1980s, the British team's approach to Everest up the Lhotse Face and the South East Ridge was known as the 'yak-route'.

In 1960, a Chinese team succeeded in scaling Everest via the pre-war British route from the north but the most significant event in Everest's post-1953 history occurred eighteen years later, in 1978, when an Italian from the Tirol, Reinhold Messner, and an Austrian, Peter Habeler, climbed Everest without oxygen. This was not without controversy: some Sherpas, including Tenzing, simply did not believe that Habeler and Messner could have done it and called for an enquiry. Others accused them of being irresponsible in pushing their bodies to the limits of what was humanly possible and encouraging other, lesser, mortals to follow in their wake. For those climbers who had argued from the 1920s onwards that it was possible to climb Everest without any 'artificial air' this, however, was a sweet victory. Two years later, to prove that there was no limit to what an élite climber could achieve, Reinhold Messner came back and climbed Everest from the north, without oxygen, on his own. It was an awesome achievement.

Messner's expeditions and the subsequent 'Alpine-style' attempts by climbers such as Britain's Stephen Venables reinforced Everest's image as the greatest challenge in mountaineering but over the last two decades its reputation has been significantly diminished by the emergence of a new phenomenon: commercial expeditions. Until the 1970s the Nepalese government only allowed one team on the mountain at any one time but today things are very different. There is no formal limit on numbers as long as each team is willing to pay the minimum $70,000 peak fee. Additionally, since the mid-1990s the Chinese government has pursued a new policy with regard to Everest, allowing as many foreign expeditions on the Tibetan side as are willing to foot the bill. In May 1996, an infamous month in which eleven people perished on Everest, there were eleven expeditions on the south side and several more on the north side. Far from acting as a deterrent, the events of 1996 only attracted more people to the mountain. In 2012, the German climber Ralf Dujmovits photographed a long line of climbers ascending the Lhotse Face. That year he estimated that there were thirty-nine expeditions on the mountain, amounting to over six hundred people.

The commercialisation of Everest and the huge growth in the numbers of trekkers and climbers visiting the area has also served to feed Everest's other negative image as 'the world's highest rubbish dump'. By the mid-1990s newspapers around the world were reporting that Everest Base Camp was piled high with human waste and that the South Col was covered in empty oxygen cylinders. After several highly publicised 'Everest Clean-Up Expeditions', much of the rubbish was carted off the mountain but the popularity of Everest probably means that this will always be a problem, unless very stringent environmental restrictions are introduced. This image of Everest as a polluted rich-man's playground is as far as you could imagine from the idea of the unassailable 'Third Pole' that prevailed in the 1950s.

If the impact of the 1953 expedition on mountaineering is complicated, it is easier to discuss its impact on the lives of the 1953 team, although even that is not quite as straightforward as might be imagined.

In 1978, when the BBC made a documentary on the twenty-fifth anniversary of the first ascent, no one looked very happy. The title of that film, *The Other Side of the Mountain*, summed up the ambivalence felt by several members of the team towards their achievement. John Hunt talked about how fame had at times estranged him from his friends and indeed from members of the team. Charles Wylie and

George Lowe revealed how the 1953 expedition had been detrimental to their careers in the army and the teaching service. Ed Hillary didn't say much but when he did appear he looked very grumpy. Twenty-four years later, in 2002, conversely, when I made a fiftieth anniversary film with Amanda Faber for the BBC, we found the team much more cheerful and very happy to talk about their Everest experiences.

The remarkable thing about the 'Everest family' is how close it stayed for so many years. As in all families there were occasional fallings-out but their comradeship set them apart from the other big Himalayan expeditions of the period. The Austro-German team that climbed Nanga Parbat in 1953 fell out spectacularly afterwards and the Italian K2 expedition of 1954 ended in lawsuits and lifetime feuds.

Everyone on the British team carried on climbing and many went on to great things. When Charles Evans led the first ascent of Kanchenjunga, the world's third-highest mountain, in 1955, George Band was one of the four climbers to get to the top. In 1961 Michael Ward led a small party ascent of Ama Dablam, the striking peak visible on the walk into Everest. Alfred Gregory climbed extensively in the Himalayas and South America. Mike Westmacott made notable ascents in Peru and Alaska and in 1993 became one of the four members of the 1953 Everest expedition to serve as president of The Alpine Club.[1]

Griffith Pugh, Tom Stobart, Christopher Summerhayes and James Morris were just as much a part of the Everest family as the climbers. James Morris left *The Times* and went on to become a leading travel writer and novelist.[2] Tom Stobart continued to work as a cameraman even after being shot in the leg in Ethiopia in 1956. Griffith Pugh's interest in high-altitude physiology flowered into a lifetime passion. In 1960 he joined Ed Hillary and Michael Ward on the Silver Hut expedition, a landmark research project. Christopher Summerhayes retired in 1955 and lived to the grand age of ninety-two.

Inevitably, with everyone so active in the mountains, there were casualties. The first was Tom Bourdillon. In the years after Everest Tom settled down to family life. He and Jennifer had two children and he continued to work as a rocket scientist for the British government. He stayed in touch with his old friends and never stopped believing that he might have succeeded in 1953, if everything had gone to plan. In July 1956 Tom Bourdillon met Charles Wylie and John Hunt at a picnic in St James' Park and talked passionately about his dream of one day of making the traverse of Everest from north to south. A week later he went to the Alps with a group of friends. While climbing the Jägihorn, in Switzerland, Tom Bourdillon and his partner Richard Viney fell to their deaths. Coincidentally, John Hunt was also in the Alps that week. He rushed over to Visp, finding the news hard to believe. When he was found, Tom was wearing the same blue and yellow check shirt that he had worn on Everest. He was buried in Switzerland.

Wilfrid Noyce was the second team member to die in the mountains. In 1962, he joined an expedition to the Soviet Pamirs, organised by John Hunt. Wilfrid and his young partner, Robin Smith, fell to their deaths while descending from Mount Garmo after a successful day of climbing. When their bodies were found, on the following day, they lay side by side. A distraught John Hunt buried Wilfrid Noyce and Robin Smith in a nearby crevasse.

After his triumph on Kanchenjunga, Charles Evans continued to climb until the early 1960s, when multiple sclerosis made it impossible. He took up sailing with great gusto until eventually he had to give up that too. For someone who had been a man of action for so much of his life it was an awful condition to develop but he dealt with it with characteristic fortitude and dignity. He died in 1995.

Inevitably, the three people whose lives were most changed by the expedition were Ed Hillary, Tenzing and John Hunt. No matter how hard John Hunt tried to persuade everyone that it was a team effort, the two who climbed to the summit got the most attention. Today in the media, 1953 is frequently referred to as 'Hillary and Tenzing's' ascent and even Hunt is left out.

It could be argued that John Hunt's life was not quite as affected by Everest as those of the summit pair. By 1953 he already had a DSO and a CBE and looked destined for high places in the army. In time, he probably would have become one of the 'great and the good' but there is no doubt that Everest gave both an immeasurable boost to his confidence and created a public profile that significantly aided him in the years that followed.

In 1956 he became the first director of the Duke of Edinburgh's Award scheme, an educational programme whose aim is to develop young people by setting them challenges both in their communities and in the natural environment. He thrived in the job and was instrumental in turning the scheme into an international institution. Unsurprisingly, his particular interest was in mountaineering and trekking and he went on several expeditions with young climbers.

After ten years John Hunt moved on to take up a very different sort of post, when in 1967 the Home Secretary, Roy Jenkins, invited him to become the chairman of another new British institution, the Parole Board. On retirement he became an active member of the House of Lords. In press and television interviews he came across as a very thoughtful and serious person but he had a strong sense of humour. In his autobiography, *Life is Meeting*, he told the embarrassing story of how, during one of his prison visits for the Parole Board, he met an inmate who greeted him warmly and recalled that they had met several years earlier in friendlier circumstances. When Hunt asked where, the prisoner replied that as a schoolboy John Hunt had presented him with a silver Duke of Edinburgh's Award.

To the end of his life John Hunt remained a passionate mountaineer. He led two pioneering British expeditions to Russia and regularly climbed in Wales and the Alps. As well as enjoying mountains himself, John played an important role in the history of the Mount Everest Foundation, the charitable trust set up to spend the money raised after the 1953 expedition. He was closely involved in its early years and continued to be involved for much of his life. In its first fifty years, the MEF[3] supported more than 1500 expeditions and distributed over £900,000 in grants.

John Hunt survived major heart surgery in 1995 but died three years later, at the age of eighty-eight; not bad for someone who had been warned by doctors sixty-three years earlier to take care on the stairs.

For Eric Shipton, the mid-1950s were difficult. He was sacked by the board of the Eskdale Outward Bound school after an unhappy affair with the wife of another member of staff. He was divorced from his wife, Diana, shortly afterwards. At his lowest point Eric spent several months working as a farm labourer, sharing a very basic cottage with another farmhand. Belatedly, in 1957 he was awarded a CBE for his contribution to the ascent of Everest. At the end of the 1950s he made the first of a series of expeditions to Patagonia, in South America. This initiated a new stage in his career as the world's pre-eminent mountaineer explorer. He wrote a well-received book about his later travels and remained an inspirational figure for young mountaineers attracted to his free-wheeling approach and his preference for lightweight expeditions. Eric Shipton died in 1977.

Ed Hillary outlived both Eric Shipton and John Hunt. The 1953 expedition unquestionably was a decisive moment in his life but many other achievements followed. His first expedition after Everest, however, leading a New Zealand team to the Barun Valley in Nepal, went so badly that at one point John Hunt was asked to write his obituary. While attempting to rescue a team member trapped in a crevasse, Ed Hillary broke several ribs. He tried to carry on until a lethal cocktail of pneumonia, dehydration and malaria forced him to retreat. Ed's performance at high altitude was permanently impaired but the episode didn't dent his appetite for travel and adventure.

In 1956 he became involved in the Commonwealth Trans-Arctic Expedition. It was led by the British scientist Sir Vivian Fuchs. Its aim was to cross Antarctica and complete the journey that Ernest Shackleton had dreamt of so many years earlier. Initially, Ed's role was limited. Fuchs and the British team were to start on one side of the continent, then motor across to the South Pole before carrying on to the other side. The New Zealanders were to build a large supply depot for the British team to use on the final leg. From the beginning Ed Hillary saw things differently. What was the point in going all the way to Antarctica just to put down a supply depot? Wouldn't it be better for the New Zealand team also to make a little detour to the South Pole?

In the end, somewhat to Vivian Fuchs and the British organisers' embarrassment, Ed and his New Zealand team reached the Pole on 4 January 1958, fifteen days ahead of Fuchs. It was a sweet victory, the culmination of the friendly Anglo-New Zealand rivalry that had been there since Everest.

After Antarctica Ed Hillary continued to enjoy the life of a global adventurer. He returned to the Himalayas in search of the Yeti, made an unsuccessful attempt on Makalu, the mountain that he had photographed from the summit of Everest in 1953, and went on an epic speedboat expedition, *Ocean to Sky*, travelling the length of the Ganges from the Bay of Bengal to the foot of the Himalayas. The expedition reached its climax with the ascent of an unclimbed mountain, which they christened Sky Peak, but in his late fifties, Ed found it very difficult to climb at high altitude. He managed to reach 18,000 ft before being stretchered off in a very weak state. He recovered and continued to visit India and Nepal but as the years went by he found himself restricted to ever-lower altitudes. He had to take oxygen on his final visit to the Solu Khumbu, the Sherpa homeland.

For much of the second half of his life, Ed Hillary led a project that was one of the other great legacies of the Everest 1953 expedition: the Himalayan Trust. It started small when, in 1960, Ed was asked if he could help the village of Khumjung to build a school. Through donations and personal favours he was able to build and staff a pre-fabricated schoolhouse. It was such a success that requests came in from villages all around the region. Ed found himself devoting more and more of his time to the building programme.

What started as a small private charity has grown into a large international organisation that has raised hundreds of thousands of pounds to build schools, hospitals, water supplies, bridges and even airstrips in the Solu Khumbu. Many of the first teachers and doctors came from New Zealand and today the Himalayan Trust has deep roots in both countries. In 1975 Louise Hillary and their daughter Belinda were killed in a plane crash near Kathmandu. This was a devastating event for Ed, his two surviving children, Peter and Sarah, and their many friends and family. It took him a long time to recover but Ed maintained his commitment to the Sherpas of Nepal to the end of his days.

The final chapter of Ed Hillary's extraordinary life began in 1985, when he was appointed New Zealand's high commissioner to India and Nepal. He remained in the post for five years and surprised himself with how much he enjoyed the work. He received the ultimate accolade in 2003 when he became the first foreigner to be granted honorary citizenship of Nepal. When Ed Hillary died in 2008, he was given a state funeral in New Zealand and mourned around the world.

Yet, in 1997, when Ed Hillary gave a speech at the Himalayan Mountain Institute in Darjeeling, to dedicate a statue to Tenzing, he described his summit partner as the 'true hero' of Everest. This was a fine tribute from someone who had achieved so much himself. In many ways, Tenzing's rise from yak herder to one of the most famous men in the world was more dramatic than either Ed Hillary or John Hunt's. Everest transformed Tenzing's life and made a huge impact on the lives of all Sherpas. However, whereas both Hillary and Hunt went on to use the fame and the confidence garnered on Everest to map out their future, Tenzing's life climaxed on the summit.

When an American foreign correspondent, Christopher Rand, visited him in the spring of 1954, he sensed that Tenzing was at a transitional point in his life. Whilst most of the other Sherpas were on expeditions, Tenzing had stayed in Darjeeling, living in a flat above a baker's shop. He had created a small museum in one room and happily showed people around, while he waited for his large house to be built.

Tenzing quickly realised that fame had a price. Some people were openly jealous of his success; others were drawn to him in the hope that he might help them financially or at least offer them a place at his table. Other than an advertisement for Brylcreem, a type of hair cream, he turned down many offers to endorse products but many businesses used his name and image without his approval. As Rand could see, Tenzing had no head for business.

Tenzing's main focus for the next two decades was India's first climbing school, the Himalayan Mountain Institute. In his speech at the opening ceremony in 1954, the Indian Prime Minister, Pandit Nehru, said his dream was that one day the HMI would produce 10,000 Tenzings. It was not long before India sent its own climbers to Everest. The first Indian expedition, in 1960, included three instructors from the HMI. Gompu, Tenzing's nephew and the youngest Sherpa on the 1953 expedition, was one of three climbers who reached 28,300 ft before stopping just short of the summit. Five years later, Gompu returned with another Indian team, which not only succeeded but also put no fewer than nine climbers on top, climbing via the South-East Ridge route.

Tenzing never went on another major Himalayan expedition. Immediately after the 1953 expedition, he said that he hoped his next challenge would be K2. In 1964 he announced a new plan to lead an all-Sherpa attempt on Kanchenjunga but neither expedition got off the ground. Tenzing's son Jamling climbed Everest in 1996 and his grandson Tashi has reached the summit twice.

In 1981 Ed Hillary and Tenzing had an unexpected meeting

in Lhasa. Ed was there as the chairman emeritus of an American team attempting to make the first ascent of the Kangshung Face of Everest; Tenzing was guiding a party of tourists. Hillary thought that he looked lonely and bored and was saddened to hear Tenzing say he envied Ed's greater freedom. In 1961, while Ang Lhamu was still alive, Tenzing took a second wife, Daku, almost thirty years his junior. Together they had three sons and one daughter.

As the decades passed, the age gap between Tenzing and his new wife, Daku, seemed to grow more pronounced. By the mid-1980s, with his children at boarding school and university in the United States, he was effectively living on his own in Darjeeling whilst Daku spent much of her time in Kathmandu. In a television interview after his death,[4] Tenzing's sister told how depression and alcohol had blighted his final years, a sad fate for someone who had been teetotal for much of his life. In 1985 Tenzing went into hospital in Delhi, suffering from pneumonia. He pulled through but died a year later.

Looking back at Tenzing's life, in the light of Hillary's comment that he was the real hero, it is impossible not to be amazed at how much he achieved. However, after Everest, he never seemed to be quite as in control of his destiny as were Ed Hillary and John Hunt. There were too many other people around him, writing his books, organising his work, trying to get him to do the things they wanted him to do.

Both John Hunt and Tenzing finished their Everest accounts with odes to the value of teamwork, a sharp contrast to the modern world, in which individualism seems to be in the ascendant. The best-known mountaineers of today are famous for their solo ascents, not for teams that they have led or been a part of. Self-sacrifice, tolerance, knowing how to take and give orders: these seem distinctly old-fashioned values. Yet the Everest expedition of 1953 epitomises and proves the value of teamwork and pulling together toward a common goal.

Bearing in mind the recent history of Everest, and its modern incarnation as a rich man's playground, it is perhaps not surprising that the achievements of John Hunt's team receive less attention today than they did in the past. Britain loves its explorers but has always had a special place for the heroic failures and the men who didn't make it back. Captain Scott, George Mallory, Ernest Shackleton, John Franklin, David Livingstone: they are the classic heroes of British exploration, who didn't have to make the transition from a life of adventure to everyday life.

In a way, the 1953 team was too successful and too organised and the fact that they made the ascent without either injury or the barest hint of frostbite made it seem almost too easy. On the release of the expedition film, *The Conquest of Everest,* some journalists were so amazed at the quality of George Lowe's high-altitude photography that they were convinced it must have been partially shot in a studio. They couldn't simply accept that he had done a really good job. Similarly, the amazing story of how James Morris got the news of the ascent back to Britain on 1 June 1953 has often been questioned, the assumption being that there must have been a lot of behind-the-scenes news management to make the announcement coincide with the coronation. The sceptics didn't want to accept it at face value: luck backed by solid preparation.

At the time the 1953 British Everest Expedition was praised as a model of good planning, good science, good teamwork, true grit and determination. All are true but several decades later it appears as a much more interesting story. It is true that John Hunt was exceptionally good at planning and logistics but there was more to his leadership than drawing up tables and schedules. He had that essential capacity possessed by all good leaders: the ability to make other people follow him and feel good for doing so.

Science played a key role in the success of the expedition, although the contributions of Griffith Pugh and the other backroom boys were not always appreciated. There is nothing more to say about grit, dedication and teamwork that haven't been said elsewhere in this book but, as in all mountaineering expeditions, good fortune played a major role.

Everest 1953 is a complex story, a mountaineering tale first and foremost, but also a narrative rich in cultural impact. Looking back on the expedition, there were mistakes, misunderstandings, injustices, controversies, cock-ups and occasional moments of comedy but in the end it was an overwhelmingly positive event that left a significant legacy. It inspired thousands of people to become climbers and trekkers, it led directly to the Mount Everest Foundation and indirectly to the Himalayan Trust and it created friendships that crossed continents and stood the test of time. To echo the *Daily Express*'s headline on 2 June: 'All this and Everest too'.

AFTERWORD

I would like to thank the many people who contributed to this book. In 2002 I was lucky enough to make a documentary for the BBC for the fiftieth anniversary of the first ascent of Everest in which we interviewed all the surviving British members of the team, family members and several journalists involved in the coverage of the expedition. My thanks in particular go to Amanda Faber, who so ably researched and worked with me on this documentary. During the course of that film we interviewed George Lowe, George Band, Charles Wylie, Mike Westmacott, Michael Ward, Joy Hunt, Jennifer Bourdillon, Pem Pem Tenzing, Tashi Tenzing, Rabindranath Mitra, Topgay, Nawang Gompu, Manindra Raj Shrestha, Peter Jackson, David Summerhayes, Jean-Jacques Asper and Ernest Hofstetter.

In the years that followed I have contacted many other family members for this book and I would like to thank them for their generous support. In particular I would like to thank Jane Ward and Jennifer Bourdillon, who have both been very generous with research materials and memories. I would also like to thank many others including: Mike and Sally Westmacott, George and Susan Band, Jan Morris, Denise Evans, Sally Hunt and Sue Leyden, John and Nick Shipton, Anna Riddiford, Norman Hardie, Bill Beaven, Suzanne and Yolande Gregory, Trevor Braham, Peter Steele, Tony Astill, Mary

Lowe, Terry Goodfellow, Russell Brice, Bill Ruthven, Ed Douglas and Ed Webster.

I'd also like to thank several people who helped me with my research into the Nepalese side of the story including David Gellner, John Whelpton, Tri Ratna Manandhar, Kamal Mani Dixit, Deepak Aryal and Pratayoush Onta. Special thanks to Yeshoda Pun, who so kindly translated several contemporary press articles for me.

Numerous librarians and archivists have helped me with this project but in particular I would like to thank Sarah Strong at the RGS, Glyn Hughes at the Alpine Club, Bruce Ralston at the Auckland War Memorial Museum, Nick Mays at *The Times*'s archive, Gabriel Swift at Princeton University, Maxine Willet at the Mountain Heritage Trust, Margaret MacMahon at the NZ Alpine Club, Kate Guthrie at the University of Otago, Jeff Walden at the BBC archives in Caversham and Theresa Lydon at BBC Television.

I am very grateful to the Writers Literary Trust for a travel grant which enabled me to research in the United States and New Zealand and to the London Library, who awarded me a Carlyle membership.

Many friends helped me by reading the manuscript and improved it immeasurably through their comments. In particular I would like to thank my old writing partner, Tim Jordan, for his suggestions, my former editor, Phillip Parker, Stephen Venables, John McAvoy, Judith Evans, Jerry Lovatt, David Presswell, Hugh Thompson and Eric Vola. Special thanks too to Ann Grand, who so ably copy-edited the manuscript.

I would also like to thank Anthony Sheil and Sally Riley at Aitken Alexander, Mike Harpley and Ruth Deary at Oneworld and Bettina Feldweg at Piper. I am as always indebted to Adam T. Burton for doing such wonderful maps and illustrations and would like to say a special word of thanks to my wonderful kids, Frank and Phyllis, for putting up with me over the course of the writing and a final word of gratitude to my darling wife Stella for all her support.

NOTES

PROLOGUE: OUR MOUNTAIN

1 In 1999 Everest was measured using GPS technology and a new height of 29,035 ft obtained. This figure is yet to be recognised by Nepal and China.

2 Sir William Goodenough to William Wedgwood Benn, 23 March 1931. India Office Library. L/P&S/12/4242 as quoted in 'Tenzing's Two Wrist-Watches', Stewart, G.T., *Past and Present*, 149

3 Sir Percy Cox to Sir Samuel Hoare, 25 May 1934, India Office Library, L/P&S/12/4242 as quoted in 'Tenzing's Two Wrist-Watches', Stewart, G.T., *Past and Present*, p. 149

1 MR EVEREST

1 Shipton, E. *The Six Mountain Travel Books*, p. 597

2 Interview, 2002

3 There are several other spellings of the Sherpa homeland - in John Hunt's The Ascent of Everest it is the 'Sola Khumbu', in Tenzing's Man of Everest it is the 'Solo Khumbu', and nowadays it is frequently written as one word, 'Solukhumbu'.

4 Shipton, E. *The Six Mountain Travel Books*, p. 598.

5 Bourdillon, T. *Diary 1951 Everest Reconnaissance*

6 Telegram E.P. Hillary to L.T. Hillary, 31 August 1951

7 Bourdillon, T. *Diary 1951 Everest Reconnaissance*

8 Letter Eric Shipton to Pamela Freston. The Alpine Club

9 Kala Patar

10 *The Times*, Everest 1951 Supplement

11 *The Times*, Everest 1951 Supplement

12 For an intriguing explanation of the footprints, see Ward, M. (1997) Everest 1951: the footprints attributed to the Yeti – myth and reality. *Wilderness and Environmental Medicine* 8(1): 29.

13 Bourdillon, T. *Diary 1951 Everest Reconnaissance*

14 Bourdillon, T. *Diary 1951 Everest Reconnaissance*

2 THE REAL CLIMBERS

1 EE/62 Memo Basil Goodfellow, 1 January 1952

2 EE/62 Draft press release, 1 January 1952

3 EE/62 Telegram 3 January 1952

4 EE/62 Memo Basil Goodfellow, January 1952

5 EE/62 Press release, 5 January 1952

6 *Daily Herald*, 6 January 1952

7 Shipton, E. *That Untravelled World*, p. 214

8 For a good brief biography of Griffith Pugh, see Ward, M.P. and Milledge, J.S. (2002) Griffith Pugh: Pioneer everest physiologist, *High Altitude Medicine and Biology* 3(1): 77

9 See Michael P. Ward and James S. Milledge. *High Altitude Medicine & Biology*. March 2002, 3 (1): 77–87.

10 EE/62 Telegram, 17 March 1952

11 EE/61 Eric Shipton, March 1952

3 THE TURQUOISE GODDESS

1 In 1951, when the New Zealand Alpine Club contacted Eric Shipton to ask if he might take some of their members to Everest, he replied that he would take any two. Eric did not realise the friction this would create among the four men of the New Zealand team who were climbing in the

Garhwal in India. One, Ed Cotter, withdrew immediately; the others – Ed Hillary, Earle Riddiford and George Lowe – argued it out among themselves. Eric Shipton later said that he would have been happy to take all of them.

2 *The Times,* 17 April 1952

3 Interview, 2002

4 Dittert, R., Chevalley. G., Lambert, R., *Forerunners to Everest* p. 92

5 Hillary, E. *Diary of the 1952 Cho Oyu Expedition,* 2 May

6 Hillary, E. *View from the Summit.* p. 119.

7 Hillary, E. *Diary of the 1952 Cho Oyu Expedition,* 15 May

8 Dittert, R., Chevalley. G., Lambert, R., *Forerunners to Everest,* p. 138

9 Subsequent climbers estimated the site of Lambert and Tenzing's high camp to be about 200 ft lower down. In an article for the *Alpine Journal* the mountaineer and cartographer responsible for the latest Everest map, Brad Washburn ('The location of Camp IX', *Alpine Journal*), listed its height as 27,265 ft. If this is the case, then Lambert and Tenzing turned back at 27,915 ft.

10 Hillary, E. *Diary of the 1952 Cho Oyu Expedition*

4 A VERY BRITISH COUP

1 *Daily Mail,* 24 June 1952

2 EE/60 Telegram Lawrence Kirwan to Eric Shipton

3 EE/90/4 Memo Tom Bourdillon, 8 June 1952

4 Letter, Eric Shipton to Pamela Freston, 6 July 1952. The Alpine Club.

5 Hillary, E.P. *Diary of the 1952 Cho Oyu Expedition,* 18 June 1952

6 EE/62 Memo Campbell Secord, June/July 1952

7 *The Blakeney Papers,* The British Library

8 The French Alpine Club had also considered applying for permission in 1953 but after an informal agreement with the Himalayan Committee had agreed to wait until 1954.

9 EE/68 Letter Basil Goodfellow to John Hunt, 10 July 1952

10 EE/68 Letter Basil Goodfellow to John Hunt, 18 July 1952

11 EE/68 Letter John Hunt to Claude Elliott, 23 July 1952

12 Shipton, E. *That Untravelled World*, p. 212

13 EE/68 Letter Claude Elliott to John Hunt, 29 July 1952

14 EE/68 Letter Basil Goodfellow to John Hunt, 12 August 1952

15 EE/68 Letter Peter Lloyd to John Hunt 12 August 1952

16 EE/68 Letter Basil Goodfellow to John Hunt, 27 August 1952

17 EE/90 Memo Basil Goodfellow, 28 August 1952

18 EE/90 Draft minutes of Himalayan Committee meeting, 11 September 1952

19 EE/90 Draft minutes of Himalayan Committee meeting 11 September 1952

20 Interview, 2002

21 The *Blakeney Papers*, The British Library

22 Letter Eric Shipton to Sir James Wordie, November 1952, The Alpine Club

23 *The Blakeney Papers*, The British Library

5 A PAPER MOUNTAIN

1 EE/68 Letter Basil Goodfellow to John Hunt, 27 September 1952

2 EE/68 Hunt, J. *Basis for Planning*, November 1952

3 Hillary, E. *High Adventure*, author's preface

4 EE/68, Letter John Hunt to Basil Goodfellow, 30 September 1952

5 EE/68/4, Letter John Hunt to Ed Hillary, 16 October 1952

6 EE/68

7 *The Alpine Journal*, Volume 98, 1993

8 The official reserves were: J. H. Emlyn Jones, John Jackson, Anthony Rawlinson, Hamish Nicol, and Jack Tucker.

9 EE/93 Letter R.W. Lloyd to Bill Murray, 29 May 1952

10 EE/93 Letter Bill Murray to R.W. Lloyd, June 1952

11 EE/93 R.W. Lloyd, *Correspondence 1952–1954, A–L*

12 LJH/16b, Letter John Hunt to Joy Hunt, 1 June 1953

6 THE KATHMANDU COLD SHOULDER

1 Izzard, R. *The Innocent on Everest*, p. 59.
2 The Public Record Office, Kew. FO 371. Letter Christopher Summerhayes to Foreign Office, 27 August 1952
3 See Ed Douglas' biography *Tenzing, Hero of Everest* and Ed Webster's memoir *Snow in the Kingdom*
4 EE/68 Cable Jill Henderson to John Hunt, 2 January 1953
5 EE/68 Letter Jill Henderson to John Hunt, 5 January 1953
6 EE/68 Letter John Hunt to Tenzing, 20 January 1953
7 Interview, 2002
8 Letter Arthur Hutchinson to Mr McDonald, 12 January 1953. Times Newspapers Limited Archive, News International. Subject Files: Everest
9 Letter Ed Hillary to Jim Rose, May 1953. Hocken Collections. New Zealand Alpine Club records. *Copies of letters from Edmund Hillary to Jim Rose*. 1951–1954. MS-1164–2/66/3
10 *The Times of India*, 10 March 1953
11 *Daily Mail*, 6 March 1953
12 EE/90/9 Griffith Pugh's report on his meeting with the Swiss Foundation for Alpine Research in September 1952. See also Christopher Summerhayes's letter to John Hunt, after his conversation with Raymond Lambert and Gabriel Chevalley.
13 EE/66/2 Letter Charles Wylie to John Hunt, 23 September 1952
14 Letter John Hunt to Gerald Norman, 10 March 1953. Times Newspapers Limited Archive, News International. Subject Files: Everest
15 EE/83 Letter Mr Band to *The Times*, 20 March 1953
16 SSC/38/14 Letter Charles Evans to Christopher Summerhayes, 17 April 1953. Royal Geographical Society
17 Hillary, E. *Diary of the 1953 Everest Expedition*. Hillary, Edmund Percival, Sir. Personal papers. Auckland War Memorial Museum Library. MS 2010/1 Folder 677
18 The Royal Geographical Society. The Papers of Sir John Hunt. LJH/1, 8 April 1953
19 Letter George Lowe to Betty Lowe, 6 April 1953. Hocken Collections.

New Zealand Alpine Club records. *Copies of letters from W.G. Lowe during Everest Expedition*. 1953. MS-1164–2/66/4

7 THE ICEFALL

1 Letter Ed Hillary to Jim Rose April 18th 1953, Hocken Collection NZAC

2 Interview George Band, 2002

3 After gender reassignment surgery in 1972, James Morris became Jan Morris. See Jan Morris *Conundrum* (1974)

4 *The Other Side of the Mountain*, BBC TV, 1978

5 The Royal Geographical Society. *Lord John Hunt Collection*. LJH/1, 14 April 1953

6 Letter George Lowe to Betty Lowe, 8 May 1953. Hocken Collections. New Zealand Alpine Club records. *Copies of letters from W.G. Lowe during Everest Expedition*. 1953. MS-1164–2/66/4

7 Letter George Lowe to Betty Lowe, 4 May 1953

8 *The Other Side of the Mountain*. BBC TV, 1978

9 LJH/1 29 April 1953

10 Morris, Jan. *Coronation Everest*

11 LJH/1 4 May 1953

12 Bourdillon, T. *Diary of the 1953 Expedition*. The Alpine Club

13 EE/91 Letter John Hunt to Edwin Herbert. (Herbert was by then the chairman of the Himalayan Committee.)

14 Evans, C. 'The First Ascent of the South Summit'. *The Alpine Journal*

15 Bourdillon, T. *Diary of the 1953 Expedition*. The Alpine Club

8 THE LHOTSE FACE

1 Hillary, E. *Diary of the 1953 Expedition*

2 Ward, M. *Diary of the 1953 Expedition*

3 Letter, George Lowe to Betty Lowe, 22 May 1953. Courtesy of Tony Astill

4 Hillary, E. *Diary of the 1953 Expedition*

5 LJH/1, 22 May 1953

6 LJH/1, 24 May 1953

9 FIRST UP

1 LJH/1, 26 May 1953

2 Letter, Charles Evans to Anne McCandless, 3 February 1953. *The Papers of Sir Charles Evans.* The Mountain Heritage Trust

3 When, a few years later, Charles Evans led an expedition to Kanchenjunga, the third-highest mountain in the world, he promised local religious leaders that if they succeeded, no one would actually set foot on the summit, in deference to their religious beliefs.

4 Bourdillon, T. *Diary of the 1953 Everest Expedition*

5 Hillary, E. *High Adventure,* p. 189

6 Hillary, E. *View from the Summit,* p. 17

7 Hillary, E. *High Adventure,* p. 196

8 According to John Hunt's plan of 7 May, George Lowe should not have been on the South Col at all. After so many days on the Lhotse Face, George should have been exhausted but he recovered quickly and was very keen to prove himself. On 21 May he persuaded John Hunt to allow him to make an additional trip to the South Col with extra oxygen and supplies.

9 Hunt, J. *The Ascent of Everest,* p. 195

10 LJH 16b 1 June 1953, letter to Joy Hunt

11 Hillary, E. *High Adventure,* p. 198

10 TO THE SUMMIT

1 Hunt, J. Unpublished review of *Man of Everest,* TLS

2 Letter Raymond Greene to Michael Ward. Courtesy of Jane Ward

3 EE/90 Press release Himalayan Committee, May 1953

4 Hillary, E. *Diary of the 1953 Expedition*

5 Hillary, E. *Diary of the 1953 Expedition*

6 Ullman, J.R. *Man of Everest,* p. 270

7 This was not the Pasang Phutar (The Jockey), whom John Hunt had sacked in April.

11 SNOW CONDITIONS BAD

1 LJH/1 30 May 1953
2 LJH/1 Letter John to Joy Hunt, 30 May 1953
3 Letter Arthur Hutchinson to Mr McDonald, January 1953. Times Newspapers Limited Archive, News International. Subject Files: Everest
4 Coronation Everest, Jan Morris, p138. In fact by the time Morris's message reached Christopher Summerhayes, it had passed through both the telegraph station at Namche Bazaar and in Kathmandu, and had been slightly modified by the operators. It read: Snow conditions bad hence expedition abandoned advance base on 29th and awaiting improvement being all well.
5 EE/90, Copy of message received from Colonel Hunt
6 Tom Bourdillon's code phrase was 'Lhotse Face impossible'
7 The Public Record Office, Kew. FO 88
8 The Public Record Office, Kew. FO 88
9 Correspondence with Terry Goodfellow, 2010
10 Interview, 2002
11 *The Times*, 4 June 1953
12 *The Times*, 5 June 1953
13 Bourdillon, T. *Diary of the 1953 Everest Expedition*. 30 May 1953. The Alpine Club
14 Noyce, W. *South Col.*, p. 208
15 LJH/1

12 WHOSE MOUNTAIN?

1 Jackson, P. *Journey to Everest*
2 *The Statesman*, Calcutta, 4 June 1952
3 *The Times*, 8 June 1952

4 The George Medal is the highest British civilian award for bravery.

5 *The Times*, 8 June 1952

6 *Gorkhapatra*, 8 June

7 *The Mail* (Madras),11 June

8 *The Leader* (Allahabad), 11 June

9 Interview, 2002

10 LJH/1

11 EE/66/4 Telegram, John Hunt to *The Times* 14 June 1953

12 The Public Record Office, Kew. FO 371

13 *Daily Mail*, 16 June 1953

14 *The Statesman*, 16 June 1953

15 In 1955, in a letter to Tenzing, John Hunt wrote that he did not mean his comment on Tenzing's limited experience of technical mountaineering to be in any way insulting. It applied equally to Ed Hillary, he added.

16 Hansard, 17 June 1953

17 Hillary, E. *View from the Summit*, p. 46

18 A military officer with a rank of Colonel was not eligible for a KBE

19 In 2002 I interviewed one of the young men who had come out to meet Tenzing. He remembered that Tenzing had confirmed that he reached the summit first but Tenzing consistently denied this.

20 *Life*, June 1953

21 Knox, R. 'Down from Everest', Punch. Rawle Knox was a journalist sent out by The Observer to cover the Everest team's return to Kathmandu. Peter Hillary, Ed's son, is not so sure about this story. Though Ed Hillary occasionally swore, this is too polished and too crude.

22 Interview, 2002

23 Unpublished dispatch from James Morris for *The Times* 22 June 1953. Times Newspapers Limited Archive, News International. Subject Files: Everest

24 *The Observer*, 21 June 1953

25 Nehru, Jawaharlal. *Letters to Chief Ministers 1947–1964*

13 BRINGING EVEREST HOME

1 A private joke between the two men: Eric watched Ed consuming pound after pound of bananas on the train back through India after the Cho Oyu expedition.

2 The National Archives, PRO 18

3 Hillary, E. *Nothing Venture, Nothing Win*, p. 167

4 EE/94 R.W. Lloyd to George Lowe, August 1953

5 *Allahabad Leader*, 3 July 3 1953

6 Interview, 2002

7 *Sunday Express*, 16 September 1953

8 *Glasgow Evening News*, 2 December 1953

9 EE/80 Letter Edwin Herbert to Alexander, 2 October 1953

10 EE/81 Memo James Morris to Lawrence Kirwan

11 These appeared in Britain in the *Daily Express*.

12 Ullman, J. R. *Man of Everest*, p. 268

EPILOGUE

1 The others were John Hunt, Charles Evans and George Band.

2 Today James Morris writes under the name of Jan Morris.

3 *Reputations: Hillary and Tenzing*. BBC TV 1998.

4 John Hunt was the second chairman of the Mont Everest Foundation (1956–7). The first was James Wordie (1954–6).

BIBLIOGRAPHY AND NOTES ON SOURCES

This book is based on three principal sources: contemporary documents held in public and private collections, interviews with expedition members and their relatives and the published accounts of the Everest team and the journalists who covered the expedition. For secondary information, I have drawn on a wide range of books and articles as well as radio, film and television coverage of the expedition and its aftermath.

ARCHIVES

The Royal Geographical Society, London:
1953 Everest Expedition Files (boxes EE/60–99)
Lord John Hunt Collection (boxes LJH 1–9)
The Papers of Sir Christopher Summerhayes

The Alpine Club, London:
Tom Bourdillon's Diary D103
The Letters of Eric Shipton B84
The Peter Steele Collection

The British Library, London:
The Blakeney Papers
The Collindale Newspaper Library

The Public Record Office, Kew, London:
Various

Mountain Heritage Trust:
The Papers of Sir Charles Evans

The Auckland War Memorial Museum Library, New Zealand:
Hillary, Edmund Percival, Sir. Personal Papers 1919–2008. MS 2010/1
Diary of the 1951 Everest Expedition
Diary of the 1952 Cho Oyu Expedition
Diary of the 1953 Expedition

Times Newspapers Limited Archive, News International
Subject Files Series: Everest

The Hocken Library, University of Otago:
New Zealand Alpine Club Records

BOOKS

Band, George *Everest, the Official History*. Harper Collins, 2003
Bourdillon, Jennifer *Visit to the Sherpas*. Collins, 1956
Braham, Trevor *Himalayan Playground*. The In Pinn, 2008
Cranfield, Ingrid *Inspiring Achievement*. The Institute of Outdoor Learning, 2002
Dittert, René, Chevalley, G., Lambert, R. *Forerunners to Everest*. Allen & Unwin, 1954
Douglas, Ed *Tenzing, Hero of Everest*. National Geographic, 2003
Evans, C. *The First Ascent of the South Summit. The Alpine Journal*
Evans, Charles *Eye on Everest*. Dennis Dobson, 1955
Evans, Charles *Kangchenjunga, The Untrodden Peak*. Hodder and Stoughton, 1956

Evans, Charles *On Climbing*. Museum Press Ltd, 1956

Gibbs, Phillip *The New Elizabethans*. Hutchinson & Co., 1953

Goswami, S.M. *Everest, is it Conquered?* Indian Press Ltd, 1954

Gregory, Alfred *Everest*. Constable, 1993

Hennessey, Peter *Having it so Good*. Allen Lane, 2006

Herzog, Maurice *Annapurna*. Cape, 1952

Hillary, Edmund *High Adventure*. Hodder & Stoughton, 1955

Hillary, Edmund *Nothing Venture, Nothing Win*. Hodder & Stoughton, 1975.

Hillary, Edmund *View from the Summit*. Doubleday, 1999

Hunt, J. Unpublished review of Man of Everest, TLS

Hunt, John *The Ascent of Everest*. Hodder & Stoughton, 1953

Hunt, John *Life is Meeting*. Hodder & Stoughton, 1978.

Izzard, Ralph *The Innocent on Everest*. Hodder & Stoughton, 1955

Johnson, Alexa *Sir Edmund Hillary, An Extraordinary Life*. Dorland Kindersley 2005

Joshi, Bhuvan Lal and Leo Rose *Democratic Innovations in Nepal*. University of California Press, 1966

Knox, R. *Down from Everest*

Koirala, Matrika Prasad *A Role in a Revolution*. Jagadamba Prakashan, 2008

Krakauer, Jon *Into Thin Air*. Macmillan, 1997

Lowe, George *Because it is There*. Cassell, 1959

Life Magazine

Maillart, Ella *The Land of the Sherpas*. Hodder and Stoughton, 1955

Malartic, Yves *La Conquete de L'Everest par le Sherpa Tenzing*. Editions du Scorpion, 1953

Morris, James *Coronation Everest*. Faber & Faber, 1958

Morris, Jan *Conundrum* Faber & Faber, 1974

Murray, W.H. *The Story of Everest*. Dent, 1953

Nehru, Jawaharlal. *Letters to Chief Ministers 1947–1964* New Delhi: Jawaharlal Nehru Memorial Fund, 1985–1989

Noyce, Wilfrid *South Col*. Heinemann, 1956

Ortner, Sherry *Life and Death on Mt Everest*. Princeton University Press, 1999

Perrin, Jim *The Climbing Essays*. The In Pinn, 2006

Rand, Christopher *The Twain Shall Meet*. Victor Gollancz Ltd, 1957

Royal Geographical Society *Everest, Summit of Achievement*. Bloomsbury, 2003

Shipton, E. *The Six Mountain Travel Book*

Shipton, Eric Earl *The Mt Everest Reconnaissance 1951*. Hodder & Stoughton, 1952

Shipton, Eric Earl *That Untravelled World*. Hodder & Stoughton, 1969

Steele, Peter *Eric Shipton: Beyond Everest*. Constable, 1998

Stobart, Tom *Adventurer's Eye*. Oldhams Press, 1958

Summerhayes, David and Jeremy Thomas *Christopher Summerhayes: Soldier, Levant Consul and Diplomat*. (n.pub), 1998

The Location of Camp XI, *Alpine Journal*

The Swiss Foundation for Alpine Research, *Everest, The Swiss Expeditions*. Hodder & Stoughton, 1954

The Swiss Foundation for Alpine Research, *The Mountain World 1953*. George Allen & Unwin, 1953

The Swiss Foundation for Alpine Research, *The Mountain World 1954*. George Allen & Unwin, 1954

Tenzing, Jamling (with Broughton Coburn) *Touching My Father's Soul*. Harper Collins, 2001

Tenzing, Tashi and Judy Tenzing *Tenzing Norgay and the Sherpas of Everest*. McGraw-Hill, 2001

Tenzing Norgay *After Everest*. Allen and Unwin, 1977

Tenzing Norgay (as told to Malcolm Barnes) *After Everest*. Allen and Unwin, 1977

Tenzing Norgay (in collaboration with James Ramsay Ullman) *Tiger of the Snows*. Putnam, 1955

Tharkay, Ang and Basil Norton *Memoires d'un Sherpa*. Amiot-Dumont, 1954

Tilman, H.W. *Nepal Himalaya*. Cambridge University Press, 1952

Ullman, J.R. *Man of Everest*, Jackson, P. *Journey to Everest*

Unsworth, Walter *Everest*. Baton Wicks, 2000

Ward M. (1997) Everest 1951: the footprints attributed to the Yeti – Myth and Reality. *Wilderness and Environmental Medicine* 8 (1) 29

Ward, M. *Diary of the 1953 Expedition*

Ward, Mike *In this Short Span.* Gollancz, 1972

Ward, Mike *Everest, A Thousand Years of Exploration.* The Earnest Press, 2003

Ward, M. P. and Milledge, J. S. (2002) Griffith Pugh: Pioneer Everest Physiologist. *High Altitude Medicine and Biology* 3 (1) 77

Webster, Ed *Snow in the Kingdom.* Mountain Imagery, 2000

JOURNALS

The Alpine Journal:

Vol 58: Tilman, H.W. *The Annapurna Himal and South Side of Everest.* May 1951

Vol. 58 : Murray, W.H. *The Reconnaissance of Mount Everest, 1951*

Vol. 59: Roch, André *The Swiss Everest Expedition: Spring 1952.* May 1953

Vol. 98: Various *Everest 40th Anniversary Edition.* 1993

The American Alpine Journal:

Vol. 8: Cowles, E. *North to Everest.* 1951

The Geographical Journal:

118: Everest: the 1951 Reconnaissance of the Southern Route

158: Ward, M.P and Clark P.K. *Everest, 1951: cartographic and photographic evidence of a new route from Nepal.*

The Himalayan Journal:

17: Houston, Charles *Towards Everest.* 1952

18: Wylie Charles *Everest, 1953* (1)

The Times (supplements):

The Mount Everest Reconnaissance Expedition 1951. December 1951

The First Ascent of Mount Everest. July 1953

JOURNAL PAPERS

Hansen, Peter (2000) Confetti of Empire: the Conquest of Everest in Nepal, India, Britain and New Zealand, *Comparative Studies in Society and History* 42: 307–32

Hansen, Peter (1997) Tenzing's Two Wrist-Watches: the Conquest of Everest and Late Imperial Culture in Britain, 1921–1953, Comment. *Past and Present* 157: 159–77

Stewart, Gordon T. (1980) The British Reaction to the Conquest of Everest, *Journal of Sport History*: 30–1

Stewart, Gordon T. (1995) Tenzing's Two Wrist-Watches: The Conquest of Everest and Late Imperial Culture in Britain 1921–1953. *Past and Present*, 149

INDEX

References to illustrations are in *italic*.

INDEX

INDEX